SOURCE BOOKS ON EDUCATION
VOL. 43

THE FOREIGN LANGUAGE CLASSROOM

GARLAND REFERENCE LIBRARY
OF SOCIAL SCIENCE
VOL. 928

THE FOREIGN LANGUAGE CLASSROOM

Bridging Theory and Practice

Edited by

Margaret Austin Haggstrom
Leslie Zarker Morgan
Joseph A. Wieczorek

GARLAND PUBLISHING, Inc.
New York & London / 1995

Library of Congress Cataloging-in-Publication Data

The foreign language classroom : bridging theory and
   practice / edited by Margaret Austin Haggstrom, Leslie
   Zarker Morgan, Joseph A. Wieczorek.
       p.   cm. — (Garland reference library of social
science ; vol. 928. Source books on education ; vol. 43)
   Papers from a conference held in Oct. 1991.
   Includes bibliographical references and index.
   ISBN 0-8153-1508-2
   1. Language and languages—Study and teaching—
Congresses.   I. Haggstrom, Margaret Austin.
II. Morgan, Leslie Zarker.   III. Wieczorek, Joseph A.
IV. Series: Garland reference library of social science ;
v. 928.   V. Series: Garland reference library of social
science. Source books on education ; vol. 43.
P51.F55   1995
418'.007—dc20   95-3040
                                                CIP

Printed on acid-free, 250-year-life paper
Manufactured in the United States of America

Contents

Introduction

In the last forty years, theories of language learning and teaching methods have evolved tremendously. In the 1950s and 1960s, under the prevailing influence of structural linguistics and behavioral psychology, the grammar-translation and audio-lingual methods were widely adopted. These methods emphasized correct grammatical forms and placed the burden of student learning on the teacher, whose function was to explain grammar and to conduct drills. In the 1970s, theoretical linguists and teachers alike began to realize that these methods failed to produce students who could use the foreign language they were studying outside of the structured confines of the classroom and language lab. This realization sparked linguists such as van Ek, Candlin, Hymes, and Savignon to speak of the need to redefine language learning in terms of what students could actually *do* with the language in real-world situations.

In 1980, Canale and Swain set forth a model for curriculum design based on the premise that communicative competence, or proficiency, is much more complex than simply memorizing and manipulating basic grammatical structures and vocabulary. While recognizing the importance of grammar, they nevertheless pointed out that language use is an interactive process that includes the simultaneous interaction of grammatical, sociolinguistic, discourse, and strategic competence (27–8). The communicative approach has inspired a variety of teaching methodologies, and there is still much debate today about issues such as the role of teacher input and of grammar in the communicative-oriented classroom. Nevertheless, those who embrace this approach, whatever their method, are committed to the notion of language use as "social behavior, purposeful, and always in context" (Savignon 1991, 273), and espouse the view that the primary goal of language teaching is to train students to "perceive and operate within real-world situations, in order to perform real-world tasks" (Swaffar 1989, 33). In the last ten years, the communicative approach has gained widespread support among theoretical linguists and teachers alike. At the same time, however, it is widely recognized that the implementation of this approach in the classroom lags far behind theory. It was our own observation of this phenomenon, and the discussion that subsequently followed, which first prompted the idea for the conference "Bridging Theory and Practice in the Foreign Language Classroom" in October 1991.

It is a curious phenomenon that at a time when the prevailing influence in linguistic theory and language teaching is one that stresses the interactive nature of language, based on the premise that "communication is not one-way, not the sound of one hand clapping, but a two-way negotiative effort" (Kramsch 1986, 368), there is often all too little communication between theorists and practitioners of foreign language teaching. Van Lier notes, "current theoretical L2 [second-language] work does not emphasize pedagogical links either as sources of data or as targets for application" (1991, 29). Explanations for this lack of dialogue are easy to find on the college and university level. The vast majority of foreign language instruction usually falls to one of three groups, none of which is primarily interested in research on language teaching. The first group is teaching assistants, whose responsibility is most often beginning and intermediate language teaching. In general, although they may be enthusiastic instructors, teaching assistants lack experience, often have little guidance or training in teaching methods, and must give priority to the courses they themselves are taking, which are usually in literature and not linguistics or pedagogy. The second group consists of faculty members who have degrees in literature or theoretical linguistics, and who are frequently either junior or adjunct faculty. In general, tenure-track instructors are hired for their past or potential publications in their areas of specialization, and tenure and promotion depend on the number of articles they publish, not on the quality of their teaching (Baltra 1992, 581). Furthermore, like teaching assistants, many have had little or no training in language teaching, since teacher training is seen, patronizingly, as being for teachers of the "lower levels"—in other words, the elementary or secondary school levels. As a result, the average Ph.D. is poorly trained for coping with beginning and intermediate language learners who are not always primarily interested in literature or theoretical linguists. The third group consists of native speakers, either tenure-track or adjunct faculty, who may or may not possess advanced degrees, but who are often not specifically trained in foreign language teaching. Members of all three groups, then, may lack the incentive and training for teaching beginning and intermediate language courses.

On the elementary, middle, and secondary school levels as well, there is too little time or administrative support for many teachers to carry out research in foreign language pedagogy. As a result, while these teachers may be versed in technique, pedagogical practices, and methodologies, the demands of preparing for, teaching, and grading papers from five or six daily classes with split ability levels, they often do not have time to carry out in-depth study of specific areas of language teaching. In addition, school administrators often encourage their teachers neither to participate in national conferences nor to conduct or publish theoretical or classroom-based research.

From the point of view of the linguist, until very recently work in the area of applied linguistics was not considered to be "real" research and only publications in theoretical linguistics counted for tenure and promotion. As Swaffar points out, "Before the present decade it was considered futile to hire applied linguists. Tradition had it that they were the least 'promotable' faculty members" (1989, 37). Although this is changing, it is still true in most colleges and universities that, as those specializing in linguistics move beyond their initial assignments as junior faculty members, they move further and further away from basic language instruction. As a result, they sometimes produce fascinating theories of language acquisition, but fail to test them on statistically valid groups of students, and at times they fail to address the practical issue of how their research can be utilized in the foreign language classroom. Furthermore, most publishing outlets still focus on technical aspects of theoretical linguistics, which are difficult for non-specialists to understand. The lack of communication between the linguist and the language teacher, then, is not one-sided and stems from a variety of causes. The effect of this division, however, is clear: Many language teachers do not receive sufficient training and too often have little incentive to pursue new developments in language teaching theory, and, as a result, fail to research or to try new approaches in their classes. At the same time, many theoreticians have lost touch with what is going on in the classroom and their work has failed to take into account the constraints that language teachers face or to provide techniques for implementing new approaches in the classroom. In light of this lack of communication, educators have increasingly pointed out the urgent need for more empirical, classroom-centered research (Nunan 1991, 180; Kramsch 1987, 29; van Lier 1991, 29).

When the three of us met in 1990 to plan the conference "Bridging Theory and Practice in the Foreign Language Classroom," our goal was to bring together representatives of both areas—language teaching and research—and through presentations and discussions create a dialogue that would encourage and facilitate exchanges of ideas and concerns. Furthermore, by publishing the proceedings of the conference, we wanted to provide an outlet in which language teachers could voice their concerns and demonstrate their classroom research in a scholarly way, thus validating their work both for themselves and for their administrations. The result, we hope, will be teachers who are more interested in the most current and effective classroom-proven techniques, theoreticians who are more responsive to the needs of the classroom, and, most importantly, a more fruitful and interesting classroom experience for students.

The articles in this volume provide some of the thoughts presented during the conference from both groups: theoreticians and classroom teachers. They unite, we believe, the best of both.

The volume begins with an important question for all curriculum developers—how to facilitate the transition from language to upper-division literature and culture courses. Schultz's article discusses some of the issues surrounding the language-to-literature transition and presents a sample lesson illustrating how literature can be used in language courses not only to enhance language learning and to encourage critical thinking, but also to provide students with tools for analyzing texts.

The next five articles focus on the learner and the learning process. Black proposes using "think-aloud" self-reporting as a means to give students insights about themselves as learners and to make them more aware of the strategies they use. She also suggests ways students can work together to develop new learning strategies. Call investigates the relationship between success in learning languages and specific personality traits. She reports the findings of a study which indicates that students who are classified as having an "intuitive" (N) orientation on Myers-Briggs Type Indicator have greater success in developing listening comprehension than students who are classified as "sensing" (S). Call's study also suggests that this difference can be explained by the more efficient strategies employed by individuals of the "N" type. The implications for the classroom are that strategy training may help students—especially "S" students—develop a higher level of listening comprehension. Kinginger examines repair strategies used by second-language learners. She finds that students prefer cope-switching into English instead of negotiating meaning in the target language. Such research has widespread implications for cooperative learning methods. Doukanari uses videotaped student role playing to demonstrate that the analysis of student discourse is valuable not only as an important tool for research, teaching, and evaluation, but also as a means to increase student strategic awareness. Waldspurger reviews recent literature that stresses the importance of the right hemisphere of the brain in early stages of second-language learning. In light of these studies, she argues for classroom activities that include not only structured drills and grammar instruction—activities that stimulate the left brain—but also activities such as music, dance, and role-playing, which involve the brain's right hemisphere.

Kassen and Gagnon look at ways to improve and respond to student writing. Based on a study of French teachers at various levels in her own university, Kassen suggests that our responses to student writing may be too grammatically oriented. While it is natural for language teachers to concern themselves with the product of students' compositions (correcting is, after all, one of the central components of the teaching profession), Kassen focuses on the interplay of the expression of meaning with other cognitive and linguistic factors and looks at think-aloud protocols in the foreign language classroom (see also Black, this volume). Furthermore, Kassen offers some concrete methods for reviewing and enhancing the process of evaluating students' written work. Gagnon proposes the publication of student texts as a motivational technique for encouraging student writing. He also provides a number of pre-writing activities that include both interactive and cooperative learning activities.

Several articles are of particular interest to teachers of less commonly taught languages. Fakhri explores the question of "which language" to teach in his paper on diglossia in Arabic. While Arabic is not a commonly taught language in American schools, it shares the problem of written versus oral form and regional koinés (dialects) with many other languages, such as Greek and Japanese. He argues that both a regional vernacular and the standard language (Modern Standard Arabic) must be taught in order for the learner to achieve true communicative competence. He includes practical suggestions for how to implement this approach. Takenoya grapples with the problem of students' inappropriate use of "address terms" in Japanese. She points out that the most popular textbooks for teaching Japanese in the United States fail to foster learner awareness of address terms and to provide adequate practice in applying knowledge of the rules of address to real-world situations. Kecskés and Papp, in a study of Hungarian students ages 14–16 who are learning English, French, or Russian as a foreign language (FL), examine the effect of FL knowledge on mother tongue development and use. Their findings suggest that FL learning significantly enhances L1 (first-language) written language development in certain cases.

Malone and Rasi discuss student oral proficiency. They have collaborated on the development and field testing of a simulated oral proficiency exam in Japanese based on the American Council on the Teaching of Foreign Languages

(ACTFL) guidelines. Of particular interest is the fact that it is able to evaluate even elementary-level Japanese learners. The authors also describe field tests that demonstrate the test's accuracy in placing those tested.

Shelly examines eight of the most popular first-year college French textbooks and finds that, in many cases, they fragment language into separate, arbitrarily defined components. She argues that since proficiency in a second language involves the constant interaction of the various components of language, more attention should be given to the interdependency of these elements and that textbook authors should reexamine the traditional chapter organization into separate sections labeled "vocabulary," "grammar," "pronunciation," and so on.

In the last article, Galloway suggests new directions for language-learning research that draw on chaos theory. She points out that traditional methods of research in foreign language-learning, such as controlled experiments and correlational studies, may actually be counterproductive, limiting rather than advancing our understanding of the learner and the learning process. This is because in their attempts to define, predict, isolate, manipulate, and control, traditional methods fail to take into account the complex nature of the individual learner and the learning process and how they may change. Galloway further argues that in order to gain a true understanding of the learner, educators should use insights from chaos theory and begin by observing and describing individual language learners engaged in the learning process over time. Finally, Galloway maintains that without such an understanding of the learner, no meaningful theory of language learning or foreign language education is possible.

These articles cover all levels, from elementary school to large universities, from commonly-taught languages such as Spanish, English, French, and German to less frequently taught languages such as Greek, Arabic, Hungarian, and Japanese. We encourage readers not to let the fact that they do not themselves study the languages in question keep them from reading the papers, since the points addressed are common to the teaching of most languages.

Several of these articles suggest that we can enhance language acquisition by making students aware of the importance of learning strategies, and by giving them training in their use. They also suggest that to be effective, teachers in foreign language classrooms must keep up to date with new methodologies, strategies, and techniques. As Chastain points out:

> Staying abreast of emerging ideas stimulates us and encourages us to try new approaches in our classes. Without new ideas we tend to become listless and unenthusiastic, and we become less and less receptive to experimentation and change. Long-held traditions and long-practiced techniques often move subconsciously and imperceptibly from subjective opinion to unchallenged assumptions. As one writer has said, the greatest obstacle to change is not ignorance but the illusion of knowledge (1986, 173).

We also hope that theoreticians, by seeing the results of actual classroom research, will be inspired to renew their work in the real classroom, taking into consideration its many constraints, which often include large numbers of students and numerous classes to teach, learner attitudes, inadequate or outdated teacher training and updating, and lack of institutional support. The intended audience for this book includes, then, language instructors, teacher trainers, curriculum designers, and teachers-in-training, as well as theoretical and applied linguists. This volume may also prove useful as a reference text in undergraduate or graduate teacher-training programs.

The need to prepare our students to live, work, and interact successfully in a world community that is now a reality, and no longer just a buzzword, must clearly be the priority of our profession. Teaching students to communicate is the instructional goal we have set for ourselves, but in order to succeed in this task, clear communication among those involved in language teaching and research must also be a primary goal. This conference and the publication of the articles that came out of it are intended to be a first step in that direction.

In closing, we would like to thank David Roswell, dean of the College of Arts and Sciences, and the members of the

Modern Languages and Literatures Department, along with the Classics Department at Loyola College in Maryland for their participation, support, and encouragement. We would also like to thank Donavan Arizmendi and Marion Wielgosz for their invaluable help in preparing the manuscript. The Maryland Foreign Language Association cosponsored the conference at which these articles were given.

Margaret Austin Haggstrom
Leslie Zarker Morgan
Joseph A. Wieczorek

NOTE

In all transcriptions of phonetic values, IPA practices are followed. For a listing of phonetic values, consult any standard linguistics text or references, such as David Crystal, *Cambridge Encyclopedia of Language* (Cambridge: Cambridge University Press, 1987), pp. 152–168.

The Foreign
Language
Classroom

Making the Transition from Language to Literature

Jean Marie Schultz

Abstract

One of the challenges in foreign language teaching is to prepare students to make a smooth transition from their lower-division language courses to their upper-division literature courses. Until recently, language instruction operated under the assumption that focusing on the acquisition of grammar and vocabulary, the fostering of speaking and reading skills, and, to a lesser extent, the development of writing skills should suffice to prepare students adequately for their upper division courses. The teaching of literature was seen as a separate endeavor; the encouragement of the higher-level critical thinking skills necessary for responding to texts at the upper division level was seen as beyond the scope of the language classroom. It is the position of this article, however, that it is never too early to introduce literature into the language classroom, and that, in fact, it is necessary to do so in order to bridge the gap between the adjacent fields of language and literature. This article proposes a multifaceted approach to incorporating literature in the language classroom, an approach that aims to encourage the development of critical thinking skills at the same time that it furthers the development of advanced writing skills (focusing on thesis statements and interpretation), grammar acquisition in context, close reading skills, and speaking skills. The article backs up theoretical discussion with a sample unit using Maupassant's short story "Le Horla" in intermediate French courses.

3

It is quite common within university language departments for the study of language and of literature to be viewed as two separate intellectual endeavors. Although mastery of a foreign language is seen as necessary to the study of literature *in the original,* the skills required for language learning are not themselves considered essential to the appreciation and interpretation of texts per se. Whereas the ability to read a work in the original language may be considered an asset to literary study, helping students develop a sensitivity to literature in general is seen as no more than cursory to language study. This view is bolstered by the approaches to literature taken by most English, comparative literature, and modern language departments, which frequently include in some form and to some degree the study of works in translation. Classical language departments tend in the opposite direction; but often, the study of Classical texts is seen as translation work and as further study of grammar, and not necessarily as interpretation.

These views of language and literature study as only tangentially related activities are at the heart of one of the challenges language departments have long confronted: how to help students make a smooth transition from lower-division language classes to upper-division literature classes. Often students who have done well in their language classes seem to have difficulty in literature courses, where their linguistic mastery is assumed to be adequate for literary analysis of texts. Barnett summarizes the long-standing dichotomy between language and literature teaching by noting that professors of literature believe "that their students should arrive in class with language proficiency as standard equipment—with proficiency defined as fluent, accurate analytical writing" (1991, 8). Although the French literature faculty at my own university hold high expectations of their students arriving from the second-year language courses, they do not expect students to produce near-native prose in their analytical essays, as Barnett implies. They do expect students' grammar to be in place, which means that there should be only infrequent patterns of error in the use of major linguistic structures.[1] A certain degree of orientation is expected in terms of students' abilities to respond to literary texts as texts in both discussion and writing. In addition, students are expected to have a sense of what constitutes an analytical essay. In other words, the foundations for advanced study should be laid in the intermediate-level language course sequence.

I have found such goals are entirely attainable at the intermediate level, provided that students receive the appropriate training; and this means, as Rice proposes, introducing work on literature early in the intermediate course. But this also means that the training students receive cannot be restricted to what Rice calls "the often endless series of questions about who did what, where, when, and, maybe, how" that characterize most elementary and intermediate foreign language readers (1991, 13).

Ironically, among the greatest impediments to closing the gap between the study of language and literature, which language-program faculty are called on more often than literature faculty to address, is the orientation of language faculty themselves. The problem has to do with the trend to view language acquisition as hierarchical and following a parallel developmental pattern in the areas of listening, reading, speaking, and writing, and the extension of this hierarchy to literature, thereby predicating the ability to appreciate and respond analytically to a literary text on sophisticated linguistic ability in the students.[2] Barnett's efforts to find a solution to the historic dichotomy between literature and language teaching adhere to this hierarchy. She proposes defining "three levels that normally exist in a language and literature department or program: first, the elementary level, where students focus on learning vocabulary, pronunciation, grammar, and the like—the language basics; second, a transitional level, where the emphasis moves from language to literature and culture, *usually in third-year college courses* [emphasis mine]; third, the advanced level, where students concentrate on literary and cultural texts and history" (1991, 10). Ironically, this emphasis on the separation of language and literature study only serves to widen the gap that already exists between the two fields because it maintains the traditional distinction between them. Adherence to the separation of the two areas suggests first of all that language learning involves primarily the mastery of discrete grammar points, and secondly, that only literature and culture are the "real" fields of study. Significantly,

Barnett's proposal does not address the question of what to do in the troublesome second year of language study. In addition, it holds problematic practical implications for advanced study. Delaying until the third year the transitional phase in which language and literature are "reconciled" not only makes it virtually impossible for students who begin their study of language as incoming freshmen to complete a French major, but it also has serious and negative ramifications for students who might like to pursue graduate work.

Put another way, adherence to fixed lines of demarcation between language and literature study makes advanced work on literature at the undergraduate level accessible to fewer and fewer students: seniors mostly, if they have begun their studies as freshmen, or other students who have had the good fortune to come from very strong high school programs or from francophone families. The added irony is that, as suggested in this essay's opening paragraph, advanced linguistic mastery is not necessarily synonymous with the ability to appreciate literature, to analyze it, or to write about it persuasively. If intermediate students can come to terms with a text—and studies show that they can—then they can deal with it *as literature*. According to Allen, Bernhardt, Berry, and Demel,

> Even the beginning learners were able to cope with 250–300–word authentic texts without experiencing debilitating frustration. This finding implies that materials developers may productively include lengthier texts in their books. Lengthier texts may well be more cohesive and, hence, more interesting, for learners. These data may help to dispel the "shorter-easier" myth. (1988, 170)

If intermediate students can read authentic literary texts in the target language, then the question becomes how to present such texts so that students receive the training necessary on both the linguistic and literary levels to help smooth the transition from lower- to upper-division work. How can literary sensitivity be enhanced, going beyond the simple plot summary level that Rice, among others, finds inadequate for advanced literary studies?[3]

To define the problem more narrowly, the question becomes: How can we enable students who may have only very little, if any, experience with literature, let alone in a foreign language, to move from their initial subjective reactions to the objective analysis characteristic of advanced undergraduate literature classes, and to express their ideas both orally and in writing? In an attempt to answer these questions, I will focus on one two-week unit done in The University of California at Berkeley's French 3 program (the first semester of the second year) that integrates reading, writing, speaking, and grammar while consciously striving to prepare students for the kinds of work they will encounter at more advanced levels of study.[4]

The unit centers on Guy de Maupassant's story, "Le Horla," about a man who has committed himself to an asylum after experiencing a number of uncanny events that he attributes to the existence of an invisible, supernatural, vampire-like being. The story is introduced in the sixth week of the semester after students have read one chapter from Goscinny's *Le Petit Nicolas*, Ionesco's "Premier conte pour enfants de moins de trois ans," Aymé's "Oscar et Erick," and Pagnol's *Fanny*. In terms of grammar, students have reviewed all verb tenses in the indicative mode by using a reference grammar with exercises. They have been presented composition lessons on semantic mapping (Schultz 1991a), outlining, thesis statements, paragraphing, and introductions (Schultz 1991b). They have been introduced to a collaborative, process-oriented approach to writing through response-group work.[5] They have been initiated into the fundamentals of textual discussion through weekly lessons focusing on pertinent vocabulary and literary concepts. During these lessons students are exposed to various basic concepts of literary analysis, generally through the use of worksheets designed to accompany the texts under study. Questions, for example, encourage students to consider the differences between the author and narrator or types of narrators (first or third person.) In order to sensitize them to an author's style, students are asked to look at the quantity and types of adjectives or verbs used in a short passage. Class discussions focus on such additional aspects of style as humor and tone; the difference between *caractère* and *personnage* is also explained.

As an initial pre-reading exercise before beginning "Le Horla," students are asked to write in French in their personal journals about an uncanny experience that either they or someone they know has had. The next day in class, students share their journal entries with two other students in group work. After the class reconvenes, each group chooses the most interesting account to be presented to the whole class (Riley 1989, 23–24).

This prereading exercise serves a number of important pedagogical functions. First, it gives students practice in writing a narrative on a personal topic, an exercise which in terms of types of required cognitive skills and psychological investment, is easier to produce than objective analytical writing (Flower 1988, 4; Schultz 1991a, 981–82; Murphy and Ruth 1988, 78–82). This preliminary writing assignment, which articulates with the basic subject of the text, acts as a kind of "advanced organizer," laying the foundation for the students' objective literary essay at the end of the unit (Fulwiler 1980; Kirby and Liner 1981; Moffett 1981, 3–26). Second, the sharing of individual accounts in small groups gives students practice in verbal skills development in a relatively informal situation—among a few peers—that Krashen has convincingly shown enhances students' language acquisition and oral performance (Krashen 1982). Once students receive affirmation in the small group, their bolstered self–esteem helps counteract any nervousness they might feel about sharing their stories with the entire group. Third, the topic of the journal entry serves a crucial function for the reading itself in terms of contextualization. As numerous studies in reading research have shown, prior familiarity with a topic is one of the major determinants for the level of reading comprehension students are able to achieve. The more students know about a topic, the better and more easily they will understand a reading selection (J. Phillips 1984, 287; Swaffar 1988; Westhoff 1991, 30). Exploring with students the possibility of the supernatural before reading Maupassant's story thus enhances their sensitivity to the issues of credibility raised in "Le Horla."

After the journal exercise, students are assigned to read "Le Horla" as homework. Over the six years this text has been in use in the intermediate program, students' initial comprehension of the general narrative situation has been found to be very high. Class discussion focuses therefore on close reading techniques, that fuse both grammar and analytical skills, mediating between "bottom-up" and "top-down" reading strategies. Thus instructors routinely concentrate on the introductions to short stories, since for this genre these passages often establish the issues that the text will attempt to resolve. "Le Horla" begins as follows:

> Le Dr. Marrande, le plus illustre et le plus éminent des aliénistes, avait prié trois de ses confrères et quatre savants, s'occupant de sciences naturelles, de venir passer une heure chez lui, dans la maison de santé qu'il dirigeait, pour leur montrer un de ses malades.
>
> Aussitôt que ses amis furent réunis, il leur dit:
>
> 'Je vais vous soumettre le cas le plus bizarre et le plus inquiétant que j'aie jamais rencontré. D'ailleurs je n'ai rien à vous dire de mon client. Il parlera lui–même.'
>
> [Doctor Marrande, the most illustrious and eminent of alienists, had called together three of his colleagues and four scholars of the natural sciences, to spend an hour with him at the clinic he was directing in order to show them one of his patients.
>
> As soon as his friends had convened, he told them:
>
> 'I am going to submit to you the most bizarre and troubling case that I have ever encountered. However, I have nothing to tell you about my client. He will speak for himself.] (from *Panaché littéraire*, edited by Cauvin and Baker, 1990, 190)

In terms of grammar, the focus in class is on the most obvious repeating structure in this passage, the superlative (*le plus illustre et le plus éminent des, le cas le plus bizarre* [the most illustrious and most eminent, the most bizarre case]). Instructors review the formation of the superlative, concentrating on placement and agreement of adjectives, the use of *de* in the structure, and the frequent use of the subjunctive (*le plus inquiétant que j'aie jamais rencontré* [the most troubling that I have ever encountered]).

The grammar lesson quickly expands to include issues of literary analysis. Comments are solicited from students on the effects of the superlatives in terms of establishing Doctor Marrande's credibility, which will have important bearing on how the reader will interpret the narrative situation. How does the use of the superlative influence our expectations of the primary first-person narrator, the patient himself? Does the superlative have an effect on the readers' receptivity to the events? These questions require interpretation, and as such, they help show students the importance of an awareness of language as an interpretive tool.

In the course of this beginning discussion students are aware early on that they are dealing with two first-person narrators (Doctor Marrande and the patient), who have very different concerns and personalities. Not so obvious, however, is the existence of a third narrator, an impersonal one who, nevertheless, offers his own interpretation of events. His existence can be brought out easily enough through examination of the passage cited above. Expressing a distinct admiration for Dr. Marrande, the third-person narrator presents him as the most preeminent and famous of psychologists. This narrator, however, also has a definite opinion about the patient, which can be noted by comparing the terms used to describe him. Whereas Doctor Marrande uses the neutral *client* to designate the patient, indicating his inability to interpret for certain the patient's mental state, the third-person narrator uses the term *malade*, as if he has already decided that the patient is insane.

Use of the close reading technique as demonstrated in the above passage thus fulfills a number of functions. It enhances students' critical reading ability by showing them how to focus on significant detail. It provides for review of grammatical points in an interesting way, and one that emphasizes its relevance for interpretation. In addition, it helps students develop the analytical skills they will need in their future study.

The close reading exercise is practiced throughout the work on the text in the form of directed group discussion exercises. Students are given a set of questions pertaining to a particularly significant passage which has been divided into short sections. Some of the questions are fairly straightforward and designed to test reading comprehension. These function also to encourage students to speak more, since the answers are easy to find. Most of the questions, however, are of a more probing and interpretive nature (see appendix). Students are put into small groups of three or four and told to discuss the questions. They are also asked to synthesize their findings, going beyond a simple summary of the passage to emphasize particularly the significance they attribute to it, and to present their findings to the rest of the class at the end of the designated time (fifteen minutes). The small group discussion exercises thus further encourage students to read carefully, to interpret passages, and to express their ideas orally. The exercise is also economical in terms of class time, allowing an instructor to cover a relatively large portion of a text in less time than general discussion would take.

Once students have come to a solid preliminary understanding of "Le Horla," instructors begin introducing them to larger issues of literary discussion. Since Maupassant's text is an example of the fantastic, instructors give students a rudimentary definition of this genre. According to Todorov's classic definition, the fantastic text presents readers with an interpretive dilemma. They must either believe the narrator's account of uncanny events and therefore admit the existence of supernatural phenomena, or they must attribute the account to some kind of hallucination, thereby putting into question the narrator's mental state (Todorov 1970, 29). After presenting this definition, instructors then ask students to reevaluate Maupassant's text according to these polarized terms.

The ensuing discussion of the narrator's mental stability or the possible real existence of an *horla* lends itself well to a debate format. The classroom can be divided in half and students asked to sift through the text looking for evidence supporting the interpretation they have chosen to defend. Time permitting, students may also be asked to switch sides and play devil's advocate. Resulting classroom debates are generally quite lively, but more importantly they train students in an important aspect of critical thinking: taking the opposing view into account. Since Maupassant's short story is an example of the fantastic, it illustrates well the necessity of considering the opposition. Thus not only does this exercise give students additional practice in speaking, but it also lays the groundwork for the composition lesson for this unit.

Two writing lessons accompany "Le Horla," one on thesis statements and one on argumentation. In the thesis statement lesson, which is borrowed from a rhetorical approach to the teaching of argumentative writing, instructors present a formula designed specifically to take opposing viewpoints into account. The formula, known as the "XYZ" thesis statement, takes shape as follows: "Although X, nevertheless Y, because Z." Here the X part of the statement presents the opposition; the Y portion, the thesis of the paper; Z presents the supporting evidence for the thesis. An example of the "XYZ" statement might be, "Although the manner in which the narrator relates his story makes him seem sane, nevertheless the details he chooses to narrate would indicate the contrary, because they are often contradictory." The "XYZ" formula lends itself very well to execution in French, yielding "Bien que X, néanmoins Y, parce que Z."[6] Because of the *bien que/quoique* type expression used in the formula, this composition lesson is combined with a review of the subjunctive using the course's grammar reference book.[7]

The "XYZ" thesis statement can also be used to set up the argumentative organization of the paper. After the introduction, the writer presents the opposition in the first part of the paper. In the next section, the writer presents his or her interpretation, countering the opposition with supporting evidence from the text. In the conclusion, the writer then reconciles the two sides, thereby formulating a dynamic interpretation of the work. This organizational format lends itself particularly well to teaching writing in French, since it is derivative of the *thèse, antithèse, synthèse* or thesis, antithesis, synthesis model that all French-educated students learn. Pointing this out makes the "XYZ" formula more interesting to students, since they are learning to write and construct an argument "as the French do," and it enhances their cultural awareness.

Because this form of argumentation is new to most American students, the presentation is backed up with two model essays, one written by the staff and one written by a student. Models play an important role in the teaching of writing, since much of the writing process is largely imitative in nature (Hillocks 1987, 74). Not only do models illustrate the composition lessons being worked on, but they also introduce students to vocabulary essential for expressing their ideas, as well as to other possible interpretations designed to stimulate further their own thinking. Professional models are useful because they can be written specifically to illustrate the lesson presented. In addition, they provide students well-written examples of the type of work that will eventually be expected of them as they continue on to advanced literature and culture courses. Anonymous student samples play an equally important role, since they illustrate the different ways other student peers have handled assignments, with varying degrees of success, thereby sensitizing students to possible difficulties they, too, may be experiencing in their own writing.

Sample essays are utilized according to two different formats in class. Particularly at the beginning of the semester when students' analytical skills are less developed, instructors lead the discussion in class, asking students to focus on thesis statements, paragraphing, statement logic, transitions, and the like. Later in the course, students analyze models as homework and in class meet in small groups to concentrate on individual paragraphs. At the end of the allotted small group discussion time, students present their critiques to the whole class, always situating their particular paragraph within the model essay as a whole.

This analysis of sample essays in class helps students learn to recognize good and bad writing, and to think of alternatives that would improve the writing. The development of this analytical ability is crucial to the continued improvement of students' writing skills. Although research shows that such ability does not significantly improve the first draft of a student's paper, it does play an essential role in the revision process (Hillocks 1987, 73; see also Chastain 1990). As students become better writers, they are able to consider their own work more objectively, recognizing and correcting flaws after having already practiced doing so on other writers' essays.

The final phase of this unit is the writing of the papers themselves. Students are assigned essay questions that typify those they may encounter in their advanced literature courses, that is, analytical interpretive questions.[8] For "Le Horla" they are given the following essay questions:

1. Dans l'histoire, le narrateur veut convaincre les collègues du Dr. Marrande de l'existence du Horla. Est-ce que son histoire est convaincante ou est-ce que le narrateur est fou? Quelles stratégies emploie-t-il pour persuader ses auditeurs qu'un être invisible existe? Est-ce que sa présentation est logique?

2. Analysez le rapport entre le Horla et le narrateur. Dans votre composition, décidez d'abord si le Horla existe ou pas. S'il existe, pourquoi a-t-il choisi le narrateur comme victime? Est-ce que le narrateur a des traits de caractère qui attirent le Horla? Pourquoi le narrateur ne peut-il pas le faire partir? Si le Horla n'existe pas, pourquoi le narrateur l'a-t-il inventé? Quels besoins psychologiques ou autres le Horla satisfait-il? Qu'est-ce que le Horla représente pour le narrateur?

3. Dans "Le Horla" les objets (fleurs, carafes, livres) jouent un rôle important. Dans votre composition analysez le rôle des objets. Pourquoi le narrateur les mentionne-t-il souvent? Dans quelle mesure contribuent-ils à la vraisemblance de la narration?

4. Le poète Paul Eluard termine l'un de ses poèmes par ces mots:

    > Entre les murs l'ombre est entière
    > Et je descends dans mon miroir
    > Comme un mort dans sa tombe ouverte.

    A la lumière de ce poème, étudiez l'apparition du Horla dans l'histoire de Maupassant.

[1. In the story, the narrator wants to convince Doctor Marrande's colleagues of the Horla's existence. Is the story convincing or is the narrator crazy? What strategies does he use to persuade his listeners that an invisible being exists? Is his presentation logical?

2. Analyze the relationship between the Horla and the narrator. In your composition, decide first if the Horla exists or not. If it exists, why does it choose the narrator as its victim? Does the narrator have character traits that attract the Horla? Why can't the narrator make it leave? If the Horla doesn't exist, why did the narrator invent it? What psychological needs does the Horla fulfill? What does the Horla represent for the narrator?

3. In "The Horla" objects (flowers, carafes, books) play an important role. In your composition analyze the role of objects. Why does the narrator mention them so often? To what extent do they contribute to the verisimilitude of the narration?

4. The poet Paul Eluard ends one of his poems with these words:

    > Between the walls the shadow is complete
    > And I descend into my mirror
    > Like a dead person into the open tomb

    In light of this poem, study the apparition of the Horla in Maupassant's story.]

For the writing of their papers, students engage in a process-approach format (Gaudiani 1981; Barnett 1989), which has been shown to produce dramatic positive results in the improvement of writing. Students are asked to bring to class two copies of the rough drafts of their papers, which they then exchange with two other students. Their homework for that evening is to analyze their classmates' compositions as their instructors might, focusing on the content, organization, and style (are sentences too long? too short? is there enough variety?), and to comment on the papers, being particularly careful to offer suggestions for improvement. The next day in class, students work in their groups, going over each others' papers. They then take home their commented copies and rewrite their papers according to the suggestions they feel are appropriate. Students turn in all copies with their final drafts so that instructors can see what changes were made during the revision process.

To sum up, then, the unit on "Le Horla" typifies an approach designed both to enhance language acquisition in the areas of reading, writing, and speaking, encouraging the mastery of grammar in the process, and also to provide students with practice in analytical interpretive thinking in French. The unit begins with a prereading/prewriting exercise through use of the journals that also encourages speaking ability. Classroom discussion is designed to enhance close reading and detailed analytical skills, and through the use of group discussion exercises, to further speaking ability. The debate format further develops speaking ability and critical thinking skills, as it prepares for actual composition lessons on thesis statements and argumentation. Grammar review is integrated both into specific writing lessons and into close reading exercises. The study of writing is backed up with the use of models. And finally, writing and speaking skills are bolstered through use of the process approach to composition that the program takes.

The unit on "Le Horla" illustrates therefore how literary works can be integrated into an intermediate program not only to facilitate language acquisition but also simultaneously to prepare students for more advanced work in the foreign language and literature department.

Appendix

Group discussion exercise for "Le Horla," paragraphs 17–30
Group I: paragraphs 17–19

- Selon le narrateur, d'où vient "l'influence fiévreuse"?
- Qu'est-ce que c'est qu'une "influence fiévreuse"?
- Est-ce que le narrateur veut quitter sa maison ou pas?
- Qu'est-ce qui le pousse à partir? Qu'est-ce qui le retient?
- Quelle est l'importance de cette hésitation?
- Quel est l'événement qui le décide à rester?
- Est-ce important qu'il appelle ses observations "un petit fait"?
- Décrivez la nuit que passe le narrateur.

- Quelles conclusions tire-t-il de la disparition de l'eau? Est-ce qu'elles sont logiques?

Group II: paragraphs 20–22

- Décrivez le test du narrateur.
- Que fait-il pour être certain des résultats?
- Est-ce un test valide?
- Pourquoi est-ce que "on" et "qui" sont en italiques?
- Est-il important que le pronon sujet passe de "on" à "qui"? Pourquoi?
- Quelle est la première conclusion du narrateur quand l'eau continue à disparaître après toutes ses tests?
- Que fait-il pour "prouver" que ce n'est pas lui qui a bu l'eau?

Group III: paragraphs 23–25

- Qu'est-ce qui disparaît?
- Quelles substances est-ce que le Horla préfère? Est-ce un indice quant à sa nature?
- Pourquoi le narrateur soupçonne-t-il que c'est toujours lui qui boit, même si ce sont des choses qu'il déteste?
- Quel est le fil de son raisonnement?
- Quelle est l'importance de ce raisonnement par rapport à la stabilité mentale du narrateur?

Group IV: paragraphs 26–29

- Que fait le narrateur pour être sûr que ce n'est pas lui qui boit les liquides?
- Dans quel état trouve-t-il les choses le lendemain matin?
- Est-ce que le narrateur aurait pu boire les liquides?
- Est-ce que quelqu'un aurait pu entrer pendant la nuit?
- Comment expliquez-vous le fait que les liquides ont disparu?

Group V: paragraph 30

- Pourquoi le narrateur choisit-il ce moment pour s'adresser à ses auditeurs?

- Selon le narrateur qu'est-ce que ses auditeurs pensent de lui?

- Imaginez l'effet sur ses auditeurs quand le narrateur anticipe leurs réactions à son récit et les formule avant qu'ils ne puissent le faire eux-mêmes. En quoi cette stratégie constitue-t-elle une manipulation de l'auditoire? Comment?

- Quelles émotions le narrateur décrit-il?

- Pourquoi le narrateur dit-il qu'il "aurait dû" décrire ces émotions? Quel est l'effet du passé du conditionnel du verbe *devoir*?

- Y a-t-il une contradiction entre ce qu'il prétend ne pas décrire et ce qu'il décrit en réalité?

- Est-ce important?

- Pourquoi met-il fin à sa discussion?

NOTES

1. Patterns of grammatical errors—that is, constant, systematic problems in major structures such as the subjunctive, conditional mode, or past tenses—are more troublesome than sporadic mistakes in less commonly used structures, and are more likely to indicate problematic linguistic mastery. For more detailed discussion of errors, see Chaudron (1988); also Wieczorek (1991a, 499–501) for discussion of error types.

2. The view of language skills acquisition as developing hierarchically and in parallel is supported by certain interpretations of the American Council on the Teaching of Foreign Languages (ACTFL) proficiency guidelines. This view is, however, highly controversial.

3. My intent in this paper is not to suggest that the only natural outcome of language study is literature. It is true, however, that most college and university language programs do have strong literature components. Often, continuing in language therefore means studying literature or advanced culture. Although the University of California at Berkeley's French department has a civilization and a graduate linguistic track, the department defines itself as primarily a literature

department. This being the case, not only at Berkeley, but at most institutions, what I propose is an approach that will not only help students master the language, but will also provide them training in the types of critical thinking skills necessary for success in foreign language literature and advanced culture classes.

4. The intermediate program (French 3 and 4) meets five days per week for fifty minutes each class period. During a given week, approximately one-and-a-half class sessions are devoted to systematic grammar review using a reference grammar. The remaining three-and-a-half sessions concentrate on a variety of interactive activities, including the study and discussion of readings such as those described in this article, small group discussions and projects, oral reports on current events, and response-group text-editing activities. Students entering the program have either completed a first-year college program or its high school equivalent. (Berkeley's first-year program uses the textbook *Découverte et Création*. The course also meets five days per week). Most students entering French 3 speak, read, and write at an intermediate-low level as defined by the ACTFL guidelines.

5. Response-group work, first developed by the National Writing Project, involves the responding to and editing of rough drafts by a group of three to five peers. Claire Gaudiani has written on use of the technique in foreign language writing courses (1981), as have Omaggio (1986) and Barnett (1989). For a detailed description of the implementation of response-group work in Berkeley's intermediate program, see Schultz (1991b).

6. In order to produce optimal results, one problematic aspect of the formula needs to be addressed. As the sample "XYZ" thesis illustrates, the statement can produce a very clumsy thesis sentence. For this reason, students are advised to use the formula as a test for the arguability of the thesis. Although the "XY" portion can potentially produce a viable and elegant thesis, the "Z" adds too much. Instructors suggest therefore that students save the "Z" for the discussion part of their paper. Thus students should try to put their theses into this format as a test, but they should consider presenting them differently in their papers.

7. Two types of grammar review are thus carried out in the program: one contextual and one systematic. The first type relies on the readings for the structures to be targeted, and thus grammar review is contextualized. The second is systematic in that it relies on the grammar book. For the systematic review, an effort is made to position the grammar chapters with regard to the readings or composition lessons so that study is made more relevant.

8. For the importance of presenting such analytical questions early in language study, see Schultz (1991b).

The "Think-Aloud" Procedure as a Diagnostic and Learning Tool for Second-Language Learners

Janis H. Black

Abstract

This study of six L2 learners' concurrent and retrospective think-aloud reports, gathered as they completed a cloze passage, illustrates the usefulness of the procedure for researchers investigating learning and reception strategies. It further suggests that thinking-aloud can have specific practical benefits for L2 teachers since it provides detailed information about learners that can form the basis for remedial courses of action. Finally, it appears that thinking-aloud can assist L2 students to gain insights about themselves as learners, allowing them to control, monitor, and refine the strategies they apply to language learning tasks.

Introduction

Recent research on strategy use by second-language (henceforth L2) learners has relied heavily on process-oriented descriptions of what L2 learners actually do when completing a task. The idea for this paper arose out of a study completed by the author that investigated the learning and reception strategies used by three successful and three less successful female first-year university students of French who were asked to *think aloud* as they completed a cloze passage, in which the task is to supply words missing from the text. The cloze procedure was chosen since it combines the learner's needs to use cognitive learning strategies[1] as well as reception strategies in solving the problems inherent to the task. (The passage used is reproduced in Appendix A.)

In completing a cloze passage, an L2 learner needs to use certain key learning strategies: making inferences, monitoring, evaluating, repeating, and looking for patterns in the language. These strategies have already been identified in earlier research (Rubin 1975, 1981; Stern 1975; Bialystok and Frohlich 1977; Naiman et al. 1978; Bialystok 1979 and 1983) as being frequently used by L2 learners in problem-solving situations. The reception strategies brought into play in the cloze procedure are some of those vital to the process of reading. They help learners derive meaning from the message, and include contextual guessing, recognizing cognates, scanning for specific contextual information, skimming for the gist, and anticipating context. These key reception strategies, used by L2 learners to access meaning, have been documented by Rubin (1975, 1981), Stern (1975), Bialystok and Frohlich (1977), Bialystok (1979, 1983) and O'Malley et al. (1985).

Benefits of the Think-Aloud Procedure to the Researcher

The technique of asking learners to think aloud as they attempt to solve problems encountered in the L2 has been used extensively in recent L2 strategy research (Hosenfeld 1977 and 1979; Block 1986; Abraham and Vann 1987; Feldmann and Stemmer 1987; Manghubai 1987; Vann and Abraham 1990). It is seen to provide a unique opportunity to probe the inner workings of a learner's mind so as to gain insight into an L2 learner's mental activity when encountering problematic situations. On the other hand, it does have the potential disadvantage of intruding upon, and therefore distorting, the problem-solving process. Certain researchers (Nisbett and Wilson 1977; Seliger 1983) view such verbal data as subject to considerable reliability problems. Bearing in mind this possible limitation, it was decided, in the research study discussed here, to combine thinking aloud and retrospective self-reporting in the six audiotaped interviews conducted with subjects. Probing or clarifying questions were used during the think-aloud only where necessary to ensure reports that were as complete as possible. At the end of the session, subjects were asked to do an immediate retrospection on the strategies or thought processes that they felt to have been most useful and effective to them on this task. These special care considerations in collecting verbal report data were implemented to reflect the recommendations of Ericsson and Simon (1980) and Cohen (1987b).

The results of the study, fully reported in Black (1993), were obtained after a detailed analysis of the transcribed think-aloud data. Specific strategies were identified and categorized using a coding procedure based on schemes proposed by Rubin (1981, 1987), Manghubai (1987) and Abraham and Vann (1987). The strategy inventory presented in Appendix B includes an example of each type of strategy found and represents the list of behaviors so far identified as being used and useful on this task. It is therefore open-ended and subject to modification as more think-aloud sessions are analyzed. Strategies were then examined in terms of the effect of (i) frequency, (ii) quality, and (iii) clustering of strategy use on performance.

Findings substantiated the hypotheses of Manghubai (1987) and Vann and Abraham (1990) that, while frequency may provide some indication of a particular strategy's usefulness on this task, it is quality of strategy use that most clearly differentiates successful from less successful item solution. Quality of strategic behavior is defined as the coherence of the thought processes engaged in by a subject while attempting to deal with a problem-solving situation. The following extracts from three of the recorded think-aloud sessions suggest how quality of strategy use can affect performance outcomes, in this case as learners attempt to solve blank 8 (correct answer is *personne/rien*):

> ___ *n'arrivait vraiment à résoudre cette difficulté* . . . well
> obviously there's a subject that belongs in there, and I
> think it might be *on* because it's A...I...T . . . third person
> singular.

> *Ils commençaient à douter de leur perception et* . . . OK now
> I'm seeing *ne* here . . . *vraiment à résoudre cette diff* . . . OK
> now *ne vraiment* I don't know if that's an expression or not,
> 'cause I don't know why there's this *ne* and there's no *pas*
> here . . . *et* something *n'arrivait* . . . OK, A...I...T . . . so if it's
> a noun or a pronoun, it would have to be *il* because of the
> ending.

> They . . . were beginning to doubt their . . . their
> understanding, and . . . no . . . nothing? really happened,
> *rien* . . . yeah you can have . . . negatives as subjects. You
> don't need a *pas* there. Nothing happened, nothing really
> happened to solve this difficulty, or something, I don't
> know what *résoudre* means, or to . . . account for this
> difficulty, I don't know. Yeah, *rien* probably sounds
> . . . OK.

Factors affecting this quality included learners' overall L2
proficiency, the organization, focus and control of their
strategies, and the clarity and coherence of their thinking.

In addition, the use of strategies in clusters was found to
consistently enrich and improve performance on this task—a
finding that substantiates the conclusions of Wesche (1979),
Rubin (1987), Manghubai (1987) and Oxford (1989). However,
success in using strategy clusters again depended greatly on the
quality of the strategies chosen, and the way in which they were
used to complement and reinforce each other. Finally, results
suggested that the more difficult the cloze deletion, the more
complex the strategy cluster needed for its solution.

To sum up, therefore, the think-aloud procedure allows
the L2 researcher to examine strategic processes that would
otherwise remain hidden, to make conclusions about specific
learner behaviors on a particular task, and to question critical
assumptions about the ways in which L2 competence is built up.

Benefits of the Think-Aloud Procedure to the Teacher

In most cases, the researcher is also the teacher, who seeks new insights and new ideas about how to help learners improve performance on L2 tasks and situations. For the L2 teacher who needs information about the processes undertaken by different learners as they seek ways of solving their problems, the think-aloud procedure provides a detailed diagnosis of the types of problems encountered, and, above all, the fundamental differences of approach adopted by different learners. In the present study, for example, it was found that two of the three successful learners favored L2-based strategies (see Appendix B for the full strategy inventory and examples of all strategies):

A2/A3: reading the text in French;

B3: monitoring and testing the sound of a possible answer;

C4: inferring an answer on the basis that it "sounds right"; and

E3: rereading in French the text immediately surrounding a blank.

This approach, however, was not the only possible path to success: the third successful learner in the study used predominantly L1-based strategies:

A1: translating to L1;

B4: checking the meaning of a possible answer by translation to L1;

C1: filling a blank initially with an inferred L1 word and then translating it; and

E2: repeating an L1 translation of the text immediately surrounding a blank.

The conclusion to be drawn from these findings is that there is not necessarily one right way to approach a task; students may be successful at a task using very different strategies.

The think-aloud reports provided detailed evidence that there are similarities as well as differences among the less successful learners. Similarities included a lack of confidence in approaching the task, anxiety when problematic situations arose, insecurity when required to risk an answer, reluctance to trust in their L2 instincts—characteristics that echo the findings of Rubin (1975), Stern (1975) and Naiman et al. (1978). It was also found that less successful subjects' approach to the task was more fragmented and disjointed. When using strategies to negotiate meaning, their attention was too closely focused on each individual word or phrase, so that the surrounding context was not implicated and integrated, and thereby remained unavailable for corroborative use (see Hosenfeld 1977, 1984; Block 1986). Less successful subjects, while acknowledging the crucial importance of understanding the passage ("I've really got to understand what's there"), nonetheless tended to produce more incoherent, fractured L1 versions of the text which often failed to connect up and convey the overall meaning of the section being worked on:

> The reaction . . . was made waiting for the professor, OK, was listening to . . . the following, commentary following.
> (Text between blanks 13 and 14; see Appendix A)

Overall, the less successful subjects had much greater difficulty distinguishing important from less important information, and keeping track of the developing picture of the text. This therefore made it increasingly difficult for them to understand, by reading, translating, or inferring, the subsequent sentences. Ironically, despite this word-for-word approach to comprehension, they were frequently inattentive to the precise detail of the message and thus found it difficult to establish a clear context that might have made filling in the blanks easier. In this way, therefore, the think-aloud procedure gives the L2 teacher a detailed picture of the types of reaction that may be characteristic of lower proficiency learners in approaching a complex L2 task.

While all the subjects in the study used a wide variety of strategies, successful subjects were able to plan and control them, monitoring and evaluating their outcome in order to refine and eventually construct appropriate final responses. This finding echoes the work of many researchers (O'Malley et al. 1985; Wenden 1986a and 1987; Rubin 1987; Oxford and Nyikos 1989) who stress the importance of metacognitive alongside cognitive learning strategies. In the present study, less successful subjects had a much less clearly defined overall plan of action:

> If it's a story or something, I'll pick out the key words and then I can tie it all around, right. But it's like, in this, you almost gotta know your vocab because if you don't know the vocabulary before, you won't be able to stick in that little word that's supposed to go in.

> I mostly remember which key words go with things . . . like I remember back to seeing that word followed by something else or that word going in front of something else . . . and I translate a lot. I translate everything when I'm reading. If I don't understand it in English, I don't understand it.

> First of all I try to translate it. I like to know what's there in my own language. But then, if I can't get that, like I'll go back and I'll look and see what looks right.

Where less successful subjects, lacking metacognitive control, relied on strategies sporadically and unsystematically, successful subjects on the other hand had planned backup strategies available for action if initial strategies failed:

> I go through it fast and fill in blanks and then I . . . see if it makes sense . . . to make sure that it sounds right. Sometimes though . . . like there's still rules sometimes that stick in my head.

Despite the similarities among less successful learners, there were also considerable individual differences. One learner, for example, was identified to be a sophisticated reader in L1. During her think-aloud session, she made a considerable effort to improve her understanding of the text by going back and refining her L1 translation. This same learner also regularly searched for cognates from L1. Another less successful learner showed signs of a developing degree of intuition for what "sounds right" in the L2, while also occasionally using syntactic analysis in order to solve cloze deletions. A single strategy-training program for less successful learners seems unlikely therefore to be effective in solving our students' problems, since different learners have different learning styles (see Politzer and

McGroarty 1985; Abraham and Vann 1987; Vann and Abraham 1990). Different learners also use different strategies that match and mirror the level and types of proficiency they have attained in L2. The corollary to this finding is that the level of L2 proficiency largely defines the strategies available to the learner, and that because of this, some strategic approaches may remain beyond the scope of reference of some learners. We, as teachers, should therefore first examine closely what our students' individual strengths and weaknesses are before we can decide on how best to help them.

To this end, the think-aloud data, when coupled with retrospective self-reports gathered mostly at the end of, but sometimes during, a session, provide an extremely detailed diagnosis of an individual learner's strengths, weaknesses, present strategic resources, and potential to be built upon. Working from an individualized learner profile, it is possible for a teacher to make specific remedial recommendations regarding strategy training or strengths to be worked on. The following is the text of the recommendation made for less successful subject Denise, whose profile reads as follows (strategies cited are described in Appendix B):

(i)   Strengths
   • has developed a certain degree of intuition about L2
   • has a certain degree of competence in syntactic analysis, as seen in her occasional successful use of deductive inferencing

(ii) Weaknesses
   • relies too much on L1 for inspiration
   • focuses on single words/short phrases—often considered in a vacuum rather than within the developing context
   • makes no conscious effort to develop the big picture in order to ease the frustration of unknown words and facilitate contextual guessing
   • has no systematic pattern of checking and evaluating

(iii)   Discussion and Recommendations

Denise's self-report substantiates the think-aloud findings of over-reliance on L1 and single-word/short–phrase type focus in her problem-solving. On the positive side, however, it is clear that this subject's developing intuitive feel for L2 suggests that she might reasonably be expected to use more B3-type checking strategies (does it sound right in L2?), in particular as a back-up strategy to her favored B4 (check via L1 meaning). Building on her other developing strength—grammatical competence—Denise might also be shown how to use B2 (check syntax/morphology) more systematically along with the other monitoring strategies.

However, her major problem lies with overall comprehension—above all, that she did not build up a schema of the passage and for this reason tended to lose track of the meaning of the text. This affected her ability to discriminate between important and less important words/phrases in the text, and her ability to guess accurately on the basis of context. Remedial lessons on the art of reading—reading in complete sentences; constantly reviewing and renewing one's picture of the developing schema by rereading and reanalyzing sentences; being prepared to infer meaning of unknown words from the context; recognizing cognates—might be recommended. Bialystok's (1983) finding that a lesson on how to infer significantly improved comprehension of reading materials suggests the potential benefit of this type of strategy training.

In this way, teachers can devise individualized strategy programs that match a subject's actual proficiency and learning style with a proposed remedial course.

Benefits of the Think-Aloud Procedure
to the L2 Learner

Finally, it is clear that the think-aloud process is of benefit not only to the researcher and the teacher, but also to the L2 learner. The retrospective self-reports gathered during the tape-sessions of this study provided information on how clearly the learner herself was able to understand the approach to language learning she was using and its possible limitations. The following is an extract from less successful subject Carol's self-report:

> See, what I tend to do, I think what the problem with me is too, where I do translate, I tend to translate in English before I leave a . . . and like, once I'm finished with one sentence, I'm like, OK, bye sentence, I'm not going to talk to you any more, like I don't connect the whole paragraph? And maybe if I did, I would tend to get the words a little bit easier. But it's just like I see each one. I don't see this as a passage. I see this as a bunch of sentences that need to be fixed up.

The fact that each subject made an accurate description of her present approach to the task, along with an acute diagnosis of its potential limitations, if any, does indicate an encouraging level of developing metacognitive awareness in these learners. This type of response suggests the importance of the think-aloud as a diagnostic and learning tool to be used by the L2 learners themselves. Thinking aloud can help learners to focus more closely on the type of problem at hand. On occasion in the study, learners talked themselves through a problem to a successful conclusion in a way that was unlikely to have happened had they worked silently. By saying aloud what they were working on and what they were thinking, they became more focused on the problem, and it was this heightened awareness of what they were doing and how they were going to manage the situation that allowed some learners to discover a correct answer in a highly learner-centered process.

This conclusion corroborates an earlier study by Block, during which the researcher found that subjects had "instructed themselves" while thinking aloud (Block 1986, 487). What follows are two examples of this process. In the first sequence, successful subject Louise moved back and forth between deductive strategies and evaluating strategies, using her syntactic knowledge and then monitoring for sound until she felt satisfied with her answer:

> *qui essay . . . pour?* no . . . *pendant.* I think *pendant* goes with the past. . . . So I think that's right. It sounds a lot better than *de . . . étudiants qui essayaient pendant?* . . . I think there's another word . . . no . . . maybe there isn't . . . *depuis!* Right . . . *depuis long . . . qui essayaient depuis long- temps.* Now which one goes with the imperfect? That's my new dilemma. Um . . . *qui essayaient* . . . I think I'll keep *depuis.* (blank 2: *depuis*)

In the second example, less successful subject Denise moved back and forth between syntactic and structural considerations and inductive inferences about the L1 meaning equivalent of the missing word, while constantly checking, via translation to L1, that the overall meaning satisfied her reading of the sentence:

> I know it's what—I just don't know how to put what there, I don't know if it would be Q...U.... I know it's referring to something up here . . . so maybe it's up here . . . hm . . . I know it's a word to refer to the news here, that he announced . . . so . . . I don't know if I could use a pronoun there, instead of what . . . but I think it's what . . . like I know what I want to say, I just don't know which word to use? . . . by what, by . . . like OK, it's the news that we're talking about . . . so if I was stuck, I might put the news in . . . like I'm not gonna leave this one blank. I'm gonna put something there. OK, I'm not sure what this word is . . . the effect produced by . . . OK it's the news . . . he just announced . . . or that he just announced. OK. I'll look up here and see . . . or maybe the headlines . . . by the headlines. I'd probably put *les manchettes* there . . . and I'd probably put q.u. there . . . that he. [Blank 19: *ce qu'/les manchettes qu'*]

In this way, Denise was able to compensate for not know- ing the French relative pronoun, *ce que*, by using her own understanding of the idea of an antecedent and slowly negotiating an acceptable alternative answer on the basis of its meaning and appropriate form.

The think-aloud technique can thus be brought into the L2 classroom so that learners consider the strategies and processes being used on a particular problem-solving task by another learner who thinks aloud in class. This might best be done in very small groups of two or three where one student does the major think-aloud while the other(s) share ideas and strategy suggestions as they work cooperatively through the problem-solving situation. Based on this exchange of resources, learners can acquire new and better strategies, particularly if they are grouped with partners with somewhat different strategic repertoires. Increasing students' strategic repertoires in this way is an extremely desirable result of learning a second language.

It should be recognized, however, that in this learner-centered process, it must be the individual learner's decision whether or not to adopt a new strategy. Clearly this choice depends first on whether the new strategy is within the range of the learner's actual L2 proficiency, and second on whether the learner personally feels a strategy's usefulness or appropriateness in the given situation. Trying out a particular strategy will not necessarily result in its regular use unless learners discover and feel for themselves the appropriateness of a particular strategic reaction. If students become aware of weaknesses or gaps in their own strategies, they may welcome the chance to try new ones. However, they may require urging and assistance in order to become accustomed to using them.

In working with students in this way, increasing their awareness of the nature of the language task at hand and their ability to make strategic choices, teachers may hope to encourage and develop more confident learners who take greater control over and responsibility for the progress of their language learning. Thinking aloud can assist L2 learners to appreciate what they can be doing to help themselves and how and why they should be doing it.

Conclusion

This study suggests that thinking aloud, a procedure already recognized as a valuable technique for the researcher, can be a powerful diagnostic and learning tool for the L2 teacher and learner. L2 teachers can use it to analyze their students' performance on a specific task and then make recommendations on types of remediation that may benefit the less confident, less experienced learner. In this way, individualized strategy training programs can be devised that match a subject's actual proficiency and learning style with a proposed remedial course.

L2 learners can benefit directly from the actual process of thinking aloud, since the procedure seems to help them focus more closely on the task at hand. It can also lead learners to develop a heightened metalinguistic awareness: while thinking aloud, they may examine and assess the strengths and weaknesses of their own problem-solving strategies—an essential first stage before any new strategies can be tried out. Thinking aloud may be done alone or in small classroom groups where the benefit to learners is in the exchange of strategic possibilities between peers. The limited experience of this researcher is that this procedure, while considered strange at first by learners, is subsequently well received once students start to understand how it empowers them with greater control over their progress towards L2 proficiency.

These findings lead us to suggest that if thinking aloud is useful in diagnosing and assisting students in context-based vocabulary exercises like the cloze procedure, then it may also be beneficial to teachers and learners in other L2 tasks. Future research may examine the usefulness of thinking aloud during other complex reading and writing tasks, while also investigating the different complexes of strategies chosen by learners in the course of these exercises.

Appendix A

The Cloze Passage

Il était une fois un groupe _____[1] étudiants qui essayaient _____[2] longtemps de comprendre la concordance des temps au passé. Ils comprenaient bien la différence _____[3] le passé composé et l'imparfait, mais chaque _____[4] qu'il fallait _____[5] utiliser, _____[6a] parlant ou _____[6b] discutant, tout s'embrouillait dans leur tête. Ils commençaient _____[7] douter de leur perception, et _____[8] n'arrivait vraiment à résoudre cette difficulté. Il fallait trouver une solution.

Un jour, le professeur est entré dans la classe, et, d'un air soulagé, _____[9] a annoncé la nouvelle _____[10], apparemment, avait fait les manchettes (=headlines) ce matin-là. Il a expliqué que l'Académie Française venait _____[11] décider _____[12] éliminer soit le passé composé, soit l'imparfait afin de simplifier l'apprentissage _____[13] français comme langue seconde. Les étudiants n'en croyaient pas leurs oreilles. La réaction ne s'est pas fait attendre et le professeur a entendu les commentaires suivants: «Ah non! Maintenant que j'ai fait tous _____[14] efforts pour apprendre les participes irréguliers, on ne va pas laisser tomber le passé composé!» «Mais alors, _____[15] imparfait, comment est-ce qu'on va exprimer la durée, l'action qui continue?» «Et _____[16] qui ai passé toute la fin de semaine à essayer de comprendre la différence entre les deux, _____[17] n'est pas sérieux!» «Je croyais _____[18] le rôle de l'Académie Française était de protéger la langue française! Ils sont devenus complètement fous!»

En constatant l'effet produit par _____[19] il venait d'annoncer, le professeur s'est mis _____[20] rire et s'est empressé de fixer la date de l'examen qui allait porter sur la concordance des temps au passé.

[Text adapted from *Vouloir . . . c'est pouvoir*, 1992 (3rd edition), Holt, Rinehart and Winston, pp. 176–177.]

B-FT Wayne

Answer Key

1 d'	2 depuis	3 entre	4 fois
5 les	6 en	7 à	8 personne/rien
9 leur/il	10 qui	11 de	12 d'
13 du	14 ces/mes/les	15 sans	16 moi
17 ce/il	18 que	19 ce qu'/ les manchettes qu'/ la nouvelle qu'	20 à

Appendix B

General Scheme of Cognitive Learning/Reception Strategies

A. Clarification/Verification of meaning/understanding

   A1. Translates into L1 words directly preceding and/or following the blank, e.g. (Blank 16: *moi*), "and something which had passed all . . . which spent all the end of the week . . . or all the weekend."

   A2. Seeks overall schema by scanning/skimming through a number of blanks, e.g. (Blanks 16 and 17: *moi* & *ce/il*), "*Et* dash *qui ai passé toute la fin de semaine à essayer de comprendre la différence entre les deux, ___ n'est pas sérieux.*"

   A3. Reads through the single blank in L2 to establish context, e.g. (Blank 7: *à*), "*Ils commençaient ___ douter de leur perception.*"

B. Monitoring: focus on form and comprehension (cognitive and metacognitive strategies)

   B1. Monitors vocabulary, e.g. (Blank 4: *fois*), "Each time. I'm thinking *temps* isn't time . . . *chaque fois qu'il fallait.*"

   B2. Monitors grammar/morphology, e.g. (Blank 5: *les*), "I don't know which pronoun you put in there to take in *le passé composé* and *l'imparfait*. I'd probably put *l'* here . . . or maybe I should put L...E...S . . . there 'cause it's talking about two of them."

   B3. Monitors sound, by testing a possible answer, or a number of options for sound, e.g. (Blank 2: *depuis*), "*qui essayaient de* . . . I don't think *de* sounds right there . . . *qui essay . . . pour?* no, *pendant?*"

   B4. Monitors specific meaning by checking the appropriateness of the possible answer by translation to L1, e.g. (Blank 10: *qui*), . . . *qui apparemment avait fait les manchettes*. OK. The professor enters the classroom . . . blah, blah, blah . . . he announces the news that appar-

ently has made the headlines this morning. . .
OK . . . yeah that seems right."

B5. Monitors general meaning by checking overall comprehension of the text or parts of the text, e.g. (Paragraph 1), "OK, so I know what the gist of the paragraph is saying."

C. Inductive Inferencing

C1. Infers L1 meaning equivalent of missing word and translates (or tries to translate) it into L2, e.g. (Blank 9: *leur/il*), "he announced to . . . wait now . . . he announced to the class . . . *a annoncé* to them, *leur* probably."

C2. Infers meaning of unknown word from cognate in L1 or L2, e.g. (*s'embrouillait*: between blanks 6 and 7), "*s'embrouillait* . . . wait now . . . I don't know . . . um . . . *brouiller* . . . I think is something like fog, so . . . to like fog your mind or whatever."

C3. Infers meaning of unknown word from context and other clues (situation, text structure, personal relationships, topic, world knowledge), e.g. (*s'embrouillait*: between blanks 6 and 7), "Uh, something happens weird in their head . . . I don't know what that word means, but I can get that from context."

C4. Infers answer on the basis of its sound, e.g. (Blank 20: *à*), "*Le professeur s'est mis* : . . . that means something . . . *s'est mis* . . . I'll just try *à rire* . . .*s'est mis à* . . . sounds . . . sounds . . . *mettre à* . . . I think that goes together."

D. Deductive Inferencing

D1. Uses syntactic/morphological knowledge, e.g. (Blank 6: *en*), "E...N . . . in speaking and in discussing. I was thinking *parlant* . . . I couldn't think what that was and then I knew that A...N...T is an -ing word and you always see *en* in front of A...N...T."

D2. Classifies, e.g. (*ne s'est pas fait attendre*: between blanks 13 and 14) "I don't understand that . . . it must be some kind of expression . . . um . . . *ne s'est pas fait*?"

E. Repetition for Retrieval

   E1. Repeats word(s) in L2 while searching for its/their
        meaning, e.g. (*il fallait*: between blanks 4 and 5), "*il fallait,
        il fallait* . . . what does *falloir* mean?"

   E2. Repeats L1 translation of text immediately preceding
        and/or following the blank, e.g. (Blank 10: *qui*),
        "OK . . . one day the prof was in the class . . . and he an-
        nounced the new . . . well, gotta be something concrete
        there . . . the new something . . . apparently . . . having
        made the headlines the day before."

   E3. Repeats in L2 known word(s) immediately preceding or
        following blank, e.g. (Blank 10: *qui*), "*il a annoncé la nou-
        velle . . . et il a annoncé la nouvelle . . . la nouvelle* some-
        thing . . . *apparemment avait fait les manchettes.*"

NOTES

1. Learning strategies, like communication strategies, are
behaviors or thought processes that directly affect and contribute to the
rate of progress in the L2. However, while communication strategies are
a means of *exploiting* a learner's competence, learning strategies are a
means of *expanding* it (Paribakht 1985).

Cognitive Aspects of Personality and Listening Comprehension

Mary Emily Call

Abstract

What makes some students better language learners than others? Part of the answer may lie in differences in the use of language learning strategies. A student's choice of strategy, in turn, may depend on his or her personality type. This study investigates the possible relationship between the intuitive personality type (as measured by the Myers-Briggs Type Indicator) and listening improvement (as measured by the Comprehensive English Language Test for Learners of English) attained during a fifteen-week English as a Second Language (ESL) course. An analysis of these two measures supports the thesis that personality variables play a role in the development of listening skills.

Introduction

What makes some students more successful language learners than others? Language teachers have been seeking the answer to this question since the focus of language learning research turned to learner variables in the early 1970s. The answer promises to be complex—an equation composed of individual traits, environmental factors, and the interactions between them. As we attempt to solve this equation, we will need to investigate the roles played by its various terms. One of these terms will represent environmental variables such as teaching style, language learning context, and cultural attitudes, among others.

Another term of the equation will represent the traits of individual language learners. Investigations of the characteristics of good language learners have yielded clues that may account for some of the differences in language learning success. Theories constructed to explain these individual differences have centered on cognitive and affective variables. Studies of cognitive variables have dealt with language learning aptitude (Carroll 1960, Pimsleur 1966, Carroll 1973) and cognitive styles (Hansen and Stansfield 1982). Studies of affective differences have included research on motivation (Gardner and Lambert 1972), personality in general (Brodkey and Shore 1976), and, more narrowly, on the personality trait of empathy (Guiora, Brannon, and Dull 1972). However, no consistent relationships between personality traits and language achievement have emerged (Lalonde and Gardner 1984).

Despite these equivocal results, the hypothesis that personality may affect learning in general, and language learning in particular, remains intuitively appealing. Perhaps this relationship is not a direct but an indirect one, mediated by other variables such as the use of language learning strategies (Gardner 1990). Recently, Ehrman and Oxford (1989) studied the relationship between language learning strategies and personality variables and found that people with a particular personality trait (people who indicate "intuitive" rather than "sensing" preferences on the Myers-Briggs Type Indicator, a personality inventory) reported the use of certain strategies that seem particularly appropriate for language learning. This is especially relevant because many scholars have attributed successful language learning (as opposed to acquisition) to the conscious use of learning strategies (Bialystok 1981, Rubin 1975, Wenden 1986b). These findings suggest a link between successful language learning and the use of strategies as well as a link between the use of strategies and personality characteristics.

If these relationships exist, it seems reasonable to hypothesize that certain personality characteristics ought to predict success in the learning of at least some language skills. The present study was designed to test this hypothesis.

Personality, Learning Strategies, and Listening Comprehension

In their study of language learning strategies and personality variables, Ehrman and Oxford (1989) used the Myers-Briggs Type Indicator (MBTI) (Myers 1962), a measure of personality based on Jungian theory, which posits that people demonstrate certain basic preferences in their cognitive and affective orientations toward incoming data. Because it measures both cognitive and affective dimensions of personality, the MBTI is an especially appropriate instrument for investigating learning. The instrument consists of four bipolar scales—introversion (I) and extraversion (E), sensing (S) and intuiting (N), thinking (T) and feeling (F), judging (J) and perceiving (P)—designed to measure cognitive and affective preferences. Preferred modes of cognitive processing are measured by the S/N and T/F scales, while affective or attitudinal variables are measured on the E/I and J/P scales. (See Appendix A for a description of each preference.) Respondents choose answers to items designed to reflect a preference, however slight, for one or the other of the two orientations. This results in a personality profile for each respondent indicated by the four letters representing his or her preference on each of the scales. Sixteen combinations of letters indicating different personality types are possible; for example, ENFP or ISTJ.

In addition to the MBTI, Ehrman and Oxford (1989) used the Strategy Inventory for Language Learning (SILL). The SILL is a self-report instrument that documents a student's use of various types of language learning strategies. These include memory strategies, compensation strategies, cognitive and meta-cognitive strategies, affective strategies, and social strategies (Oxford 1990).

Ehrman and Oxford (1989) found that certain personality characteristics were associated with the use of particular types of language learning strategies. Most interestingly, they found that intuitors (people whose preferred mode of learning is to look for relationships and possibilities in incoming information) tended to employ the language learning strategies of searching for meaning and constructing formal models. These are the kinds of strategies that are believed to underlie fluent listening and reading (Carrell and Eisterhold 1983).

Recent research in listening comprehension suggests that cognitive models, called schemata, frame our understanding of linguistic input (Long 1989). Since these models are culture-specific, language learners who can construct new schemata quickly and easily should be more successful at learning to listen accurately than those who feel discomfort when they must react quickly to linguistic input, without time to reflect on details.

From this evidence, it seems reasonable to expect that (N's) would do better than S's (the polar opposites of N's) on measures of listening achievement over the course of a semester of English as a second language study. Therefore, the present study was undertaken to test the hypothesis that people who demonstrate an MBTI preference for searching out patterns in incoming data and forming hypotheses about it (N's) will learn to make sense of rapidly fading auditory-linguistic input more quickly than people who focus on the sensory aspects of the sounds (S's). Specifically, the null and research hypotheses were these:

H_0 The listening improvement scores of intuitive (N) students will not be different from the listening difference scores of sensing (S) students.

H_1 The listening improvement scores of intuitive (N) students will be significantly ($p < .05$) higher than the listening difference scores of sensing (S) students.

The Study[1]

To determine their progress in listening, a group of ESL students was tested at the beginning and at the end of a fifteen-week term of study. The magnitude of a student's improvement in listening skill was measured by subtracting the first listening score from the second. To determine their personality characteristics, the students were asked to respond to the MBTI. The listening improvement scores of the N's were then compared with the listening improvement scores of the S's to determine whether or not they were significantly different.

Nineteen women and fifteen men ranging in age from eighteen to more than thirty-six years participated in this study. Twenty-five (73.5%) of these students spoke Spanish as a native language while the remaining nine (26.5%) spoke either Russian, Gujarati (an Indic language spoken in northwestern India), Chinese, Japanese, or Thai. They were placed in one of four levels of ESL classes on the basis of the structure section of the Comprehensive English Language Test (CELT) (Harris and Palmer 1986) and a writing sample. Twelve of the students (35%) were enrolled in ESL I, nine (26.5%) in ESL II, nine (26.5%) in ESL III, and four (12%) in ESL IV.

Most of these students were enrolled as part-time students in the Weekend College at Montclair State University and took classes only on the weekend (Friday night through Sunday afternoon). The ESL curriculum emphasizes the four skills of listening, speaking, reading, and writing.

On the first day of class students were given the listening section[2] of the CELT, Form A; during the last two weeks of class (fourteen to fifteen weeks after the first test), Form B of the listening section of the CELT was administered. Listening improvement scores were determined by subtracting each student's score on the first listening test from his or her score on the second listening test.

In order to familiarize them with personality variables, the students were assigned a simple reading about the MBTI adapted from *Type Talk* by Kroeger and Theusen (1988) and were asked to participate in the study by agreeing to take the test. Almost all the students who were in classes during this term agreed to be tested. MBTI scores were collected during the last half of the term and reported to the students by the researcher, who asked the students to validate the results by reading short paragraphs describing their personality types. There was general agreement, and no disagreement, about the "fit" of the descriptive paragraphs.

Table 1: Student Data

| ESL Level | Native Language | | Totals |
	Spanish	Other	
I	11	1	12
	M=5 F=6	M=0 F=1	
II	5	4	9
	M=4 F=1	M=2 F=2	
III	5	4	9
	M=1 F=4	M=2 F=2	
IV	4	0	4
	M=1 F=3	M=0 F=0	
Totals	25	9	34

Note: M=male   F=female

Data Analysis and Results

Of the 34 students, only seven (21%) were N's, while 27 (79%) were S's. (These are roughly the proportions of N's and S's thought to occur in the population at large—25% and 75% respectively [Kiersey and Bates 1978]). A t-test for difference of means had been planned prior to this finding, but since the sample included so few N's, the requirements for this procedure were not met. The median was judged to be the best measure of central tendency, so, the Median test was used to test the hypothesis in place of the t-test (Hatch and Lazaraton 1991). The median of the listening improvement scores was 2, as can be seen in Table 2 below. (See Appendix B for the raw scores.)

Table 2

Rank Ordering of Listening Improvement Scores																	
										0*							
							3*	2*		0							
							3*	2		0							
16*	13	10					3	2		0	–1	–2	–3				
16	13	10	9*	7*	5	4	3	2	1	0	–1	–2	–3	–5	–6	–8	–9

* Scores of N's

Five of the seven N's and nine of the twenty-seven S's were above the median, as can be seen in Table 3 below:

Table 3

Median Test Table			
	N's	S's	Total
Above	5	9	14
Below	1	15	16
Total	6	24	30[1]

[1] This number *excludes* four scores equal to the median, 2.
z score computed on data = 1.97 $p < .025$
z score needed to reject at $p < .05 = 1.64$ (one-tailed test)

The median test score computed using these data was 1.97, which is significant at the .025 level, allowing the rejection of the null hypothesis and the acceptance of the hypothesis that the listening improvement scores of N's are significantly higher than those of S's.

In an effort to understand this relationship in greater depth, a post hoc factor analysis was performed on the data. Two factors appeared in both the principal component analysis and in the varimax rotation (see Tables 4 and 5).

Table 4: Factor Matrix

Principal Component Analysis (PCA) Extraction		
	Factor 1 (PCA)	Factor 2 (PCA)
CSS/N*	.68847	.24708
DIFFLIST**	.14338	.89958
CSE/I	−.57373	−.04489
CST/F	.62670	.05715
CSJ/P	−.66121	.54545

* The CS in these terms refers to continuous score, while S/N,
E/I, T/F, and J/P have the MBTI values used throughout
this paper.

** DIFFLIST refers to the difference in listening scores between
CELT Form A and CELT Form B.

Table 5: Factor Matrix

Varimax Rotation		
	Factor 1 (VR)	Factor 2 (VR)
CSS/N*	.70769	.18498
DIFFLIST**	.22268	.88330
CSE/I	−.57545	.00622
CST/F	.62930	.00129
CSJ/P	−.61017	.60200

* The CS in these terms refers to continuous score, while S/N,
E/I, T/F, and J/P have the MBTI values used throughout
this paper.

** DIFFLIST refers to the difference in listening scores between
CELT Form A and CELT Form B.

Since correlations above .30 are considered significant in factor analysis studies (Hatch and Lazaraton 1991), these tables show two factors, each correlating significantly with various personality or listening scores. The first factor correlates significantly (positively or negatively) with continuous scores on all the MBTI personality scales, but it does not correlate highly with listening scores; thus, it can be inferred that this factor does not reveal anything about the relationship of personality and listening skill. The second factor correlates with continuous scores on the judging/perceiving scale *and* with listening scores, suggesting a link between J/P preference and listening skill. The factors computed by each procedure are highly correlated with one another, as can be seen in Table 6:

Table 6

Factor Transformation Matrix		
	Factor 1 (VR)	Factor 2 (VR)
FACTOR 1 (PCA)	.99605	−.08878
FACTOR 2 (PCA)	.08878	.99605

This degree of correlation lends credence to the reliability of the procedures.

Discussion

Although the relationship between listening skill and personality characteristics, as measured by the MBTI, cannot be generalized on the basis of this small sample, these results support H_1, which states that N's should have significantly higher listening difference scores than S's. They also complement Ehrman and Oxford's (1989) findings that N's use more strategies that underlie comprehension and Long's (1989) contention that schemata (and, by extension, schema formation) underlie listening skills. In this sample, the people who demonstrate an MBTI preference for intuition appear to be more skillful listeners, possibly because they seek to impose meaning on incoming data and, therefore, are better able to comprehend and respond to auditory linguistic input. These results also support the hypothesis that personality plays a significant, but unspecified, role in language learning.

In addition, the factor analysis performed on the data indicates a possible relationship between the J/P scale and listening skill. Since the majority of the students preferred J, this seems to indicate that a search for closure characteristic of J types is beneficial to developing listening skill. This is intuitively plausible:

Given the rapidly-fading nature of auditory input, those who prefer to bring searches to decisive closure quickly may place themselves at a competitive advantage over those who do not have this preference. However, extreme caution must be exercised until these findings are replicated. First, the sample size was minimally adequate. Second, this correlation may be an artifact of the dispersion of this body of data. Since a larger proportion of the subjects were J's (73%) than in the general population (about 50% according to Keirsey and Bates 1978; 55–60% according to Myers and McCaulley 1985), a spurious correlation between this variable and the factor identified by the principal component analysis and varimax procedures may have been computed. Repeated sampling might show such a correlation in most groups that are disproportionately J's but not in more balanced samples. Thus, a replication of this study is necessary, controlling for this variable by selecting a sample in which J's occur as frequently as in the population at large. If, under these circumstances, factor analysis continues to demonstrate a correlation between J/P preference, listening scores and the unidentified factor, then a theoretical explanation of that factor will become necessary.

Implications for the Language Classroom

This study suggests a link between an MBTI preference for N (rather than S) and skill in developing listening comprehension. Since listening comprehension is a schema-based activity (Long, 1989) and since N's naturally use strategies that are conducive to efficient schema building (Ehrman and Oxford 1989), this link may be taken as evidence for the efficacy of using strategies that promote schema building and the discovery of patterns in spoken language in order to learn to make sense of auditory linguistic input. Since students can be trained in the use of strategies that are appropriate for given language skills (Oxford 1990), one implication of this study is that language teachers should consider training their students to use the strategies that underlie efficient listening. (Oxford [1990] gives excellent suggestions for teaching students to use strategies in the second or foreign language classroom.) While those students who are intuitives may already be using these strategies naturally, several scholars (Bialystok 1981, Rubin 1975, Wenden 1986b) suggest that they will benefit from bringing their intuitive strategy use into consciousness. Such training will most clearly benefit sensing students, whose natural propensity is to concentrate on the details and lose the "big picture"—a process that is disastrous from the point of view of comprehension. Strategy training and practice in listening to authentic input while using strategies consciously may help all students develop a higher level of listening skill.

Conclusion

The empirical results of this study permit us to conclude tentatively that personality can play a role in successful language learning, and that this role is probably mediated through the intervening variable of language learning strategies. Although these findings must be taken as preliminary, they do suggest that employing this scientific paradigm promises to be a useful and productive method for exploring the relationship between affective variables and language learning.

Appendix A

Descriptions of MBTI Preferences

There are four bipolar scales on this measure of personality. The first two are designed to measure cognitive preferences. The sensing/intuitive (S/N) scale determines preferred orientation toward new situations or new information. People who prefer the sensing function tend to focus on the immediate sensory aspects of the world and often have keen powers of observation and handle details well. On the other hand, people who prefer the intuitive function tend to see the patterns and possibilities in new information and try to relate it to what they already know. They often ignore details and focus on the "big picture." About 75% of the U.S. population prefer S and about 25% prefer N (Keirsey and Bates 1978).

The second cognitive scale, thinking/feeling (T/F), is concerned with decision making. People who prefer thinking make decisions based on impersonal logic and are concerned with justice and fairness. On the other hand, people who prefer feeling make decisions on the basis of personal or group values and consider the impact of their decisions on the people involved. While the U.S. population demonstrates equal preferences for T and F, about 66% of U.S. males prefer T and about 66% of U.S. females prefer F (Kroeger and Thuesen 1988).

Next come the variables associated with attitude, extraversion/introversion (E/I) and judging/perceiving (J/P). Jung's theory characterizes extraverts as people who are energized by being with other people. Sociability and the ability to communicate well are attributes typical of extraverted people. On the other hand, introverts are people whose interests are centered on the inner world of ideas. They typically seek solitude and privacy to recharge their batteries. About 75% of the U.S. population prefer E, while 25% prefer I (Keirsey and Bates 1978).

The second set of attitude variables, judging and perceiving, has to do with orientation toward the outer world. This orientation, implicit in Jung's work, was made explicit by Myers and Briggs as they were developing the inventory. People who prefer the judging attitude like to make plans and to organize activities. They seek to bring closure by making decisions and often seem organized and purposeful. On the other hand, people who prefer the perceiving attitude are tuned in to new information and often put off making decisions because of the impact that new information might have. Perceivers are often viewed as being spontaneous and flexible. Kiersey and Bates (1978) report that about 50% of the U.S. population prefer J, while Myers and McCaulley (1985) estimate the percentage to be 55–60%.

Appendix B

Student	1st Listening Score	2nd Listening Score	Listening Improvement Score
1	24	25	1
2	17	27	10
3	22	22	0
4	20	18	−2
5	21	23	2
6	12	19	7
7	10	26	16
8	10	23	13
9	12	22	10
10	23	25	2
11	21	18	−3
12	21	34	13
13	35	35	0
14	33	31	−2
15	37	39	2
16	18	22	4
17	38	30	−8
18	43	46	3
19	31	34	3
20	35	38	3
21	27	27	0
22	42	41	−1
23	39	30	−9
24	32	32	0
25	22	16	−6
26	37	42	5
27	43	43	0
28	40	35	−5
29	32	41	9
30	11	27	16
31	38	35	−3
32	33	32	−1
33	45	48	3
34	44	46	2

Raw Scores and Listening Improvement Scores for Each Student

*Listening Improvement Scores were obtained by subtracting the first listening score (CELT Form A) from the second (CELT Form B).

NOTES

1. The assistance of the following students in tabulating and analyzing the data is gratefully acknowledged: Debra Agnese, Patti Babcock, Arlene Berkowitz, Sean Fagan, Carol Gottlieb, and Carol Hudzik.

2. The listening section of the CELT consists of fifty multiple-choice items divided into three subsections. The first subsection requires test takers to select the best answer to a question they have heard. The second requires them to paraphrase a statement and the third requires them to listen to a short conversation and draw a conclusion based on it. The test takes about thirty minutes to complete. There are two forms (A and B) of the CELT.

3. Continuous scores are linear transformations of preference scores and are computed for E, S, T, and J by subtracting the numerical score from 100 and for I, N, F, and P by adding the numerical score to 100. This transformation allows correlations to be performed on the preference data (Kroeger and Thuesen 1981).

Task Variation and Repair in the Foreign Language Classroom

Celeste Kinginger

Abstract

This article describes the outcome of a study examining repair in conversations among American classroom learners of French as a foreign language. The study involved recording, transcription, and analysis of two different conversation types representing extremes in a hypothetical continuum of classroom styles, from more "natural" to more "instructional." Interpretation of the data was guided by tools for conversation analysis, analyzing repair in terms of self- versus other-initiation and completion. Findings demonstrate that "instructional" activities produce greater amounts of the other-initiated and -completed repair, which is typical of teacher-led classroom interaction. In more "natural" tasks, repair in the second language and the resultant interactional risk are often avoided altogether in favor of code-switching. These findings suggest that certain activities considered beneficial for developing discourse competence may not produce the desired results, and that the linguistic and cultural homogeneity of many foreign language classes has an impact upon the negotiation of meaning in small group and pair work.

Introduction

This article describes the outcome of a study examining repair in conversations among American classroom learners of French as a foreign language. This observational study involved recording, transcription, and analysis of two different conversation types representing extremes in a hypothetical continuum of classroom styles, from more "natural" to more "instructional" (Kramsch 1985). Interpretation of the data was guided by tools for conversation analysis developed by Sacks, Schegloff, and Jefferson (1974). The study's results show variation by task type in the resolution of conversational problems, and suggest some ways in which the larger contexts of learning may influence the quality of classroom discourse.

The Significance of Repair
in Second-Language Research

Due to the widespread use of techniques involving small group and pair work, a good deal of recent research on classroom language acquisition focuses on the nature of discourse in interactions among learners. Much of this research examines the resolution of conversational trouble sources, or *repair*. Beyond the fact that repair is a very common feature of classroom talk, and therefore deserves the attention of any researcher interested in classroom second-language (L2) use, investigations of repair are significant in several research perspectives.

Researchers approaching repair from a psycholinguistic perspective view certain types of repair as productive for the development of grammatical competence. Starting from Krashen's (1982) view of "comprehensible input" as a necessary and sufficient condition for second-language acquisition (SLA), Long (1983) proposed that interaction enhances the delivery of input by matching it with the individual learner's particular needs. In other words, interactive work toward achieving comprehension promotes SLA.

Observation of this work has led to the identification of certain interactional features (e.g., clarification requests, comprehension checks, repetitions) regrouped under the category "negotiation of meaning." A number of studies have compared the quantity of this negotiation in various tasks and participant configurations, ultimately suggesting that learner/learner interaction presents certain advantages in the gathering of comprehensible input and in the control of morpho-syntactic form that will theoretically ensue (Long 1983, 1985; Long and Porter, 1985; Porter, 1986; Pica and Doughty, 1985a, b; Doughty and Pica 1986; Gass and Varonis 1985). There has been some criticism of this quantitative approach to the assessment of meaning negotiation within interaction types, suggesting that a narrow focus serves to obscure the overall qualities of learner participation in talk (Aston 1986). However, this does not negate the potential validity of Long's original hypothesis concerning the importance of interaction and of the repair that exists within interaction.

A different perspective on repair is adopted by researchers and theorists concerned with the limitations of the classroom as a setting for the development of discourse competence (e.g., Kramsch 1985; Savignon 1983; Widdowson 1979). Participation in everyday conversation requires an ability to attend to and resolve speaking problems of all types (e.g. one's own and others'). Unfortunately, opportunities to engage in conversational discourse, including repair, are conspicuously absent from much of classroom discourse. An unequal distribution of power among the participants often leads to a situation in which the teacher becomes the fulcrum for interaction. Furthermore, since teachers are considered responsible for the quality of talk, they tend to provide large amounts of corrective feedback as a matter of routine (McHoul 1978; van Lier 1988). In other words, students typically have their speaking problems resolved for them instead of learning to cope independently. In this perspective, one of the functions of learner/learner talk in the L2 classroom is to provide opportunities for engagement in communication via conversation, including practice in conversational repair.

The Study

Design

The design of this study was influenced by Kramsch's observations in her 1985 article on "discourse options" in the L2 classroom. In this paper, Kramsch proposes that classroom styles exist on a continuum, ranging from most instructional to most natural. The instructional end of the continuum is characterized by fixed roles, teacher-oriented tasks, and a twofold focus on accuracy of facts and on content, which in the case of many language classes consists of facts about language forms. The natural end of the continuum is characterized by negotiated roles, group-oriented tasks, and a focus on the process and fluency of the interaction. Learners typically have long experience and strong expectations of what it is like to participate in classroom talk and, as Kramsch explains: "Despite their good intentions at increasing the amount of communication in the classroom, students and teachers have often fallen short of their goal because their style of interaction has remained at the instructional end of the continuum." (1985, 181).

Tasks

This study was designed to explore the types of repair adopted by learners of French as they performed two activities typical of their classroom work. The data were selected from the data base in Kinginger (1990), a study that examined the overall qualities of interactive work in thirty-two conversations of four task types. Preliminary observation in the research sites (classrooms) allowed the researcher to select tasks which were part of the classes' instructional routine. The two tasks under consideration here represent the two ends of Kramsch's continuum: 1) The more "instructional" task included is known as the "conversation card." Speaking in French, two learners are to ask and answer a series of questions displayed on cards in English. The questions are designed to illustrate the use of the vocabulary and grammatical structures of the current lesson. A third learner holds a card with the correct questions in French and monitors the accuracy of her companions' utterances. 2) The more "natural" task included in this study is an in-class discussion, in French, of a group collaborative assignment, where the outcome of the discussion will ultimately be graded.

Participants and Settings

Each of the tasks was performed by two pairs of learners in each of four classes, resulting in a data base of eight conversations for each task. Two of the classes observed took place at a large public midwestern university, while the other two took place at a small, private college on the East Coast. At both schools, a proficiency-oriented methodology was promoted in initial and ongoing teacher education.

The participants were enrolled in intermediate-level (second-year) classes. They were audiotaped as they spoke, and the tapes were transcribed using a transcription system adapted from van Lier (1988). (See the appendix for a description of the transcription system.)

Analysis

In this study, analysis is guided by the comprehensive framework for the study of repair initially developed by Schegloff, Jefferson, and Sacks (1977). Discourse modifications are said to be triggered by "trouble sources," and these modifications are referred to as "repair." Repair sequences consist of three parts: 1) production of the trouble source, 2) initiation of repair, and 3) completion of repair. Attention to a trouble source may be initiated by the same speaker who produced it and who is then referred to as "self." Such attention may also be initiated by another participant in the interaction, who is then referred to as "other." Within this framework, there are four basic trajectories through which a repair sequence may be realized:

1) Self initiated/self-completed (the speaker who produced the trouble source initiates and completes the repair). Self-initiated/self-completed repair may be expected to occur in learner classroom discourse where the learners

are provided sufficient time to attend to and resolve their own speaking problems.

2) Other initiated/self-completed (the interlocutor identifies the trouble source, and the producer of the trouble source completes the repair). Other-initiated repair is in general far more frequent in classroom discourse than in the conversations studied by Schegloff, Jefferson, and Sacks (1977). Indeed, it is a preponderance of other-initiated repair provided by the teacher that characterizes much of teacher-led classroom talk. An additional feature of classroom repair noted by van Lier is the presence of intra-turn/other-initiated repair, in which a learner's turn is, in essence, interrupted by the other for the purpose of drawing attention to a trouble source.

3) Self-initiated/other completed (the speaker who produced the trouble course identifies it and repair is completed by the interlocutor). This repair type is treated cursorily by Schegloff, Jefferson, and Sacks (1977), perhaps because it is a fairly rare occurrence in everyday conversation. In the classroom, however, learners often solicit help in coping with repairables. This is accomplished in a variety of ways; for example, through direct appeal for assistance, or through "try marking" (i.e., "the candidate item, or suspected trouble source, may be offered with tentative (rising) intonation . . . and may be preceded by hesitation markers and pauses, and followed by a brief pause" (van Lier 1988, 202).

4) Other-initiated/other completed (the interlocutor both identifies the trouble source and completes the repair). Other-initiated/other-completed repair, whether it occurs as an intra-turn utterance or in the next turn, may also be expected to occur far more frequently in classroom talk than in conversation. This repair type may in fact be peculiar to educational contexts, or other contexts where participants are considered "not yet competent in some domain" (Schegloff, Jefferson, and Sacks 1977, 381).

Within their description of informal conversations, Schegloff, Jefferson, and Sacks (1977) describe certain preference structures, and most notably with regard to repair, a "massive preference for self-repair." The organization of repair sequences is such that every opportunity is provided to "self" for resolution of conversational trouble sources. In fact, most trouble is dealt with at its source. Other-repair, when initiated, is delayed and/or modulated (e.g., the "other" will take the blame for the repairable by claiming nonunderstanding or failure to hear). The presence of this preference for self-repair has also been demonstrated for conversation between native speakers and nonnative speakers (Day, Chenoweth, Chun and Leppescu 1984) and for nonpedagogic conversations between nonnative speakers (Schwartz 1980).

This preference has been related to the concept of concern for preservation of "face" (Goffman 1967), the self-image that a member of society wishes to maintain and to present to others (Brown and Levinson 1978). In polite conversation, participants' mutual concern for the preservation of face requires that explicit attention to others' faults or mistakes be avoided.

As suggested above, preference structures for the organization of foreign language classroom repair may be expected to differ in important ways from the structures observed in informal interaction. These differences have to do with differing goals or expected outcomes. In informal interaction, for example, a goal of mutual comprehension and respect implies constant efforts to maintain face. In the classroom, this requirement is often suspended in favor of maintenance of formal accuracy in the speech.

Results: Conversation Cards

This is clearly the case for the group work observed as the participants in this study carried out the more instructional activity called "conversation cards." These interactions divide neatly into question and answer cycles. As learners attempt to produce the questions and answers required for completion of the task, learners in the role of monitor contribute to turn construction (the way in which talk is structured), while scrutinizing the accuracy of the forms produced.

In the first example (figure 1), we see a case of intra-turn/other-initiated repair. Ann is answering a question about joining the Peace Corps, and is interrupted in midutterance by Cindy, the monitor, because she has failed to produce an article of the correct gender.

Figure 1

1) Ann: OK. Si je faisais partie de la Corps=
[OK. If I participated in the (incorrect gender) Peace Corps=]
2) Cindy: No, du.
[No, in the (correct gender)]
3) Ann: =du Corps de Paix?
[=in the Peace Corps?]

In ordinary conversation, an interruption of this sort would likely constitute a face-threatening act. Here, however, the goal of the interaction is the production of correct language. The monitor's responsibility for the quality of the language carries with it a right to initiate repair that overrides other considerations, including interactional rules of politeness.

Sometimes, the learners in the role of monitor can become a bit overzealous, as is the case in the second example. Abby is asking her partner where she spent her childhood, and Caleb is the monitor. In turn #1, Abby produces an instance of another common repair type in these interactions: self-initiated repair with try marking (interrogative intonation) directed at the monitor. In turn #2, Caleb takes her up on it, mistakenly "correcting" her possessive pronoun toward a nonnative form. Abby then tries again before Caleb realizes his error in turn 4. Caleb responds to Abby's explanation with an evaluative comment typical of teacher talk.

Figure 2

---

1) Abby: Où est-ce que tu as passé, uh, ton? enfance?

[Where did you spend, uh, your? childhood?]

2) Caleb: Pas ton.

[Not ton.]

3) Abby: uh . . . ta?

[Uh . . . ta?]

4) Caleb: Oh. Tu as raison! Ton enfance!

[[Oh. You are right! Your childhood!]

5) Abby: Parce que . . . enfance . . . commence . . . avec . . . um, e.]

[Because . . . enfance . . . starts . . . with . . . um, e.]

6) Caleb: Très bien. Très bien.

[Very good. Very good.]

A final example from the conversation cards shows the collaborative construction of turns via self-initiated/other-completed repair. This process creates a situation in which the construction of a question about the disadvantages of foreign travel takes nine turns from the questioner and the monitor, Betsy and Cindy respectively. In each of her turns, Betsy implicitly requests feedback from the monitor on the form of the question constructed thus far.

In these interactions generally, the monitors enjoy a greater interactional status than do the other two participants, by virtue of the information they hold in the form of cards with correct versions of the questions to be asked. Accordingly, most of the talk is subject to repair and the monitor tends to participate very actively, producing a preponderance of "other" involvement in the resolution of conversational problems.

Figure 3

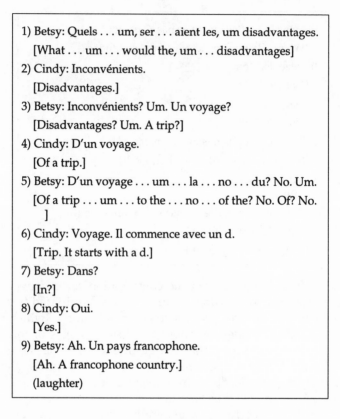

1) Betsy: Quels . . . um, ser . . . aient les, um disadvantages.

[What . . . um . . . would the, um . . . disadvantages]

2) Cindy: Inconvénients.

[Disadvantages.]

3) Betsy: Inconvénients? Um. Un voyage?

[Disadvantages? Um. A trip?]

4) Cindy: D'un voyage.

[Of a trip.]

5) Betsy: D'un voyage . . . um . . . la . . . no . . . du? No. Um.

[Of a trip . . . um . . . to the . . . no . . . of the? No. Of? No.
]

6) Cindy: Voyage. Il commence avec un d.

[Trip. It starts with a d.]

7) Betsy: Dans?

[In?]

8) Cindy: Oui.

[Yes.]

9) Betsy: Ah. Un pays francophone.

[Ah. A francophone country.]

(laughter)

Results: Discussion of a Collaborative Assignment

In the second task, the learners are working on a collaborative assignment involving the achievement of group consensus, where the focus is on the establishment of social relationships and the exchange of meaning. The types of conversational trouble sources encountered, and their treatment, are fundamentally different from those of the conversation card task. For considerations of developing grammatical ability, what is most interesting about these data is the nature of other-involvement in repair. As might be expected, when the "other" initiates repair, it is for the purpose of obtaining clarification or repetition of a previous utterance. In other words, this task promotes the interactive work identified as "negotiation of meaning" by SLA researchers. In terms of developing discourse competence, it is interesting to note that the learners tend to achieve clarification by adhering to basic rules of politeness. In figure 4, Rose obtains a repetition of Pete's utterance in this manner.

Figure 4

---

1) Pete: Est-ce que tu vas aller à l'étrangère pour étudier?

[Are you going to go abroad to study?]

2) Rose: Excusez-moi? Excusez-moi?

[Excuse me? Excuse me?]

3) Pete: Est-ce que tu vas aller à l'étrangère pour étudier?

[Are you going to go abroad to study?]

4) Rose: Non.

[No.]

An additional fact of interest about these interactions is the tendency for learners to complete repair by code-switching from French to English and back. In contrast to learners of mixed first language background who are learning English as a second language, these learners may opt to avail themselves of commonalities in language and culture. In this way, they may avoid the interactional risk and the disruption of conversational rhythm and topic development created by prolonged repair sequences. In the next example, Nathan requests a repetition or clarification of Kevin's utterance in turn #4. Kevin opts for immediate clarification of his meaning by switching to English.

Figure 5

---

1) Nathan: Je voyagerai en France la semaine prochaine.
   [I will travel in France next week.]
2) Kevin: Ah oui?
   [Ah yes?]
3) Nathan: Et-oui. Et c'est possible de-
   [And yes. And it is possible to-
4) Kevin: Tu vas aller là?
   [You are going to go there?]
5) Nathan: Pardon?
6) Kevin: Are you going there?
7) Nathan: Oui.
   [Yes]

A great deal of the repair in these conversations centers around missing lexical items. Again, a common strategy for the resolution of this problem is code-switching. In the final example, Leo abandons his attempts at circumlocution in favor of simply stating what he means in English. May interprets this as a request for assistance, and attempts to help by coining a word.

Figure 6

---

1) Lew: Oui toute ma famille est est venue d'Allemagne
   mais beaucoup de notre, uh, beaucoup de choses que
   nous que nous faisons . . . customs. Habits.

   [Yes my whole family came came from Germany but a
   lot of our, uh, a lot of things that we that we do . . .
   customs. Habits.]
2) Mary: Uh, coustumes?
   [((word coinage))]
   ((laughter))
3) Mary: Oui je comprends.
   [Yes I understand.]

Discussion

This study has explored task-related variation in the resolution of conversational trouble sources by classroom learners of French. The two tasks under consideration do not represent the many possibilities for classroom styles that might exist closer to the center of Kramsch's classroom style continuum (from "instructional" to "natural"). Rather, they were selected to illustrate interaction at the extremes of the continuum. This approach demonstrates both advantages and disadvantages of particular task foci for the development of communicative ability.

The conversation-card task is recommended to foreign language teachers because it is believed to allow participation in conversational interaction without a corresponding sacrifice of formal accuracy. Unfortunately, it is not clear that either one of these goals is attained by the participants in this study. Whereas face-to-face conversational interaction requires means of attending to and resolving one's own trouble sources, what occurred in the talk observed here was a marked reliance on repair provided by the participant whose role most resembled that of a teacher. Indeed, the style adopted by the participants falls very near the instructional end of Kramsch's continuum. In any case, repair is not based upon normal conversational intentions (i.e., making oneself clear). Rather, since the point of the interaction is to guess the forms on the monitor's card, repair revolves around this goal. The status of "error" falls on all forms which do not match the official version of questions, including forms which are otherwise comprehensible and/or grammatically accurate.

In American foreign language teaching, the impetus to experiment with strong versions of communicative teaching tends to momentum in a maze of conflicting ideas about how communicative ability is acquired. At issue is what Savignon has called "the tension that presently exists between the encouragement of second language use, or functional proficiency, on the one hand, and a renewed emphasis on discrete points of sentence-level grammar, on the other." (1985, 130). The conversation-card task is an example of recent attempts to combine these two conflicting

pedagogical objectives into one activity type. This attempt, as we
have seen, results in interactions among learners which bear little resemblance to conversation. Rather, the activity is very much
a discrete-point grammar translation exercise embedded in the
discourse patterns of the traditional classroom. Many learners
and instructors, equating participation in this kind of talk with
"learning French," no doubt remain unaware that participation
in conversation requires abilities beyond the formulation of accurate sentences.

In the meantime, conversational interaction among
learners is clearly desirable, yet the foreign language classrooms
studied here presented specific challenges as settings for such
interaction. The participants in this study share not only a
common native language, but also a good deal of common
experience as students at their respective schools. At the very
outset then, holding a conversation in French is a rather unusual
thing to do. The more "natural" task type does appear to present
certain advantages: learners engaged in the types of interactive
work considered productive of SLA while practicing discourse-
level strategies necessary for involvement in polite conversation.
However, frequent code-switching reflects the fact that French is
not logically necessary for communicative exchange. Having
reached an impasse, these learners simply did not have to take
the interactional risk of appearing incompetent. Rather, they
often chose to express their idea in English, then get on with the
conversation.

In terms of psycholinguistic perspectives on repair in
interactive work, there is an interesting contrast here between
this situation and that of learners who have mixed first-language
backgrounds. The subjects of American studies in SLA, including
most of the studies on group work, have been learners of English
as a second language (e.g., Doughty and Pica 1986; Gass and
Varonis 1985; Pica 1987, Pica and Doughty 1985a, 1985b; Porter
1986; Schwartz 1980; Yule 1991; Yule and McDonald, 1990).
These learners typically do not share a common linguistic and
cultural background, and so must rely more heavily upon their
second language for communication among themselves. It is
precisely this which creates a need for the meaning negotiation
considered productive of optimal input and, by extension,

second-language development. The extent to which the results of these studies can be generalized to the foreign language context remains in question.

It is important to note, however, the ever-increasing linguistic and cultural heterogeneity that charaterizes the American classroom (Kramsch 1993). This fact will inevitably alter contexts of communication in ways that are particularly significant to language educators and that must be taken into account when evaluating the implications of research results.

Meanwhile, in order to develop conversational competence, it is probably the case that learners need at least some involvement in conversational work. The results of this study suggest that learners are able, albeit in a limited way, to provide each other with opportunities for such interaction. The limitations of classroom group work for attaining conversational competence reside not only in possible provision of ungrammatical input, but also in the fact that the interactions in question usually are not examples of cross-cultural communication. The ideal approach to development of conversational ability would balance opportunities for student involvement in conversation itself with efforts to promote understanding of cross-cultural variation in conversational style.

Appendix

Transcription Conventions

The transcription system employed in this study includes the following conventions:

1) The symbol = is used in two different ways:

    a) If a speaker's turn is interrupted, usually by a listener's response during a pause, = is inserted at the beginning of the pause and at the point at which the speaker resumes.

    b) If inserted at the end of one speaker's turn and the beginning of another's, = indicates that there was no overlap between the two turns.

2) Long pauses, of five seconds or more, are indicated with an ellipse: . . .

3) Intonation is marked in one of three ways:

    ? : rising intonation, not necessarily a question

    ! : strong emphasis with falling intonation

    . : falling (final) intonation

4) A hyphen indicates an abrupt cutoff with level pitch.

5) Double parentheses indicate transcriber's comments.

Translations of the learners' contributions in French are provided in brackets. Because of the nature of the learners' talk, these translations are of necessity approximations.

Applying Discourse Analysis to Students' Videotaped Performances
A Recent Methodology, a New Beginning

Elli Doukanari

Abstract

Discourse analysis has been applied extensively to native speaker conversations, but has not yet received wide recognition and application to second-language (L2) learners' discourse. This study addresses the significance of discourse analysis in L2 classroom research where the teacher-researcher can analyze data and draw conclusions, even in the absence of the traditional control group. The article provides practical examples of a way that discourse analysis may be used as a methodological tool to interpret L2 phenomena. Using the students' videotaped performance in a Greek class as data, I demonstrate how the students' own output can serve as valuable input or resource of input in L2 teaching.

Introduction

Earlier research has focused on quantitative analysis as the prominent methodology to assess second language teaching and learning. Although quantitative measures are undoubtedly valuable, there is a growing need for a more qualitative approach to classroom research, for which discourse analysis could be useful as a methodology. Discourse analysis has been applied extensively to native speaker discourse and conversations by researchers such as Chafe (1980), Erickson (1984), Tannen (1984), Schiffrin (1994), and others, but it has not yet received wide recognition and application to second-language learners' discourse. This may be partly attributed to the fact that in the field of language teaching, the validity of discourse analysis is disputed in cases where either there is lack of a control group, or teacher-researchers have not yet become familiar with the use of discourse analysis as a tool in linguistic research. Discourse analysis is a vast area and one of the least defined in linguistics, and this may be another reason for its lack of recognition.

Discourse analysis is an interdisciplinary field that is based on a number of academic disciplines different from one another, such as linguistics, anthropology, philology, sociology, communication, rhetoric, philosophy, and artificial intelligence. According to Tannen, "discourse analysis has been criticized by some reviewers for its heterogeneity: for not reflecting a monolithic theory and a consistent method of analysis. . . . Discourse analysis will never be monolithic because it does not grow out of a single discipline" (1989, 7). As a result of this interdisciplinary nature of discourse analysis, there are different approaches to it, namely pragmatics, speech act theory, ethnomethodology, interactional sociolinguistics, ethnography of communication, and variation theory. It is important to clarify that not all of the approaches developed initially as means of analyzing discourse. Particular issues have led certain approaches to resort to discourse analysis. For example, pragmatics primarily focuses on speaker meaning at the level of utterances (usually sentences) rather than text. But since utterances are situated in context (including text), it is often necessary for pragmatics to provide means to analyze discourse. Although these approaches often overlap in their ways of analyzing discourse, they differ in the work of various researchers. The varying approaches to discourse provide different theoretical and metatheoretical assumptions on what constitutes text and context, structure and function and discourse and communication. The various approaches to discourse also hold different beliefs about methods for collecting and analyzing data. The debate in discourse analysis is what kind of method to use, what constitutes data, and what is a valid proof. Schiffrin (1994) provides extensive insights on the above issues related to discourse analysis.

The usefulness and application of discourse analysis on second-language research is indicated in Larsen-Freeman (1980), Kramsch (1981), and others. There is, however, still a question on the part of applied linguists and teachers on how discourse analysis can be applied to nonnative discourse. In classes in discourse and conversational analyses, a question often raised by applied linguistics graduate students is how discourse analysis can be used as a methodology to assess language teaching and learning. It is clear that more studies based on practical applications are needed in order to (a) emphasize the significance and applicability of discourse and conversational analyses theories to second language teaching research, and (b) enable and train graduate students and language teachers to use discourse analysis as a methodological tool in order to analyze and interpret classroom discourse.

This study addresses the significance of discourse analysis in second language classroom research where the teacher-researcher can analyze data and draw conclusions, even in the absence of the traditional control group. The study provides practical examples of a way that discourse analysis may be used as a methodological tool in order to interpret second language phenomena. For this, discourse analysis is applied using my students' videotaped performance in a Greek class as data to demonstrate how the students' own *output* can serve as valuable *input* or *a resource of input* in second-language teaching.

Originally, I videotaped student performances in search of communicative activities in the language classroom.[1] In the less commonly taught languages such as modern Greek, where a paucity of adequate teaching materials is more apparent than in the more commonly taught languages such as English, Spanish, or French, the students' videotaped performances can be especially useful to supplement teaching materials which lack communicative activities. As Lonergan (1984) suggests, student performance on video may be used to foster language learning. By carefully examining the data of the videotaped activities, I recognized that in addition to the pedagogical significance of videotaped student performances, the application of discourse analysis to those data is also of great importance to the researcher for methodological purposes.

Data Collection and Significance

The subjects of this study were four American students (three males and a female), all in their twenties, from one of the intermediate Greek classes at the School of Languages and Linguistics, Georgetown University. The researcher, a native speaker of Greek, was their instructor. The subjects were assigned role-play tasks in front of a video camera. The term role-play is used throughout this paper to refer to the activity during which the students were given a scenario title (a scene at a Greek restaurant), a language function (how to order food at a Greek restaurant), and a set of roles (the waiter and the customers).

It is important to emphasize that prior to videotaping, the students were prepared accordingly, and rehearsed the role-play.[2] The videotaping took place in a conference room at Georgetown University. Although one might expect that a new environment would make the students more uncomfortable, this did not appear to be the case in the present study. On the contrary, in an environment different from the classroom where they were usually taught and tested, the students stated that they felt more comfortable. This may be also attributed to the fact that the students were accustomed to environments other than the language classroom; i.e., on several occasions, lessons were conducted outdoors, or the students were taken to the same conference room for other language activities.

Five different takes were done in order to make the students more comfortable before the camera and to practice different characters and plots. The students were instructed that during each take, the performance should not be interrupted for any reason, to assure a more coherent interaction. Students were given the opportunity to repair their performances in subsequent takes. Of course, the detailed procedures followed for the videotaping are important not only for methodological purposes but also for pedagogical reasons. However, this constitutes a topic of its own and is discussed in Doukanari (1995).

Role-playing in front of a video camera became a fun activity and gave the students the opportunity to use the target language for the purpose of communication rather than to test their knowledge of the language. This resulted in a collection of data as "natural" as possible for a foreign language class. In discourse analysis, the collection of "natural" data is preferred by a number of researchers because it elicits spontaneous, ordinary, and unconstrained flow of speech. The researcher as an observer and analyst can use context in its broadest sense to explain the presence of certain linguistic forms in discourse, rather than just concentrating on overt meaning (Linde and Labov 1975, Tannen 1984). "Natural" is placed in quotation marks because the presence of the video camera may somehow hinder the production of natural speech. However, since a tape recorder or video camera is necessary, discourse analysts are forced to restrict themselves to data collected in as natural a way as possible. The fact that the conversation participants are second-language learners and therefore more conscious about the language, and the technicalities related to the role-play (e.g., role-play is acting and specific roles and functions are assigned) may also interfere with the production of "natural" speech. However, role-play is not as controlled as other classroom activities, such as drills and question-answer exercises.

Role-play as an activity is of *pedagogical* importance because it provides students with the opportunity to move beyond the structured exercises which are based on sentence-level syntax to a more communicative activity that elicits more free speech and creates interaction among them. Role-play is also useful to the researcher for *methodological* purposes because as an interactional activity, it results in a collection of data that involve more spontaneous and "natural" discourse. The selection of a particular *task* is also important for the discourse analyst; for example, ordering food at a restaurant does not require only certain language structures, but is a give-and-take interaction among people that involves personal, social, and cultural values. The utterance of a student determines the language and expression of the other students, leading to production of discourse. Conversation is dynamic, and meaning is constantly negotiated. When we videotape our students' performances, we capture this dynamic nature of interaction in a particular context in which the conversation takes place. The sitting arrangement, gestures, and other nonlinguistic and paralinguistic phenomena always accompany language.

Discourse Analysis as a Methodological Tool

Wagner-Gough and Hatch (1975) address the need for a more global analysis of language learning that looks beyond the sentence grammar, taking into consideration the interactions in which learners engage. In this study, the videotaped student interactions constitute data that are transcribed and analyzed to interpret language learning phenomena.

In discourse analysis, the entire transcribed discourse or conversations are analyzed depending on the specific phenomena that the researchers are concerned with, such as discourse markers, turn-taking, turn-giving, repair, peer input, or other linguistic and paralinguistic phenomena. Analysts disagree on the details of transcription systems; for example, Sacks, Schegloff, and Jefferson (1974) have a different transcription system from Tannen (1984, xix). It is important, when transcribing discourse, to choose a transcription system and to be consistent with the conventions of that system. The examples in this paper follow Tannen's (1984) "Key to Transcription Conventions."[3]

Schiffrin (1994) describes two main analyses of discourse: the structural and the functional. Structurally-based analyses of discourse assume that the textual structure consists of smaller linguistic units (constituents), which have particular relation-ships with one another and which can occur in a restricted set of often rule-governed arrangements. These structurally-based analyses extend methods of linguistic analyses that have been useful for lower levels of linguistic description, such as clauses and sentences. Functionally-based analyses view discourse as a socially and culturally organized way of speaking through which particular functions are realized. Those functions are not limited to tasks that can be accomplished by language alone; rather, they can center upon explicitly non-linguistic tasks such as maintaining interaction or building social relationships. Although structural linguistic regularities can be examined in functional analyses, the focus of analysis tends to be the way patterns of talk are used by participants for certain purposes and result from the application of communicative strategies in a particular context. A functional analysis to discourse is used in the present study.

Analysis and Discussion

In this section, I demonstrate a way that functional discourse analysis may be used in order to draw conclusions about language learning. By using the functional approach to discourse analysis, as mentioned above, we do not look only at the language structures students use, but we are also concerned with strategies used to interact and communicate with each other. We look at the way students project themselves, and their understanding of cultural and social values.

In the examples throughout this chapter, the original Greek text appears transliterated in bold on the first line. The second line is a gloss (a word-for-word translation). The third line is an idiomatic translation. Dots preceding or following conversational segments indicate that the segments are part of a larger text. Underlined utterances indicate points for discussion.

In the following examples, the teacher-researcher is interested in the different ways that the students' output serves as input to their fellow students. In example I, two of the students portraying the customers, Yiannis and Renée, discuss the food they are going to order. Following their discussion, Demetris, the waiter, enters the scene and takes their order.

Example I

. . .

1. Yiannis: **Ti   na paroume. oum.**
               What to   take.   hmm.
               What should we order. hmm.

2. Renée: **Souvlaki?**
               Souvlaki?
               Souvlaki?

3. Yiannis: **A   nai. to souvlaki   thanai   kalo.**
               Oh yes. the souvlaki   must be good.
               Oh yes. the souvlaki must be good.

4. Renée: **Horiatiki,**
               Country style (salad),
               Greek salad,

5. Yiannis: **A. nai malista. a kai mia feta,**
               Oh. yes yes.   oh and one feta,
               Oh. yes yes. oh and one feta cheese,

6. Renée: **Nai.**
               Yes.
               Yes.

7. Yiannis: **kai mia feta. kai... ti   tha   pioume.**
               and one feta. and... what shall we drink.
               and one feta cheese. and... what shall we
               drink.

8. Renée: **E   krasi.   kokkino.**
               Um wine.   red.
               Um wine. red.

9. Yiannis: **Endaxei.**
               Okay.
               Okay.

10. Demetris: **Oriste.   ti   tha   fate?**
    [waiter]   Your pleasure. what will you eat?
               Yes. what will you eat?

11. Yiannis: **I despinis, thelei.. souvlakia, mia horia-,**
               The miss,   wants.. souvlakia,   one cou-,
               The lady, wants.. souvlakia, one Gr-,

12.   <u>mia horiatiki   salata, kai mia feta.</u>
        <u>one country style salad, and one feta.</u>
        <u>one Greek salad, and one feta cheese</u>.

13.   <u>kai to   krasi pou theloume einai..</u>
        and the <u>wine</u> that we want is..
        and the <u>wine</u> we want is..

14.   <u>theloume na pioume kokkino krasi.</u>
        we want <u>to drink   red   wine</u>.
        we want <u>to drink red wine</u>.

. . .

In the above example, Yiannis projects himself as a Greek gentleman, where he asks the lady he accompanies to the restaurant, Renée, what she would like to eat. The request is followed by a negotiation of the students on what they want to order. The negotiation is achieved through a conversational kind of discourse, by using questions and statements. Throughout this segment, we can detect different strategies that allow for each student's output to become an input for the others. I focus only on one of the many important discourse strategies observed: *repetition*.

According to Tannen, "each time a word or phrase is repeated, its meaning is altered" (1987, 576). In this example, Yiannis repeats the word *souvlaki* (line 3), following Renée's utterance (line 2). The first time the word *souvlaki* is used by Renée, a *suggestion* is made for the kind of food desired. When the other student (Yiannis), however, repeats the word, he makes an *agreement* to order that particular dish. Thus, by repetition, the meaning of the utterance is altered and serves a different function. A suggestion leads to an agreement.

After the two students negotiate what they want to eat, Yiannis uses Renée's output as well as his own to place their order (lines 11–14). Thus, Yiannis takes the segmented conversational discourse, and by repetition of utterances used during their negotiation, transforms it into a more holistic discourse, which takes another meaning and fulfills the function, *to order food*. We have seen in this example how through repetition, the students' utterances display each time a different meaning and serve a different function, from making a suggestion, to making an agreement, and consequently ordering food. By using different strategies such as repetition, each student's utterance, which is an output, is received by another student as an input, which is utilized to create another utterance (output) to be used again as an input, and so on.

Tannen further argues that repetition also creates coherence. Repetition "not only ties parts of discourse to other parts, but ties participants to the discourse and to each other, linking individual speakers in a conversation" (1987, 584), and sending a metamessage of rapport between the participants, thus creating interpersonal involvement. Swain (1985) suggests that, in second-language learning, the message should not only be conveyed, but conveyed coherently and appropriately. In the above example (I), by repetition, not only do the students negotiate meaning, but they also create at the same time appropriate and coherent discourse and establish rapport, thus creating interpersonal relationships, which ties in with Swain's (1985) and Tannen's (1987) claims.

In example I, Yiannis and Renée (the customers) agree on everything without creating any conflict. There were other instances throughout the videotaping, however, where student-created conflicts arose; for example, by not agreeing on the food and drinks they would order. Thus, in the different takes, the students are given the opportunity to communicate by providing each other with valuable and coherent input, by creating conflicting and nonconflicting situations, and by projecting different selves, all in order to build interpersonal relationships.

The functional approach of analyzing discourse, which focuses on the way students project different selves and how they interact with each other, enables us as teachers and discourse analysts to see ways that student output becomes input for fellow students. An important issue is raised here. The *peer repetition* that frequently occurs in student output becomes a significant input strategy, and consequently facilitates learning. This ties in with previous studies that recognize peer repetition as an important process for L1 and L2 learning. For example, Watson-Gegeo and Gegeo (1986) observe that the Kwara'ae (Melanesian people of Malaita, Solomon Islands), speaking an Austronesian language, use in their caregiver speech certain kinds of *repetitive routines* to teach small children language, sociocultural knowledge, and interactional behavior. Thus, repetition, as an input strategy, plays an important role in language teaching, learning, and acquisition.

Repetition has been identified as a distinctive feature of audiolingualism. With the emergence of the communicative approach to language teaching, repetition has been misinterpreted by language teachers as a mechanical technique that hinders communication in the second language. One of the drawbacks of audiolingualism, however, is not repetition per se, but the overemphasis and restriction of repetition to the sentence level, rather than viewing repetition as part of discourse. According to Tannen, "repetition is a resource by which conversationalists together create a discourse, a relationship, and a world" (1987, 601). Since studies have shown that repetition is a major ingredient in native speaker discourse, and plays an important role in L1 and L2 learning, then repetition, especially peer repetition, should constitute a major strategy in communicative language teaching, in order to enable students to communicate by creating coherent discourse and to establish interpersonal relationships in the foreign language.

Using discourse analysis, we can also compare different takes. Example II contains parts from the second and fifth takes. In this case, we observe that *peer correction* also occurs in the students' output and becomes an input. During the videotaping of the role-play, again through repetition, students indirectly correct each other through the natural flow of the conversation. For example, during the second take, one of the students, Renée, rather than ordering *paidakia* (spareribs), orders *pedakia* (children). During the fifth take, however, after listening to two of the other students in the previous takes pronouncing the word correctly, Renée picks up the appropriate pronunciation, as is clearly illustrated in example II below.

Example II

Second take

. . .

15. Demetris: **Oraia,   kai seis mandam?**
    [waiter]   Beautifully, and you madam?
                 Good, and you madam?

16. Renée: [she laughs] **pedakia, se parakalo,**
                 [she laughs] <u>children</u>, please,
                 [she laughs] <u>children</u>, please,

17.   **kai ena soupa.**
                 and one soup.
                 and one soup.

. . .

Fifth take

. . .

18. Yiannis: **Ego tha paro paidakia.**
                 I   will take spareribs.
                 I will have spareribs.

19. Renée: **<u>Paidakia</u>? ohi. um mbrizoles.**
                 <u>Spareribs</u>? no.   um steak.
                 <u>Spareribs</u>? no. um steak.

. . .

Throughout the different takes, Renée's fellow students use the word *paidakia* with its correct pronunciation. Therefore, by repeating the word several times, they indirectly correct Renée, who by the fifth take picks up the correct pronunciation immediately repeating it after Yiannis through the natural flow of the conversation. Whether peer correction was intended or unintended in this case is difficult to determine. What is obvious is that fellow student output—that is, the repeated use of the problematic word—has provided Renée with useful input which she utilizes to correct herself.

At this point, a question arises on the part of the discourse analyst. Renée laughs before she orders "children" (line 16), so it might be that she has pronounced the word incorrectly in order to create a humorous situation. However, through more careful examination of the whole transcription of the five takes, it became apparent that Renée had mispronounced the word in other instances prior to the fifth take, none of which indicated any voluntary attempts on her part to make a joke. This was verified in another classroom activity where the students were given the opportunity to analyze their own discourse, at which time Renée revealed that she had picked up the correct pronunciation from her fellow students. This is another important part of discourse analysis as a methodology. As discourse analysts, we need to take into consideration the whole discourse and may interview the participants to verify an interpretation of discourse which is questionable.

In the above example, by concentrating only on repetition, we have seen how student output is available as input to fellow students and how that input is acquired. Corder (1967, 165) suggests that input is "what is available for going in" and intake is "what goes in." Through discourse analysis, it becomes obvious not only how the students' output serves as input (e.g. through repetition), but whether it becomes an intake as well. According to Hatch and Long:

> Discourse analysis has provided us with a look at the "teaching syllabus" available to the learner outside the classroom. It shows us that the learner receives language which is simplified in many ways. However, it is difficult to say precisely what the learner learns about language in such exchanges. Our claims must be tempered with caution. Yet, it has opened avenues for investigating second language acquisition. (1980, 34–35)

Even though Hatch and Long recognize the contribution of discourse analysis to second language acquisition, they caution researchers as to the claims they make on language acquisition through the application of discourse analysis. Example II carefully demonstrates how input becomes an intake. This was shown: (a) by taking the actual discourse of the students' performance as a starting point; (b) by a thorough examination of all five takes of the whole discourse; (c) by taking into consideration nonlinguistic and paralinguistic phenomena; and (d) by interviewing the participants when deemed necessary. For example, when Renée used the incorrect pronunciation of the word *paidakia* (spareribs) and ordered *pedakia* (children), the fact that the word was accompanied by laughter was also taken into consideration. After all, the activity of role-play in front of a video camera is entertaining and there was a possibility that Renée already knew the correct pronunciation of the word, but might have changed it to make a joke. Therefore, an interpretation based on language alone and on partial examination of discourse might affect the credibility of the researcher's claims. Hence, I considered it necessary in this case, to examine the discourse in its entire entity, both to take into consideration nonlinguistic and paralinguistic phenomena and to interview the student in order to confirm my findings.

Through the above examples, the kinds of peer input available are observed, such as *peer correction through repetition*. This illustrates how discourse analysis as theory and methodology can be combined with theories and methodologies of language teaching in order to interpret second-language phenomena occurring in our student interactions. Throughout the analysis, I also observed other phenomena such as students *simplifying their output* to make it more comprehensible to their fellow students, thus providing each other with what Krashen (1985) calls the "*i + 1*" comprehensible input needed for acquisition to occur. In other instances, student output served as *recycled input*; for example, in response to Renée's question whether coffee was available at the restaurant, Demetris (the waiter) gave directions to a nearby café and fulfilled another language function, how to give directions. Thus, by his output, Demetris provided his fellow students with recycled input given by the teacher in previous lessons.

The students' videotaped performances can also be used in later activities in the classroom. An activity which can be used later is what I call the evaluation stage (Doukanari 1995), where students and teacher evaluate the student performance by using the videotape as reference to analyze their discourse. The evaluation stage is similar to Di Pietro's (1987) debriefing stage. Di Pietro, since he does not videotape the students' role-play, suggests that students at this stage recall the utterances they used during their performance. But, according to Tannen, "'reported speech' is not reported at all but is creatively constructed by a current speaker in a current situation" (1989, 105). That is, a dialogue is recreated rather than reported. One can imagine how much more difficult it is for foreign language learners to recall a dialogue that occurred during a performance. Therefore, the videotape can be used for reference to the actual data in a particular context, rather than trying to recall what was said during the interaction.

During the evaluation stage, one of the problems identified by the students was that some of them had referred to the word *nero* (water) in the singular and others in the plural, which is illustrated in example III.

Example III

. . .

20.	Yiannis:	**Na mas ferete kai... nera?**
		To us you bring and... waters?
		Will you bring us... water?
21.	Demetris:	**Malista** [he leaves]
	[waiter]	Yes. [he leaves]
		Of course. [he leaves]
22.		[he returns] oriste to nero.
		[he returns] here is the water.
		[he returns] here is the water.

. . .

Some students argued that the word *nero* (line 22) is only used in the singular and others that it can also be used in its plural form *nera* (line 20). This gave the teacher the opportunity to explain how the word *nero* can be used in either its singular or plural form, in that particular context and in other contexts. Therefore, in the evaluation stage, the videotape serves as a *resource of input* to be analyzed in the language classroom. In a way, the students use discourse analysis together with the teacher to evaluate and benefit from their performance. Therefore, in this case, not only does discourse analysis serve as a methodology, but it is also used as a *classroom activity*.

In this study, in order to demonstrate a way that discourse analysis may be applied to interpret language learning phenomena, I have investigated how student output serves as input to fellow students. Teachers may also use discourse analysis to investigate other, more specific phenomena, such as the way students utilize information they have learned about greetings, and how they give directions.

Concluding Remarks

I have demonstrated how discourse analysis of our students' videotaped performances can be useful as a methodology and even as a classroom activity. Discourse analysis can be used by the teacher-researcher as a methodology through careful examination of the transcription based on the videotape itself. In order to use discourse analysis as a methodological tool, teachers also need to be familiar with the theories of discourse analysis and the different ways of analyzing discourse, which combined with their knowledge of language teaching theories will enable them to interpret classroom discourse phenomena. As Widdowson (1978) suggests, if we are seriously interested in a communicative approach to language teaching, we need to consider the complex nature of communication and discourse, and the abilities involved to create discourse. Discourse analysis can also be used as a classroom activity where students and teacher work together by carefully analyzing and evaluating the students' videotaped performances and therefore initiate conversation and detect and provide solutions to language, social, and cultural problems in that particular context.

Analysis of *native* speaker discourse enables us to design foreign language syllabi, materials, and teaching activities. However, the teacher-researchers need to add to their knowledge, that analysis of the *foreign* language learners' discourse is also useful to diagnose student problems, evaluate their progress, and detect patterns of learning. This methodology can be used by comparing control and experimental groups, but as we have already seen, it can well be used to draw conclusions even in the absence of a control group.

Larsen-Freeman (1990) addresses the need for a language teaching theory. I would like to suggest that discourse analysis, especially functional analysis, can help build on such a language teaching theory. Language is not only morphemes, words, clauses, and sentences bound to a text, accompanied by grammatical, syntactic, and semantic rules. Language is also bound with psychological, social, and cultural nature, an issue that the functional analysis of discourse takes into account. How many of us as language teachers face the frustration of providing our students with rules that can very well be followed and applied to the exercises found in our teaching materials, but when we have our students watch a TV interview, or engage in activities such as conversation time and student role-play, we discover that the exceptions to the rules are more numerous than the rules themselves? Language is not so clear-cut; it is complex and dynamic, constantly changing according to participants and situations. This is why videotaping our own students' discourse and carefully analyzing it is a useful methodology in language teaching.

The groups we teach are usually not the same in terms of proficiency levels, needs, and cultural backgrounds. Each group will face different language problems, even if the task is the same. Therefore, becoming familiar with the activity of videotaping, which pedagogically serves communicative purposes and in addition constitutes data for linguistic research, as well as becoming familiar with discourse analysis as a theory and methodology, will enable us to fulfill the specific needs of each individual class.

In this article, I do not suggest that discourse analysis based on student videotaped performances is the only way of building teaching theories and designing classroom activities. But it can serve as another building stone for language teaching, learning and communication.

NOTES

Special thanks to John Staczek and Heidi Hamilton, Department of Linguistics, Georgetown University, for sharing much of their valuable time to provide me with useful comments. I would also like to extend my thanks to my students of the 1989 Intermediate Greek class, and to Jackie Tanner, director of Language Learning Technology, School of Languages and Linguistics, Georgetown University, and her staff, for videotaping my students' performances and thus making this study possible.

1. For information on communicative language teaching, see, among others, Widdowson (1978), Littlewood (1981), and Nunan (1989).

2. Prior to the videotaping, the students were provided with cultural information about Greek food and restaurants, as well as gestures and other paralinguistic phenomena that may occur in an interaction between a waiter and customers. The students were also given a language frame illustrating formulaic expressions exchanged in a restaurant. Subsequently, the students were given a menu to practice names of Greek foods. The students also listened to dialogues of native speakers ordering food, and worked on exercises. The preparation for the videotaping activity is discussed in more detail in Doukanari (1995).

3. The transcription conventions used in this article are:

.. noticeable pause or break in rhythm (less than 0.5 second)

... half second pause

. marks sentence-final falling intonation

? marks yes/no question rising intonation

- marks a glottal stop or abrupt cutting off of sound

, marks phrase-final intonation (more to come)

[brackets] mark comments on quality of speech and context

Stimulating the Right Brain in the Second-Language Classroom

Theresa A. Waldspurger

Abstract

Methodologies abound in second-language (L2) learning, but few of them are deeply rooted in neurological and/or psycholinguistic theory. One such theory deals with brain lateralization and the role the right hemisphere plays in learning a second language. It is generally believed that the primary language centers are located in the left hemisphere; the right brain, in contrast, is not considered to be a fundamental influence in verbal expression. Some researchers believe, however, that the right hemisphere may play a larger role in language learning than previously thought, and that stimulating the right brain while acquiring a second language can lead to a greater degree of success in L2 acquisition (McCarthy 1987; Seliger 1982; Schneiderman and Wesche 1983; Schneiderman 1986; Scovel 1988). This article discusses classroom methods and activities which can stimulate the right brain in order to harness and amplify L2 learning potential.

It has long been assumed that in over 95% of the human population, language comprehension and production is predominantly controlled by the left cerebral hemisphere, as has been repeatedly borne out in aphasia studies. In recent years, however, researchers have found more evidence which ascribes a significant—if still subordinate—role to the right hemisphere with respect to language processing. There have been an increasing number of studies in which aphasics with *right* hemisphere lesions have demonstrated language deficits (Chary 1986; Joanette et al. 1990). Specifically, studies of both normal subjects and aphasics with right brain lesions have shown that the right brain plays a definite role in the processing of a number of linguistic phenomena. These phenomena include prosody (Joanette et al. 1990; Behrens 1985); normal discourse, such as indirect questions, irony, humor, inferences, storytelling, speech acts, and other contextual cues (Molloy et al. 1990; Joanette and Goulet 1990; Joanette et al. 1990); lexical semantics, including differentiating between connotative and metaphorical meanings of words (Brownell 1988), listing nouns in related semantic fields (Joanette and Goulet 1988), and polysemy (Chiarello 1988); and recognition of letters, word patterns, and other visual material, especially complex symbols such as two-word Chinese characters (Keung and Hoosain 1989; Joanette et al. 1990). Even in young children, the right hemisphere has been shown to contribute to language learning (Peters 1981; Bakker 1981). Children who have had one of their cerebral hemispheres removed suffer significant language deficits, despite the theory that the remaining hemisphere can take over early in life. Children with only their left hemispheres remaining have problems with visual receptive skills necessary for reading and apparently better processed by the right hemisphere (Dennis and Whitaker 1977).

All of these studies point to the possibility that there are certain linguistic faculties which are processed, at least in part, by the right hemisphere. These abilities include linguistic and emotional prosody such as stress, rhythm, and intonation; the processing of letters and word patterns necessary for efficient reading skills; contextual cues that provide cohesion and coherence in discourse; and certain aspects of lexical semantics, especially the processing of concrete words that create strong images and formulaic, emotional, high-frequency language such as swear words or the days of the week.

The left hemisphere is often characterized as analytic, sequential, and field-independent, while the right hemisphere is usually described as holistic, parallel, and field-dependent. Goldberg and Costa (1981), after detailed anatomical studies of the brain, found that these two contrasting modes of processing are due to different neuroanatomic structures and the asymmetrical organization of the brain's hemispheres. The right hemisphere possesses a greater neuronic capacity with which to process *multiple* modes of representation in a cognitive task. The left hemisphere, on the other hand, excels in tasks which require a *single* mode of representation. They found that trained musicians, expert Morse code operators, and native language speakers exhibited a distinct right ear advantage in dichotic listening tests, suggesting left hemisphere dominance for their respective tasks. Untrained musicians, novice Morse code operators, and second-language learners, however, displayed a left ear advantage, signifying greater right hemisphere participation. Goldberg and Costa conclude that in the beginning stages of learning a highly complex system, such as language, the right brain participates more; as proficiency increases, that is, as language processing becomes more automatic or routinized, the left hemisphere takes over.

Accepting then, that the right hemisphere indeed plays an early and continuing—if ultimately subordinate—role in language processing, we now turn specifically to the right brain's involvement in adult second-language learning. A number of studies indicate that languages learned after childhood are less left-lateralized, or more ambilateralized, than native languages, suggesting that the right hemisphere is more active in processing second languages (Galloway 1978; Obler 1981; Albert and Obler 1978; Scheiderman and Wesche 1983). Genesee (1982) claims that the right hemisphere plays a larger role in bilinguals who acquire their second languages (1) in adulthood and (2) in informal contexts. Sussman et al. (1982) conducted a number of finger-tapping experiments with mono- and bilinguals. In these experiments, subjects were asked to read passages, describe pictures, and recite formulaic language while tapping the index fingers of either their right or left hands as fast as they could. Most monolinguals were disrupted only while tapping their right index fingers, showing a clear left brain dominance for language. Bilinguals, in contrast, were more disrupted when tapping with their left index fingers, and they had more trouble with their second languages than their first languages, showing a lesser degree of lateralization in their second languages. Sussman et al. conclude that bilinguals tend to have greater right hemisphere participation in second language processing, especially when the second language is acquired in adulthood.

In light of these studies, much speculation has been posited concerning exactly how the right brain contributes to second language learning. Schneiderman (1986) suggests that a second-language learner, in order to decipher an unfamiliar linguistic code, must rely on all available linguistic and extra-linguistic cues. The right hemisphere, with its holistic-parallel processing style, is the optimal hemisphere for this type of undertaking. Thus, the right brain is most useful in the early stages of second-language learning—after an initial reliance on holistic linguistic and extralinguistic aspects such as intonation, formulaic language, gestures, situational context, and other chunking techniques, which are best processed by the right brain, then the left brain can begin to break these chunks down into their constituent parts.

Galloway and Krashen (1981) and Carroll (1981) take this reasoning a step further by claiming that in *formal* language-learning situations, such as occur in most classrooms, the right brain's involvement, and thus language acquisition, may be retarded due to the preponderance of "learning" as opposed to "acquisition" activities. Carroll suggests that the combination of highly structured classroom situations with the adult penchant for analytic learning may reduce or at least mask right hemisphere involvement, hence stifling language learning. These researchers suggest that the solution may lie in the development and utilization of teaching strategies that will specifically harness the right brain's potential, especially in the early stages of second-language acquisition. Albert and Obler (1978) declare that a higher degree of right brain involvement may mean the difference between those language learners who achieve some measure of bilingualism and those who forever remain monolingual.

In response to this problem, the remaining part of this article mentions a number of teaching models and activities, many already commonly used, which stimulate the right hemisphere as well as the left in the second-language classroom.

The first method, which has been specifically developed with right brain processing in mind, is the 4MAT model for teaching, created by Bernice McCarthy in the 1980s (McCarthy 1987). It is a general learning method which can be used for any subject at any grade level or age. 4MAT integrates individual learning styles with left and right brain processing modes. McCarthy based the 4MAT model on the work of David Kolb, who defined an axis which divides all learning styles on two continua: one of perceiving information, from concrete to abstract, and one of processing information, from active to reflective. Parallel to Kolb's four learning styles, McCarthy has distinguished four basic types of learner, each with an associated learning style: imaginative learners, analytic learners, common sense learners, and dynamic learners (see Figure 1). McCarthy stresses the importance of subjecting all students to all four types of learning styles, regardless of their individual styles. Unfortunately, formal education has traditionally favored analytic learners, who tend to excel in relatively passive classroom settings where recall and memorization of abstractly presented facts constitute the bulk of learning.

In addition, McCarthy further divides each learning style into a left brain mode and a right brain mode. As previously mentioned, the left hemisphere, which is the one usually accessed in traditional classrooms, processes information in an analytic, sequential, discrete, objective way, while the right hemisphere processes information in a visuospatial, holistic, gestalt, subjective manner. Due to this relative dichotomy, McCarthy maintains that *both* left and right modes should be equally activated in any learning situation. While the left brain is dominant in activities that involve verbal, analytical, structural processing, such as formal grammar instruction and discrete-point test-taking, the right brain excels in activities which incorporate visual, spatial, and holistic processing. Specifically, the right brain is stimulated by music, dance, movement, and emotion, modalities that are often neglected in the classroom.

McCarthy asserts that activities that center around images, patterns, visuals, realia, movement, role-playing, rhythm, poetry, art, experimentation, and intuition all stimulate right brain processing. She concludes that when both teachers and curricula address all four types of learners and both halves of their brains, then all individuals will not only be able to learn confidently and successfully, but they will also be able to help each other to learn as well.

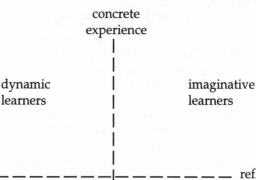

Figure 1. 4MAT's Four Types of Learners (adapted from
    McCarthy 1987)

A specific right brain mode activity fitting the 4MAT scheme is the jazz chant. Jazz chants have been developed by Carolyn Graham at the American Language Institute of New York University. Jazz chants are "the rhythmic expression of

Standard American English as it occurs in situational contexts" (1978, ix). They are short dialogues set to a steady beat and rhythm which draw students' awareness to the international patterns of English. Primarily geared toward familiarizing students with rhythm, stress, and intonation, they also help build listening comprehension and vocabulary. With their musical, repetitive, rhythmic nature, jazz chants stimulate the right hemisphere as they contribute to second language-learning.

There are many other activities that teachers can use to stimulate the right brain. Drama activities such as role-play, simulation, mime, and improvisation (Jones 1982; Livingstone 1983; Dougill 1987) draw upon extralinguistic features such as gestures and facial expressions as well as paralinguistic features such as rhythm, intonation, and tone of voice, all of which evoke the emotional, visual right brain. The use of literature (e.g., poetry, short stories, essays) in the second-language classroom also involves the creative, intuitive side of the brain (Hill 1986; Maley and Duff 1989), as does integrating realia and pictures with more traditional language learning activities (Maley et al. 1980; Jerald and Clark 1983). Using maps and signs, going grocery shopping, telling jokes, composing songs and letters, organizing scavenger hunts and demonstrations, talking on the telephone, and drawing and discussing pictures are all activities which inspire the creative, intuitive, emotional right hemisphere as well as the analytical, verbal left.

A well-known and often-used model of language teaching that also specifically addresses the brain's right hemisphere is Total Physical Response, or TPR. TPR is a popular method of language teaching developed by psychologist James Asher (1966). The theoretical basis for TPR is that learning can be facilitated by coupling physical actions with spoken language, namely imperatives. Asher claims that recall is greatly enhanced when motor activity accompanies learning (Asher et al. 1974). Based on experiments with splitbrain cats and humans, Asher claims that while the left hemisphere expresses itself verbally, the right is more adept at expressing itself through pictures and actions (Asher 1981). According to Asher, if language input is directed via the right hemisphere through physical activity, there will be an increase in comprehension and long-term memory, resulting in successful language learning. Thus, he attributes the success of TPR to its strong stimulation of the right brain.

A method that is dissimilar to TPR yet also encourages right brain participation is the Silent Way (Gattegno 1976). Caleb Gattegno first printed his Silent Way materials for English, Spanish, and French (1962). Since then, his word charts, Fidel charts, and Cuisenaire rods have been used to teach dozens of languages. These materials stimulate the right brain because they are primarily visual-spatial. The Fidel charts consist of small rectangular blocks of different colors arranged in rows, with each rectangle representing a single sound of a language. A horizontal line separates the vowel sounds at the top from the consonant sounds below. Similarly, the word charts are organized, color-coded *visual* presentations of the spellings and words of a language. The Cuisenaire rods, which can be used to teach any language, are colored rods of varying lengths that can create visual representations of building plans, cars, people, clocks, calendars, and numerous other figures. The use of these materials builds associations in the brain between the colors and rods and the sounds and words of a language, thus serving to facilitate language processing via the right as well as the left hemisphere.

Lozanov's Suggestopedia also addresses both halves of the brain. Lozanov views second language learning from an aesthetic perspective; his heavy use of emotional and artistic stimuli, such as background music and exaggerated rhythm, intonation, and ballet-like movements of the instructor, all serve to harness the power of the entire brain, including the emotional and artistic right hemisphere. By stimulating both the analytic, objective left brain and the holistic, subjective right brain, Lozanov claims to facilitate the suggestive process and utilize a much larger portion of the brain than is addressed in traditional language learning. Thus, the student's learning ability should be heightened to an astounding degree, providing her with "hypermnesia"—supermemory—which enables her to internalize large chunks of the new language in a much shorter time (Lozanov 1978; Stevick 1980). Kraetschmer (1986) considers Suggestopedia to be the strongest evidence of second-language learning success due to right brain involvement.

The preceding methods and activities have all been used for a number of years and have all achieved some measure of success. This article is not meant to be an evaluation of *whether* they are effective methods, but rather *why* they are effective. That is, what these methods and activities all have in common is that they activate both the left and the right cerebral hemispheres, which may lead to higher success rates in the second-language classroom.

In sum, second-language education has become more interested in recent years in the fields of psychology and neuro- and psycholinguistics. Indeed, without a detailed neurological account of how individuals learn, second-language teaching and learning theories cannot be considered complete. Similarly, this article would not be complete if it did not mention some researchers' words of warning. Obler et al. (1982) and Kraetschmer (1986) both discuss methodological aspects that are often ignored in lateralization experiments: Age, handedness, gender, method of second-language acquisition, level of proficiency, and even socioeconomic status are but a few of the variables that must be carefully controlled and analyzed when testing for cerebral dominance. Furthermore, Seliger (1982) and Scovel (1982) caution against blindly accepting the results of neurolinguistic experiments, which often conflict with each other and may not yet accurately measure or reflect true language processing. Despite these caveats, many researchers agree that, although in most instances the right hemisphere is still linguistically subordinate to the left, it nevertheless exhibits significant linguistic prowess and therefore should be equally stimulated in the second-language classroom.

Responding to Foreign-Language Student Writing
Expanding Our Options

Margaret Ann Kassen

Abstract

The role of writing in today's communication-oriented language classroom has been influenced greatly by research into second-language acquisition and the writing process. Despite these influences, studies show that foreign language (FL) teachers continue to emphasize formal accuracy in their markings of student writing. This article presents further insights into teacher response to student writing from a case study of twelve French teachers. The findings suggest that in order to communicate better their views about writing to their students and to achieve their communicative goals. FL teachers need to use a variety of feedback options that encourage comments on content as well as form. Several such commenting techniques are detailed.

Introduction

Our understanding of what it means to teach writing in a foreign language has been greatly enhanced by recent research in two fields: the writing process and second-language (L2) acquisition. From the first area, we have learned to view writing not merely as "writing down" but as the complex interplay of cognitive processes by which writers discover and create meaning (Emig 1971; Flower & Hayes 1981; Osterholm 1986). L2 acquisition research, the second field, has demonstrated that learning a language is not simply habit formation; rather it involves the expression of communicative intent as mediated by various competencies, including grammatical, sociolinguistic, discursive, and strategies (Canale & Swain 1980; Hatch 1983). Meaningful, purposeful, contextualized language use is an essential component of numerous models of second-language acquisition, including those based on input (Krashen 1982; Krashen and Terrell 1983), output (Swain 1985) and interaction (Brumfit 1984).

The communication-oriented pedagogies used by many of us in the field today draw on the research into writing and language acquisition in significant ways. We strive to balance our treatment of writing along with the other language skills. We recognize that our students, "even at the beginning level, can write for communication if the tasks they are asked to carry out are realistic, meaningful, occasioned by need, and appropriate to their level of linguistic sophistication" (Terry 1989:44). We try to provide students with the opportunity to do more than just transcribe or write down in the target language. As the ACTFL proficiency guidelines suggest, we encourage students to create with the language and to go beyond the word and sentence level to the paragraph and discourse level. We recognize that, as Byrnes (1983:34) points out, "the skill of learning to communicate successfully is fostered at least equally well by making students conscious of the characteristics underlying coherent and cohesive writing."

Our enhanced understanding of writing and our awareness of its benefits to language learners combine with our own experiences as writers to make us more appreciative of the many demands involved in creating and communicating meaning through writing. While we may be aware of and share such views, there is considerable evidence that second-language teacher feedback tends to focus on surface level features, particularly errors. Two surveys, one of high school foreign language (FL) teachers (Applebee 1981) and one of university FL and ESL students (Cohen 1987), suggest that teachers comment most on grammar and mechanics and least on ideas and organization. Two studies of university level ESL teacher comments (Zamel 1985; Cumming 1985) also found that teachers attended primarily to surface level features. Only one out of ten teachers in Cumming's study focused on content and other discourse level features.

A recent case study that investigated the response of French teachers to writing of their students (Kassen 1990) supports these earlier findings but offers additional insight into FL teacher response. It is the purpose of this essay to examine some aspects of this case study and other related studies as they pertain to the focus on form in teacher response to student writing. To conclude the discussion, a review of several feedback techniques, which allow teachers to respond in ways that are consistent with current views of writing and second-language acquisition, will be summarized from the professional literature.

Case Study

Twelve university-level French teachers, four at each of the three traditional levels of instruction (beginning, intermediate, and advanced) were asked to mark one class set of their students' papers in their normal fashion. The teachers were also requested to think aloud as they marked three of the papers. Concurrent verbal reports such as these have been used in various studies of the writing process and in Cumming's (1985) aforementioned study of ESL teacher commenting as a method of gathering data on thought processes involved in a task (Ericsson and Simon 1984). The "think aloud" protocols were audiotaped and later transcribed. After the data were collected, the participants were interviewed about their views on writing. The interviews were also recorded and transcribed.

Two general patterns emerged in the procedures for marking papers (Figure 1).

If no rewrite . . .	If rewrite . . .
Teacher corrections	Error code (with error identification)
Marginal/end comments in French or English	
Final grade, letter or number	

Figure 1. Feedback Techniques Employed by Twelve University-Level French Instructors with Beginning, Intermediate, and Advanced-Level Student Writing

If no rewrite was required of the student, the teachers in the study provided corrections of errors and occasionally identified errors with a code. If rewrites were to follow, the teachers signaled the errors and used a code to identify error types. In both cases, rewrite or not, marginal or end comments in French or English were frequently offered, and letter or number grades were consistently given.

Analysis of the think-aloud protocols and the written comments revealed that the teachers responded to four main concerns: grammar, vocabulary, mechanics and content. A portion of transcribed and analyzed protocol is included in Appendix A at the end of this essay. Table 1 presents a ranking of the three most frequent comment types at the three levels of instruction for oral and written comments.

When responding to beginning level student writing, the teachers commented most often about grammar, followed by vocabulary and mechanics. This pattern was obtained for both the comments made out loud and those written on the students' papers. At the intermediate and advanced levels, grammar received the most attention orally and in writing, with vocabulary ranking second. However, the third most frequent comment type varied according to whether comments were made aloud or in writing. In writing, mechanical errors were marked third most frequently, as they were at the beginning level. In the think aloud protocols, however, content-directed comments were made more frequently than ones on mechanics.

Table 1. Hierarchy of Frequency of Concerns of Twelve University-Level French Instructors on Student Compositions

Level	Written comments	Think aloud
Beginning	G V M	G V M
Intermediate	G V M	G V C
Advanced	G V M	G V C

G=Grammar, V=Vocabulary, M=Mechanics, C=Content

In the follow-up interviews, the participants at all levels indicated that they considered the writing tasks they had assigned to be opportunities for students to express themselves freely and to communicate their ideas. Three-fourths of the teachers stressed clarity as an important element in good writing. More than half expressed concern about helping students to develop audience awareness, or as one participant called it, "le souci de communiquer au lecteur."

Discussion

This study found evidence in support of earlier claims that teacher feedback to student writing tends to focus on form. Unlike previous studies, this investigation offered the insight that teachers are also concerned with their students' ideas and that they do see writing as communication. Yet these views, revealed in the think aloud protocols and in the interviews, contrast strikingly with the emphasis on surface-level features in the written comments. While it is possible that the teachers mentioned their interest in ideas when talking with students in (or even outside of) class, the message the students saw on their papers dealt with form, not content, even at more advanced levels of instruction. This apparent contrast is perplexing. Why was the written feedback so focused on surface form? Why was there so little written response to ideational content?

Zamel (1985) suggested that L2 teachers focus on error because they view themselves essentially as language teachers rather than writing teachers. Language teaching has a long tradition of correcting learner errors and identifying errors for learners to correct. (See Walz 1982 and Chaudron 1988 for reviews of error correction.) Samples of error codes are readily available in professional literature (Omaggio 1986). Despite the widespread popularity of written error correction strategies, results of research into such techniques are somewhat mixed and are not strongly in favor of these techniques.

In a study of intermediate-level university students of German, Lalande (1982) found that students who rewrote their compositions correcting errors that had been identified by a code and then tallied their errors on an error awareness matrix, made significantly fewer grammatical and orthographic errors on a writing posttest than did those students who had rewritten their compositions incorporating teacher-provided corrections. These findings are somewhat limited, however. First, the design of the study did not permit for a comparison of the error code and error awareness treatments separately, and secondly, the study, which was restricted to concern for accuracy, did not consider other aspects of writing quality or student affective reaction to the treatments.

Other studies that included both surface accuracy and additional variables relating to writing quality do not support Lalande's conclusions. Semke (1984) examined the effect of four types of commenting on intermediate-level German journal writing. She found that students receiving comments on content alone tended to write significantly more than those who received corrections, corrections and comments, or error codes. None of the treatments resulted in increased accuracy. Her study also provided some evidence for increased language proficiency and more positive attitudes toward writing in the group that received only content-directed response. Robb, Ross and Shortreed (1986) studied the effects of feedback types including error corrections and error codes on the writing of university-level English as a Foreign Language students. They found that writing fluency seemed to increase with practice regardless of feedback type and that none of the error-directed feedback types in their study affected accuracy. They concluded that teachers' time "might be more profitably spent in responding to more important aspects of student writing" (p. 91). Goring Kepner (1991) compared the effects of two types of feedback, message-related comments and error correction with rule reminders, on intermediate Spanish journal writing. She too found that students receiving error corrections did not produce fewer errors than those receiving comments only on content. Furthermore, those students who received content-oriented comments demonstrated significantly greater ideational quality as measured by proposition counts.

Studies such as these lend support to what first-and second-language writing experts have emphasized: the need for teacher feedback to communicate a more authentic view of writing to students (Brannon and Knoblauch 1982; Dvorak 1986; Zamel 1985). They stress the importance of feedback that helps student writers see ways to improve their texts. They draw a clear distinction between the revision process, where the student writer re-reads the text, considering higher-level goals such as topic, audience, and intentions, and the editing phase, where relatively low-level, surface concerns are addressed. By studying writer protocols, they have found evidence that an early focus on form may distract student writers from fully developing their ideas.

Given the presence of these recommendations in the professional literature and the French teachers' own stated interest in communication, why did they respond so infrequently in written feedback to areas of concern that are thought to be of greater importance to the writing process, areas they themselves tended to comment on while thinking aloud? While there are no precise answers to this question, one possibility was suggested by Cumming (1985). Because the ESL teachers he studied who used error identification techniques tended to focus on errors while the teacher who responded orally focused on content, he was led to posit that feedback techniques might impose constraints on the marking process. Similarly, the markings of the French teachers, who responded using teacher corrections and error identification, were specifically directed to errors of form. Could error-directed marking techniques by their nature focus the teacher's attention on surface level concerns and, as a result, limit the likelihood of addressing discourse-level issues?

Some evidence supporting this notion is found in the responses of three of the French teachers in the case study. A beginning level teacher noted the inadequacy of her error coding system for dealing with sentence level concerns:

> I've never used a notation for syntax; I guess I'll look one up. You know, I tell them about their syntax, but I don't really have a notation that tells them to pay attention to the syntax.

At the advanced level, one teacher was frustrated by his self-imposed use of an error code.

> I should've put over in the margin *t*; is it *t* for tense? I forget. Or *f* for form. I guess I need to get my stupid sheet and see what it is, what my markings are that I'm supposed to be using.

Another advanced level teacher responded consistently to content and style. When asked to explain this aspect that differentiated his response from that of his colleagues', he attributed his attention to these concerns to the evaluation system he had developed. The first draft was graded for a maximum of fifty points, and the rewrite contributed the remaining fifty points according to the following criteria:

> Conformité au sujet (10 points)
> Richesse de structures et de vocabulaire (20 points)
> Style (20 points)

The evaluation sheet, which was filled in for each student, served to direct the instructor's comments and the student's attention to discourse level as well as surface level concerns.

Implications

Though as language teachers we may not view ourselves as writing teachers, we recognize the need to develop writing skills as part of today's emphasis on communication across all the modalities. The work of both first- and second-language experts provides us with support for not limiting our role to that of proofreader or "fixer-upper" of our students' texts. We second-language teachers can take an active role in responding to students' writing in ways which encourage learners to develop their abilities to think and to communicate their ideas effectively in writing.

The kind of feedback we use is only one component of our writing program, but it is one that is clearly visible to our students, indicating, implicitly or explicitly, what we think is important about their writing. There is considerable evidence that focusing our comments on errors does not have a beneficial effect on our student's writing. In view of this research and in light of the possible constraints imposed by error-directed feedback, it becomes important for us to consider other ways to mark student writing that are more consistent with our current understanding of the composing process. We need to become acquainted with a variety of feedback techniques that encourage us to respond to student writing beyond the surface level.

Several feedback options drawn from the professional literature lend themselves to this goal and others advocated by writing experts. These options will be described and, whenever possible, sample formats will be provided in the Appendices at the end of this essay. First, holistic and analytic scoring, two types of evaluative feedback designed to give or justify a grade, will be examined. Even though these techniques treat writing essentially as a product, they do offer the advantage of allowing for evaluation of more than grammatical accuracy. The overview continues with options that focus on intervention in the writing process and those that are interactive in nature.

Holistic Scoring

In holistic assessment, a text is scored for its overall impression compared to preestablished norms. Because readers' judgments may vary widely and thus bring the reliability of this technique into question, researchers recommend reducing subjectivity in scoring by training several raters and by using clearly stated descriptions of the most important criteria to judge. Holistic scoring is frequently used in evaluating placement essays. The rating used for the Advanced Placement Exams in French range from 9 (superior) to 1 (incompetent), with one floating point awarded for coherence and/or exceptional creativity or organization. Each numerical rating is accompanied by descriptions of the vocabulary use, grammaticality, and style characteristic of that level (see Johnson 1983, as cited in Terry 1989).

Analytic Scoring

An analytic approach to writing evaluation breaks writing into a number of component parts and allows for assessment of each of these parts. Examples of analytic scoring are found frequently in professional literature. Gaudiani (1981) proposes evaluating grammar/vocabulary, stylistic technique, organization, and content on a scale of A to F. Heaton (1975, as cited in Terry 1989) focuses on grammar, vocabulary, mechanics, fluency, and relevance, with score ranging from 1 (the equivalent of an F) to 5 (the equivalent of an A). The components of the widely used EL Composition Profile (Jacobs et al. 1981) are weighted to reflect the instructional context: content, 30 points (Maximum); organization, 20 points; vocabulary, 20 points, language use, 25 points; and mechanics, 5 points. While this type of scoring may suggest the oversimplified notion that good writing is equal to the sum of the parts, it nonetheless offers advantages to both teachers and students alike. The specified criteria allow teachers to mark papers more reliably, and students are provided with input regarding identifiable aspects of their writing.

Checklists

Checklists offer considerable flexibility in that they may be developed to address a combination of both sentence-level concerns and more global issues. Items on a checklist may be coordinated with course or assignment objectives. The sample checklist provided in Appendix B was developed specifically for a response to a penpal's letter and includes questions on surface and discourse level concerns. Magnan (1985) proposed checklists that follow the more long range goals of the proficiency movement's functional trisection. When checklists are developed in conjunction with the writing task and presented to students prior to writing, they help guide students during the writing process. When used for evaluation, they offer students positive feedback on what has been successfully accomplished (Knapp 1972).

Written Comments

Another type of feedback that can be used during and after the writing process is commenting in the margins or at the end of the student text. Writing experts offer several guidelines on commenting. First, they stress the importance of writing comments and questions that help students gain insight into reader response. Secondly, out of concern for learner attention span and teacher marking time, it is suggested that teachers limit the quantity of comments (Raimes 1983). To provide a balance to teachers' comments and to minimize students' negative reactions to teacher remarks, it is recommended that comments mention students' strengths as well as weaknesses.

Despite the potentially positive value of comments, research has also identified several areas of concern about commenting. Teachers' comments often prove difficult for students to understand (Brannon and Knoblauch 1982). More explicit comments with direct suggestions for revising have been found to be more effective than implicit feedback (Ziv 1984). A teacher may unknowingly comment in ways that take students away from their original intentions and focus them instead on the teacher's own goals. A final caution is based on the evidence from the case study reported on in this essay. The use of comments does not necessarily result in feedback that directs students to process-oriented concerns. While most of the participating French teachers also wrote end or marginal comments, these remarks were focused on errors of form.

Oral Response

Teachers can also make oral comments about students' papers (Patrie 1989). As with written comments, oral comments may be made during the writing process and afterwards. Similar to the manner in which the teachers in the case study thought aloud as they marked, teachers can tape record their oral feedback for students to listen to at home. As the data presented here and in Cumming's study suggest, oral response techniques may facilitate comments on content and other higher-level concerns.

Conferencing

One-on-one conferences, in which the student writer and the teacher talk about what has been written or about what the writer wants to say, offer the possibility of increased teacher-student interaction. Conferences can take place at any time during the writing process. Though lengthy discussions may seem impractical in many teaching contexts, even very short conferences before, after, or during class may be helpful to students. A recent case study of ESL writing conferences (Goldstein and Conrad 1990) points to the central role that active participation and negotiation by the student writer play in the effectiveness of this technique.

Peer Editing

Students themselves offer another avenue for feedback when they comment on each other's writing between drafts. Advantages of peer editing as summarized by Chaudron (1984) include (1) students practice reading critically, a skill they can apply to the revision of their own texts as well, (2) the input provided by other students is at the same level of development and interest as the learner, and (3) the teacher has additional time for instruction and assistance. To maximize the appropriateness of peer feedback and to reduce student concern about its value, those who employ this technique recommend providing guidelines for the editing process (see sample in Appendix C). Checklists, guiding questions, and open-ended statements such as "The main idea of this paper is . . ." are techniques for structuring the peer editing sessions for greater success.

Dialog Journals

Perhaps the most interactive type of writing is dialog journals. In this technique, the teacher and the student maintain a running "conversation," with each participant taking turns as reader and writer. The focus is on meaningful communication in a low-anxiety context without overt error correction (see example in Appendix D). Despite the absence of direct corrections, teacher input plays an important role; research has found that the most effective input is personalized, expands on the student's chosen topic, requests replies, and is at a level slightly above the individual student's level. Reported student gains from this type of writing include increased writing fluency, higher interest level, improved correctness of student writing, and better reading comprehension (Kreeft et al. 1984; Peyton 1990; Semke 1984).

Conclusion

Research on writing, language acquisition and teacher feedback on L2 writing has suggested the need to expand our options for dealing with student writing. The techniques discussed here help us communicate to our students that good writing is more than just error-free writing. By employing feedback that views writing in its richness and complexity, we language teachers can share in the goals of the Writing Across the Curriculum movement (Klein 1990; Morocco and Soven 1990). As we join forces with educators across a variety of disciplines we present our students with a unified and clear message: Writing is a powerful learning and thinking tool as well as a means of communication.

Though we have begun to gain insight into the issue of providing feedback to FL students on their writing, many important questions remain: What do students actually do with teacher feedback? What are the effects of different types of feedback on student writing? Are certain feedback types more effective than others in dealing with particular aspects of student writing or at different levels of language proficiency? When investigating these questions and others like them we in the language teaching profession will continue to benefit from the fruitful interplay of research and practice.

Appendix A

Excerpts from Two Think Aloud Protocols

The underlined portion is the student text read out loud by the teacher. Boldface type indicates emphasis given by teacher. For responses made orally but not in writing, the comment type is set off by slash marks (/ /).

G = grammar, V = vocabulary, M = mechanics, C = content, O = organization

Intermediate Level

Evelyn

C   7 <u>Il a beaucoup d'amis intelligents</u>. Alors, c'est vrai? They talked about them smoking and stuff like that and I don't think that's too intelligent (writes "C'est vrai? p. 162 1. 4?" above). I know exactly. <u>Il a beaucoup d'amis **intelligents**</u> (broken line under intelligents, -1 in right margin)

M   8 <u>Animus considère </u>(changes direction of accent; -1 for this error or the one before?)

C   9 <u>Anima comme une ignorante</u>. Du début? Ça a été toujours vrai? (writes "du début?" above; later adds "à la fin?"; -1 in right margin)

G   10 <u>Elle n'est pas très intelligente et elle n'a pas une bonne education</u>, pas de (adds "de" above une, -1 in left margin)

V   11 <u>bonne **formation**</u> (writes "formation" over education, -1 in left margin)

Jacques

/O/   5 <u>Il était en Suisse pour ses vacances</u>. Alors, je vois que déjà dans ses premières lignes d'introduction, elle situe bien les choses. Les personnages, le lieu.

/C/   6 <u>Sa vie avait été difficile. Son médecin</u> . . . Donc elle a fait un bilan des années écoulées à ce moment là,

   7 et puis, une anecdote que nous avons vue en classe.

V   8 <u>Son médecin lui a dit qu'il a besoin du repos. . . . une réserve</u>. Évidemment, c'est un anglicisme pour dire qu'il a réservé une chambre.

Appendix B

Composition Checklist

	Yes	Some-times	No
Content			
Did you provide the information requested?			
Did you include some questions for your penpal to answer?			
Vocabulary			
Did you use a variety of vocabulary?			
Did you check the spelling of words you were unsure of?			
Did you use *aller* to talk about how you/your penpal are (feeling)?			
Structures			
Did your adjectives agree with the nouns they modified?			
Did you select the appropriate possessive adjectives (*mon, ma, mes,* etc.)?			
Other Concerns			
Did you use the appropriate friendly letter form?			
Did you address your penpal with the informal *you*?			

Appendix C

Peer Editing Guidelines

The following questions were used in an intermediate-level university French class to guide the peer editing of a composition in which students had written the text of a travel brochure for their hometown or state. The worksheet has been translated into English for this Appendix.

A. Exchange compositions with a partner. Read the composition through once or twice and answer the following questions.

1. What attitude is communicated in this text? Cite several specific words or phrases that reflect this attitude.

2. What is the main idea of each paragraph? Are there any paragraphs where you have difficulty trying to decide what the main idea is?

   paragraph 1 _____

   paragraph 2 _____

   paragraph 3 _____

3. Is there something else not mentioned that would be useful or interesting to read about?

4. Do you now want to visit this town or state? Why or why not?

B. Now read the text again and complete the chart below.

Structure	No Problems	One/More Errors	Examples
a. adjectives			
b. articles			
c. verbs present tense imperative			
d. other concerns			

C. Complete the following sentences.

    1. What I liked best about this composition is _____

    2. The most important thing to change is _____

Appendix D

Dialog Journal

Intermediate-Level Spanish

Student:

Yo tengo una familia muy grande. Tengo cuatro hermanas y tres hermanos pero no somos de los mismos padres. Sin embargo, seis de mis hermanos viven en la misma casa.

Todos de mis hermanos se llevan bien algunas veces, pero no nos llevamos todo el tiempo. Cuando luchamos todos de nuestros vecinos junto con nuestros padres corren y esconden. Somos malintencionados y violentos cuando nos luchamos casi insignificante sujetos, por ejemplo ropa, comida, yo amigos.

Teacher:

Debe ser muy interesante tener tantos hermanos (yo soy hija única). Aun en mi familia pequeña, había momentos en que nosotros tampoco estábamos de acuerdo. Discutíamos también sobre asuntos como la ropa, el transporte, mis quehaceres, etc.

Si pudieras escoger, ¿qué preferirías, una familia grande o una pequeña? Pienso que tienes ciertas ventajas con todas las posibilidades de compartir experiencias en tu familia, pero también veo algunas desventajas. ¿Qué piensas? En tu opinión, hay un tamaño pefecto para una familia?

La production écrite en langue seconde par le recueil de textes

Michel Gagnon

Abstract

In this article, the author demonstrates how first-year second-language students develop their writing skills by writing and publishing their own books. This approach to second-language writing is presented in a ten-step process that combines communicative activities and cooperative learning. This project has been used successfully for the last five years.

Rédiger un texte organisé et sans faute dans une langue seconde demande énormément de travail; le nombre d'heures qu'il faut investir à l'apprentissage d'une langue exige beaucoup d'efforts. D'où l'importance de bien gérer son temps; les enseignants de français langue seconde en sont bien conscients, puisque l'apprentissage de cette langue exige un minimum de quatre cents heures d'étude. Dans la société québécoise d'aujourd'hui, l'apprentissage de l'écriture devient de plus en plus important; l'urgence de donner une formation adéquate en ce sens à nos immigrants s'avère incontournable. Les **classes d'accueil** disposent d'un double mandat (Germain 1990); insertion à l'école française des immigrants d'âge scolaire et intégration à la collectivité francophone du Québec. Les classes d'accueil existent pour enseigner le français aux nouveaux immigrants inscrits dans les écoles primaires et secondaires et vivant en terre québécoise, quelle que soit leur nationalité d'origine. Le projet présenté dans le cadre de cet article vise les élèves d'accueil de niveau secondaire; par contre, on peut l'adapter pour l'utiliser dans les classes de niveau primaire. Conformément à l'objectif linguistique et culturel des classes d'accueil, l'élève qui a suivi avec succès ce stage intensif en français se verra intégrer aux classes régulières pour y poursuivre sa scolarité, au même titre que les Québécois d'origine. L'élève issu des classes d'accueil aura étudié le français à raison de quatre à cinq périodes de cinquante minutes par jour; il aura également eu des cours de mathématiques, d'éducation physique et d'initiation à la vie québécoise. Ce qui caractérise les classes d'accueil est leur grande hétérogénéité; chacune des ethnies composant une classe d'accueil de dix-neuf élèves présente ses particularités dont l'enseignant doit tenir compte, car tous ne sont pas forcément rompus à la calligraphie du français ou à sa phonétique. Chacun aborde donc la langue française à partir de son propre système linguistique. Les valeurs sociales, les croyances religieuses et les habitudes scolaires propres à chaque ethnie font des classes d'accueil un milieu fort intéressant pour les enseignants, car ils y côtoient une belle diversité planétaire. Par exemple (Pinsonneault 1985), l'enfant cambodgien obéit à un code de politesse qui le force à baisser les yeux quand il s'adresse à quelqu'un; pour l'enfant indien, la famille forme un tout, de sorte que l'autonomie personnelle n'est pas une valeur courante; l'enfant asiatique porte un très grand respect pour l'enseignant.

Par ailleurs, l'apprentissage et l'acquisition de l'écriture du français en classe d'accueil reposent sur une période d'étude de dix mois, soit la totalité d'une année scolaire. Cela peut paraître long, mais pour en venir à maîtriser le code écrit de la langue française et bien réussir les travaux scolaires une fois intégrés en classe régulière, il s'agit d'une courte période de temps pendant laquelle les élèves doivent étudier de façon intensive. A cet égard, il est important de souligner une importante étude du Collectif de recherches interculturelles à l'Université de Sherbrooke, qui dégage plusieurs ombres au tableau de l'accueil; une faible maîtrise du français, peu d'orientations normatives, peu de concertation entre les intervenants et une vision réductionniste de la problématique de l'apprentissage de la langue (Beauchesne et Hensler, 1987). Une vision tronquée de l'apprentissage de la langue ne peut être que néfaste pour l'élève; pour bien enseigner la langue, il faut la voir dans son contexte global, rattaché au besoin de s'exprimer. Il est plutôt rare que les élèves issus des classes d'accueil obtiennent de bons résultats, au niveau de l'expression écrite, en classe régulière (Therrien 1990); en effet, la recherche menée par Michel Therrien a permis de constater de graves lacunes, chez les élèves allophones intégrés aux classes régulières, dans les aspects suivants: orthographe lexicale et grammaticale, morphologie verbale (temps et formes), termes incorrects ou impropres et aussi la syntaxe. À la troisième année du secondaire, au niveau de la cohésion, on a relevé de nombreuses répétitions et des erreurs de pronominalisation. La concordance des temps est aussi source de nombreuses erreurs. L'enseignement qui existe maintenant dans les classes d'accueil ne semble pas permettre aux élèves d'intégrer les classes régulières de français en douceur, bien qu'il soit permis de croire à la bonne volonté et à la disponibilité des enseignants. Malgré cette apparente bonne volonté de tous et chacun, on signale à l'accueil une population grandissante d'élèves présentant des problèmes de retard scolaire (Proulx 1988). La situation demande donc une certaine rectification.

Le projet exposé ici propose une façon de remédier à la situation, tout au moins de façon partielle; si on pouvait, dans le cours des dix mois de l'année de francisation des immigrants, maximiser l'apprentissage de la langue écrite en créant, entre autres, des habitudes de rédaction et des réflexes de révision, serait-il possible d'assurer une meilleure transition entre la classe d'accueil et la classe régulière?

Le but de cet article consiste à présenter une approche de l'enseignement de l'écriture qui puisse donner aux apprenants les outils nécessaires pour intégrer sans trop de heurts la classe régulière. Il va sans dire que si l'apprentissage du français se fonde sur des bases solides, les matières autres que le français présenteront moins de problèmes pour l'apprenant; que ce dernier soit en mathématiques, en sciences physiques ou dans

quelque cours que ce soit, il se confronte toujours à la langue
seconde.

Cette stratégie d'intervention pédagogique, loin de pré-
coniser le retour à l'enseignement de la grammaire pour la grammaire, reconnaît l'urgence de bien la posséder; par l'instauration
d'un cadre pédagogique communicatif et significatif, on peut
renforcer la compréhension du code de la langue française (Besse
et Porquier 1984). Il est également possible de valoriser le
français par des activités collectives où la pédagogie de la
coopération ("cooperative learning") amène l'apprenant à
devenir l'agent de son propre apprentissage. Une plus grande
circulation des textes écrits par les élèves accroît l'importance
accordée au geste d'écrire. Ce projet propose de publier, dans un
recueil, les textes des élèves; bien que le résultat ne soit pas
nécessairement volumineux, il constitue quand même, ne
l'oublions pas, un pas de géant et un objet de fierté pour ces
élèves.

L'élaboration d'un recueil consiste également en un
moyen de "séduire" le jeune immigrant face au français, de le
rendre plus ouvert au fait français d'Amérique du Nord. La
conscience linguistique des immigrants par rapport à notre
langue a aussi besoin d'être relevée.

Donc, la démarche pédagogique proposée consiste à
publier, sous forme de recueil de textes, les productions écrites
des élèves de la classe; cette publication devrait avoir lieu vers la
fin de l'année scolaire, au moment où les élèves ont presque
terminé les dix mois réglementaires du stage en accueil. Plus tôt
serait sabrer dans la qualité des textes; il importe de considérer
cette publication comme apothéose d'une année scolaire bien
remplie; de cette façon, l'enseignant, sous toute probabilité, aura
couvert l'ensemble du programme du ministère de l'Education.

Ce projet s'articule autour d'une hypothèse générale et de
trois hypothèses de travail; ces hypothèses constituent le lien
entre la recherche théorique effectuée pour cet article et la
pratique vécue en classe depuis maintenant cinq ans. Ces hypothèses sont une conséquence logique et possible de la théorie et
son application pratique.

Hypothèse générale: La production écrite, dans l'apprentissage d'une langue seconde, s'acquiert mieux dans le cadre d'un enseignement interactif.

Le processus rédactionnel qui se fixe comme base théorique et la communication en contexte naturel mène à une rédaction de qualité; c'est ce que la théorie moderne porte à croire. Un contexte d'apprentissage communicatif, s'appuyant sur des situations de communication authentiques et permettant la collaboration entre élèves-écrivant, risque fort bien de déboucher sur une production écrite de qualité supérieure.

Trois hypothèses de recherche

1. Une consigne de rédaction significative pour l'apprenant produit un texte de meilleure qualité, quant au fond et à la forme.

L'hypothèse générale vient en réaction avec une conception plus traditionnelle de l'acte d'écrire, selon laquelle l'enseignant donne aux apprenants le sujet de la composition, en mettant ainsi de côté leurs intérêts particuliers. Il est difficile pour un élève, à plus forte raison en période d'apprentissage, et de surcroît en classe d'accueil, d'écrire une composition sur un sujet qui lui est étranger. On pourrait en déduire que pour produire un texte expressif, l'apprenant doit avoir vécu quelque chose; à moins d'exception, l'enseignant ne peut pas connaître la totalité du vécu de chaque apprenant. De la même façon, il serait difficile de produire un texte informatif sans avoir des informations précises à communiquer. Or, laisser à l'apprenant le choix de son sujet de texte expressif peut éliminer ce genre de situation. Graves (1984), un chercheur qui a travaillé à un important rapport sur l'enseignement de l'écriture, disait ceci: "Until students feel they have some information to convey, it is difficult for them to care about writing or to feel they can speak directly and with authority (72)."

A plus forte raison en situation de classe d'accueil, il semble évident que les élèves aient quelque chose d'intéressant à raconter; les conditions sociales ou politiques qu'ils ont connues, les différences culturelles qu'ils apportent ainsi que leur vision du monde ne sont là que quelques aspects qui peuvent intriguer l'éventuel lecteur et éveiller chez lui une certaine empathie (Noël-Gaudrault 1990). L'acte rédactionnel devrait viser le partage de connaissances. Chaque apprenant possédant un vécu différent de celui de son voisin, il est certain que ce qu'il ou elle aura à raconter sera nouveau pour le lecteur; chaque auteur devient alors un "spécialiste" qui partage avec le lecteur un peu de son vécu. Les suggestions de l'enseignant peuvent surseoir à une éventuelle panne d'inspiration de l'écrivant ou mettre un terme à une période d'errance. D'ailleurs, il en va de même pour la rédaction de textes informatifs; l'apprenant produira un texte de meilleure qualité s'il s'y intéresse. Graves (1984) insiste: "Students can improve quickly with skilled, personal attention that concentrates on what they know and can tell others (63)."

2. La publication du texte de l'apprenant incite à une plus grande performance.

Autre motivation importante, le recueil de textes qui résulte de cette démarche sera en circulation à travers toute l'école et la bibliothèque en aura quelques exemplaires en consultation ou en prêt; l'apprenant, avec la publication de son texte expressif, devient plus conscient qu'il sera lu par d'autres personnes que son professeur. En classe d'accueil, les élèves ne voient guère plus que deux ou trois enseignants, parmi lesquels seulement un revendique la responsabilité de leur enseigner à écrire. Soudainement, le public s'élargit avec la perspective d'une publication prochaine; or, l'acte d'écrire ne signifie plus la même chose. Il sera publié, lu par des étrangers, peut-être même par les dirigeants de l'école et quelques autres enseignants; la motivation à mieux écrire serait ainsi créée (Seiferling 1981, 70).

D'ailleurs, on peut y déceler les bases du concept de la pédagogie de la coopération, selon laquelle les élèves acquièrent mieux les contenus d'apprentissage s'ils sont en situation active plutôt que passive (Adams et Hamm 1990). De plus, des recherches ont semblé démontrer certaines constantes dans cette méthode d'enseigner. Par exemple, qu'un apprentissage né de la pédagogie de la coopération peut améliorer le rendement scolaire autant chez les plus faibles que chez les plus forts;

qu'une équipe composée d'élèves d'ethnies différentes démontre plus de tolérance et de compréhension (Webb 1982). C'est un apport non négligeable, surtout en classe d'accueil, là où plusieurs ethnies se retrouvent ensemble dans une même classe. Le défi consiste à les faire travailler en équipe, de sorte que l'importance porte sur la consigne à réaliser, plutôt que sur une compétition entre individus.

3. L'enseignement dit communicatif et la pédagogie de la coopération amènent une plus grande compréhension des notions grammaticales.

Le traitement de la grammaire, à travers tout ça, conserve bien sûr une place importante, mais pas de tout premier plan. Au lieu de servir d'objectif en soi, la grammaire prend plutôt un rôle secondaire, plus utilitaire. Il a souvent été démontré qu'en-seigner les règles de grammaire hors de tout contexte significatif ne sert pas à grand'chose et qu'il n'y aurait que peu de transfert d'acquis (Besse et Porquier 1984). Ne l'oublions pas, trois courants de pensée existent habituellement à ce sujet en didac-tique des langues; l'approche naturelle, selon laquelle l'en-seignant ne devrait pas apporter de corrections lors de l'énoncia-tion et laisser les apprenants découvrir la grammaire par eux-mêmes (il n'existerait pas de lien entre la correction grammati-cale et l'acquisition de la langue (Terrell 1987)); de la grammaire implicite ou inductive (Besse et Porquier 1984); et, bien entendu, de la grammaire explicite selon un modèle traditionnel (Vigner 1984).

La place de la grammaire, dans ce projet, se situe plus ou moins au milieu de ce continuum; il n'est pas utile de donner de cours magistraux sur les règles du fonctionnement de la langue française; en classe d'accueil, la grammaire devrait être incidente, pas oubliée. L'apprenant devrait, dans l'esprit de ce projet, émettre des hypothèses sur le fonctionnement de la langue. L'erreur ne constitue pas une bavure irréparable; on y voit da-vantage un moyen de confirmer ou d'infirmer une hypothèse préalable. La tolérance de l'enseignant face à l'erreur peut con-tribuer à mettre en confiance et à faire voir la possibilité de s'ex-primer dans un français même approximatif. L'enseignant, qui voit plus loin que la faute immédiate, laisse l'apprenant parler en ne mettant pas de barrière affective entre eux (Terrell 1987). Ne l'oublions pas, en situation de classe d'accueil, il importe que l'apprenant en vienne à dire ou à écrire quelque chose, quelque fautif que ce soit. L'importance devrait être mise sur la communication. Ensuite, il est toujours temps d'apporter des correctifs; par conséquent, le fait de pouvoir s'exprimer est loin d'être négligeable. Par ailleurs, en ce qui concerne la rédaction d'un texte en vue du recueil, la récurrence de l'erreur peut être une indication que l'enseignement n'a pas atteint tous ses objectifs; voilà peut-être le signe qu'il vaudrait mieux faire un retour, apporter un élément de structuration. L'approche communicative propose que l'enseignement des notions grammaticales se fasse en contexte significatif et non dans la vacuité (Besse et Porquier 1984). Par exemple, l'enseignant peut recenser, à l'aide des brouillons, les erreurs les plus grosses ou les plus fréquentes; les transcrire à l'intérieur de leur contexte sur une feuille, distribuer la feuille et donner aux apprenants la consigne de trouver ce qui ne va pas dans chacune des phrases. Cette consigne peut se faire en groupe ou en équipe, suivi d'une plénière. Dans le cas du travail d'équipe, l'enseignant peut avoir recours à la pédagogie de la coopération; chacun des membres de l'équipe y va de son interprétation, tente de convaincre les autres à l'aide d'une grammaire ou d'un dictionnaire et lance la discussion. Il va sans dire que la discussion peut porter sur des erreurs qui n'en sont pas, mais au moins il y a discussion et émissions d'hypothèses. Le retour en plénière peut éliminer toute mésentente ou confirmer certaines hypothèses.

Sommaire de la partie théorique

La pertinence du sujet de rédaction, la compétence de communication et l'apprentissage des règles de grammaire en contexte significatif forment les bases théoriques du projet d'écriture présenté ici. De manière moins théorique, les étapes de réalisation du recueil de textes nécessitent tout de même un investissement de temps assez important pour l'enseignant et les apprenants. Loin d'être une recette miracle, ce projet vise trois objectifs:

a) rendre l'élève capable de produire des textes expressifs et informatifs;

b) établir un pont, par la publication du recueil, entre les immigrants et les locuteurs natifs;

c) mieux comprendre le fonctionnement de la langue française.

Ce projet de rédaction collective en classe se veut un instrument qui puisse apporter un élément de changement afin que l'enseignement de la production écrite, en classe d'accueil, puisse répondre aux besoins exigeants de la société québécoise et de ses institutions scolaires pluriethniques. Le projet de rédaction en classe d'un recueil de textes s'articule autour de dix étapes.

Les Dix Étapes de Réalisation du Recueil

1. Développer l'habileté à rédiger un texte

De toute première importance, l'habileté à produire un texte est à la base de ce projet; toutefois, avant que les apprenants n'acquièrent cette habileté, il faut tout d'abord les motiver. Il est à noter que la clientèle des classes d'accueil ignore généralement jusqu'à la signification du mot "bonjour" avant leur arrivée en classe. Tous peuvent reconnaître que la motivation ajoute à la performance (Seiferling 1981, 71); la motivation est donc vitale à la réalisation de ce projet. Une bonne façon de motiver les élèves consiste à leur montrer le recueil de l'année précédente, ou un autre recueil préférablement produit par des élèves; la conceptualisation du résultat final stimule l'apprenant. De plus, quand les élèves constatent que leurs textes seront probablement lus par d'autres, ils prennent le geste d'écrire plus au sérieux et tendent à produire de meilleurs textes.

Outre la motivation, un climat de confiance doit régner dans la classe; l'enseignant doit être perçu comme une personne ressource qui apporte aide et conseil. Je crois qu'on atteint ce climat de confiance, à tout le moins partiellement, en adoptant une attitude de tolérance face à l'erreur; ne l'oublions pas, il s'agit probablement de leur tout premier texte écrit dans une langue étrangère. Il faut éviter de créer des barrières affectives entre l'apprenant et son apprentissage de l'écriture.

Aussitôt que possible, on peut leur donner de courtes consignes de rédaction, normalement vers la fin octobre ou au début novembre, pour les élèves qui ont commencé leur apprentissage en septembre. Par exemple, l'enseignant peut donner la consigne de résumer les activités de la fin de semaine sous forme de journal de bord à l'aide de courtes phrases. L'agenda que plusieurs écoles font acheter aux élèves peut servir à cette fin. Ceci, bien sûr dans le but de créer l'habitude d'écrire, de sorte que la rédaction que ce projet exige ne soit pas une brique qui leur tombe sur la tête.

La prise de conscience de la place importante du verbe dans la phrase, ainsi que de la structure Sujet-Verbe-Complément comme base de rédaction élimine une partie importante des problèmes de phrases sans fin ou qui n'en finissent plus. Le verbe, comme le veut le cliché, constitue le moteur de la phrase.

Il faut également enseigner, à l'aide de courts textes, la structure du texte; l'introduction, le développement et la conclusion sont à la base de toute rédaction. A cet égard, le manuel de l'élève de la méthode *Intermède* en fait une bonne présentation (Hardy et Joly 1991).[1] De plus, plusieurs élèves provenant de pays où la scolarisation est accessible ont déjà été sensibilisés à cette réalité.

Tout au long du projet et même avant, si possible, il est bon que les apprenants prennent l'habitude de réviser leurs textes avant de les présenter à l'enseignant; une panoplie d'outils, tels que les dictionnaires, les grammaires et autres documents de consultation doivent être mis à la vue et consultés, et ce dans la mesure de l'évolution des élèves. Il ne suffit pas d'inviter les élèves-écrivant à "bien réviser" leur texte avant de le remettre aux enseignants; nombreux sont les élèves qui croient que leurs textes ont atteint leur version finale et ultime lors de la remise à l'enseignant (Barnett 1989). Il est permis de proposer quelques stratégies d'interventions pédagogiques en espérant qu'elles puissent remédier à la situation. Bisaillon (1992) propose des pistes intéressantes à ce sujet; l'expérience de Gangi (1986) a démontré que l'enseignement systématique de la révision, au moyen de questions guidant les étudiants dans le processus de rédaction, s'est révélé très efficace, occasionnant à la moyenne des examens recensés d'augmenter de dix-huit points après avoir subi une révision systématique. Le réflexe de réviser son texte entraîne une conscientisation (Rutherford 1987) à la grammaticalité de la langue et met en évidence l'importance de la grammaire pour la bonne compréhension du fonctionnement de la langue. Par contre, il serait injuste d'espérer une révision en profondeur, compte tenu de la force des élèves; plutôt, il faut viser l'élimination des erreurs dont ils sont conscients. Les erreurs de pluriel, par exemple, peuvent être évitées par une révision assez brève.

2. Donner des thèmes de textes expressifs et annoncer l'élaboration d'un recueil de textes

L'enseignant peut montrer un recueil de textes produit par d'autres élèves, s'il y a lieu, afin de donner une idée du produit fini. Egalement, ceci a l'avantage de mettre les élèves sur la piste. La pédagogie de la coopération offre des possibilités intéressantes pour le choix de sujets de rédaction; par exemple, une équipe peut avoir comme consigne de présenter leur pays. Il arrive souvent qu'un pays ait plusieurs représentants; alors, chaque équipier est responsable d'un dossier différent sur ce même pays; par exemple, l'élève A s'occupe de parler des activités parascolaires alors que l'élève B traite de la vie à l'école. Quand les brouillons sont terminés, un retour en équipe permet de discuter et de voir à ce qu'il n'y ait pas de chevauchement dans les textes.

La pédagogie de la coopération, dans ce projet, a une portée bénéfique et souhaitable en ce sens que les membres de l'équipe peuvent s'entraider et collaborer à un but commun: la rédaction ou la correction d'un texte.

3. Correction sélective du texte

En laissant visibles certaines anomalies de syntaxe, on peut ainsi respecter l'esprit et la couleur du travail de l'élève tout en évitant une asceptisation qui rendrait les textes invraisemblables. De plus, l'enseignant peut restreindre ses commentaires, afin de laisser libre cours à l'inspiration des jeunes auteurs (Murray 1984). Il serait difficilement vraisemblable de lire des textes, dans le cadre de ce projet, qui démontrent une parfaite maîtrise de la grammaire; les élèves provenant des classes d'accueil ne sont que des nouveaux "usagers" de la langue française. La correction individuelle (avec chaque élève) permet d'expliquer et de cerner la plupart des fautes; il faut éviter de remettre une feuille tachée de rouge car ça n'a aucun sens si l'élève ne comprend pas ses fautes. On retrouve ici une variante intéressante de la pédagogie de la coopération, en ce sens que l'enseignant prend le temps, avec chaque élève, de voir comment on peut améliorer le texte en question. Il s'agit là bien sûr d'une intervention qui prend énormément de temps, car il arrive à l'occasion des textes carrément médiocres. Il importe, dans ces cas-là, de dégager le fil, ou la "voix" de l'auteur; c'est difficile et parfois impossible. Quand l'enseignant l'a trouvée, cette "voix," il peut y aller doucement avec le marqueur rouge pour ne pas la noyer; c'est ainsi qu'on peut garder la couleur originale du texte, même si le style est à la limite de la norme. Il convient bien sûr d'éliminer toute faute d'orthographe; les élèves seraient eux-mêmes scandalisés de voir leurs textes publiés avec des erreurs.

4. Rédaction du propre

Permettre un deuxième ou un troisième brouillon selon les élèves; n'oublions pas qu'un premier texte dans une langue étrangère est un "événement" en soi et qu'il faut laisser le temps de le rédiger. La révision joue un rôle très important; l'apprenant doit acquérir le réflexe de se relire. En relisant, il peut revenir sur une phrase qui lui paraît suspecte; la révision occasionne une interaction de l'auteur avec son texte et permet de l'améliorer (Murray 1984).

5. Atelier d'écriture assisté par ordinateurs (facultatif)

L'enseignant a tout le loisir d'avoir recours à la salle d'ordinateurs de son école, en autant que cette dernière en possède une et qu'elle soit utilisable. Il est extrêmement frustrant pour l'enseignant et pour les élèves de travailler sur ce projet dans une salle d'ordinateurs peu adéquate ou désuette. Par contre, si la chose est possible, le logiciel de traitement de texte doit avoir été présenté préalablement, afin d'éviter toute perte de temps. Il est presque essentiel que l'enseignant connaisse le fonctionnement d'au moins un logiciel de traitement de texte. Chaque élève devrait avoir sa propre disquette sur laquelle il peut conserver la totalité de ses textes. Il a ainsi le loisir d'y retourner à volonté. L'ordinateur aide les élèves à mieux voir leur texte et peuvent en modifier la forme à volonté (paragraphes, centrer le texte, justifier les marges, ou carrément opter pour une présentation qui défie toute convention); de plus, la notion même de paragraphe devient plus concrète en ce sens que l'élève les voit et peut les changer de place à volonté. Il en va de même pour l'introduction, le développement et la conclusion.

6. Impression du "premier" texte final et correction

Maintenant, ce sont les coquilles et fautes de frappe qui devraient disparaître, tout en gardant à l'esprit que le texte doit conserver sa couleur originale: révision avec l'élève.

7. Retour au traitement de texte et impression du texte final

Ici, l'élève a conservé son fichier (texte) sur sa disquette personnelle et peut y retourner à volonté.

8. Mise en page et organisation picturale

On peut laisser ici libre cours à l'imagination d'un ou d'une "artiste" de la classe. Pour découvrir cette perle rare, on peut faire dessiner, par exemple, une page couverture qui reflète le thème du recueil par tous les élèves; choisir les quatre ou cinq meilleures et ensuite faire voter (secrètement, bien sûr!) les autres élèves pour trouver celle qui leur plaît le plus. Pour ce qui est de la mise en page, je m'en occupe habituellement, mais rien n'interdit l'initiative des élèves.

9. Impression du recueil, mise en place de publicité

La publicité revêt une importance capitale, car c'est grâce à elle que des dizaines de lecteurs se précipiteront à la bibliothèque pour lire avec passion le nouveau recueil de textes de la classe d'accueil! On peut avoir recours à l'affiche murale (haute en couleur) qui met en évidence la date de publication et de disponibilité du recueil; aussi, une ou deux mentions dans le bulletin des annonces de l'école quelques jours avant et quelques jours après l'événement. A noter que si l'école ne possède pas sa propre imprimerie, les frais d'impression, pour une trentaine d'exemplaires, peuvent monter jusqu'à cinquante dollars, selon le type de reliure choisi.

10. Distribution

Tout d'abord aux auteurs, qui méritent bien chacun une copie, et aussi à la bibliothèque pour consultation; il est également à conseiller d'en envoyer une copie aux directeurs ou directrices de l'école pour qu'ils et elles aient l'occasion de venir souligner le travail des élèves participants au projet de recueil de textes.

Conclusion

La pédagogie de coopération prend également une dimension de première importance dans l'enseignement en milieu multiculturel; diverses études ont démontré (Slavin et Madden 1979) qu'une éducation ou une sensibilisation au multiculturalisme n'améliorait pas une attitude raciale négative; plutôt, le fait de travailler ensemble *à la réalisation d'un but commun à l'équipe* contribue à réduire, chez les élèves, le degré de conscience des différences ethniques. A plus forte raison en situation de classe d'accueil, cette approche vaut son pesant d'or, car nul n'est à l'abri des préjugés.

La réalisation de ce projet est grandement stimulante; le sentiment de satisfaction que les élèves ressentent devant le produit fini vaut à lui seul tous les efforts fournis; par contre, le temps nécessaire à sa réalisation est le témoin de grands progrès dans l'apprentissage des élèves. Ce progrès n'est que partiellement visible dans le recueil, celui-ci étant écrit avant la fin de l'année scolaire. Les derniers mois et particulièrement les six ou sept dernières semaines d'enseignement constituent la période idéale pour la réalisation de ce projet; la relation prof-élève, à ce point, possède toutes les chances d'être à son meilleur. Les en-

seignants des classes d'accueil savent que passer une année scolaire avec le même groupe (et avoir vécu avec lui son choc culturel) suffit à créer une atmosphère détendue où la créativité
tend à mieux s'épanouir, et ce malgré les contrariétés
administratives. Je crois qu'on peut enseigner plus efficacement
le français en passant par le coeur de l'apprenant; la langue
française, nous dit-on, symbolise la langue de l'amour; pourquoi
ne pas en profiter?

NOTE

1. Il s'agit du matériel didactique conçu pour l'enseignement
dans les classes d'accueil; la référence se trouve en bibliographie.

Arabic as a Foreign Language
Bringing Diglossia into the Classroom

Ahmed Fakhri

Abstract

This article argues for the replication of the diglossic situation of Arabic in the Arabic as a foreign language (AFL) classroom by integrating the teaching of Modern Standard Arabic (MSA) and a regional vernacular. The purpose of this integration is for the learner to achieve authentic communicative competence. Suggestions for integrating the two language varieties are made. These include the matching of language skills with language varieties and the use of Community Language Learning for practicing the regional variety. Problems of language interference and language testing which may result from this approach to teaching AFL are also discussed.

Introduction

The evolution of foreign language pedagogy toward proficiency-oriented instruction and the growing emphasis on developing communicative competence in the language learner (Omaggio 1986) have presented foreign-language teaching professionals with many new challenges. One of these challenges is how to deal with the extreme language variation that often characterizes the language to be taught. In many instances, communicating appropriately in the target language (TL) requires the mastery of two structurally distinct varieties of that language. Joseph (1988) discusses this issue with respect to the teaching of French as a foreign language. He observes that the widening structural gap between modern French and what he terms "New French," the informal spoken variety, presents French methodologists with the pedagogical dilemma of how to handle these two varieties. He identifies and evaluates several options available to French teachers, ranging from the focus on a single variety to the simultaneous or sequential presentation of both varieties (Joseph 1988, 32–35).

Teaching Arabic as a foreign language (AFL) represents an even more extreme case, given the diglossic situation of the Arabic language (Ferguson 1959; Abu-Absi 1991). In general, Arabic speaking communities employ two separate linguistic varieties, Modern Standard Arabic (MSA) and a regional vernacular variety (e.g., Egyptian Arabic, Syrian Arabic, or Moroccan Arabic), both of which are functionally and structurally distinct. MSA is the formal, "prestigious" variety used mainly in writing, whereas the regional vernacular is reserved for informal everyday transactions. Even though MSA and the regional vernacular exhibit important overlaps with respect to grammatical structure and lexicon, in many instances the structural and lexical differences are so important that they obscure the relatedness of the two varieties. The following examples from MSA and Moroccan Arabic (MA) exhibit a high degree of relatedness between the two varieties.[1]

(1) raža9a rražulu mina lmadrasati (MSA)

(2) ržə9 rražəl mən lmədrasa (MA)

[returned the man from the school
the man returned from school]

The MSA sentence (1) and the MA sentence (2) have the same word order and the relatedness of the lexical items is fairly obvious, the main differences being the inflections used in MSA (e.g., *u* at the end of *rražulu* [the man] to indicate nominative case) and vowel reduction in MA (e.g., MSA *mina* 'from' becomes *mən* in MA).

On the other hand, the substantial lexical differences between the following semantically equivalent sentences render them mutually unintelligible.

(3) 'uri:du Ta:ba9an bari:diyyan min faDlak (MSA)

(4) bġit wahəd tənbər 9afak (MA)

   [I want a stamp, please]

Note, for example, that the word for stamp in MA is *tənbər*, a loanword from French (*timbre*), but in MSA it is *Ta:ba9an bari:diyyan*, literally "stamp postal."

The question, then, for teachers of AFL is how to deal with this type of extreme variation. Which Arabic variety should be taught? Should the students be exposed to both MSA and a regional vernacular? The advantages and disadvantages of teaching one Arabic variety or another have been debated for quite some time. After a succinct discussion of various options available to AFL teachers, Mansoor reached the conclusion that "MSA should be taught side by side with the colloquial" (1959, 95). More recently, AFL professionals such as Ryding (1991) have proposed the adoption of a mixed variety, a sort of middle Arabic that is less formal than the standard variety but not as casual or stigmatized as the vernacular variety.

The present study reexamines the issue of what type of Arabic is suitable for the AFL classroom and argues that the integration of MSA and one regional vernacular is still the most desirable option. It also explores ways for achieving this integration. The reexamination of this issue is motivated by two related factors. First, the decision as to which language variety or varieties should be taught must be informed by recent developments in foreign-language teaching pedagogy, which favor communicative, proficiency-oriented approaches. The pedagogical merit of a particular solution to the problem at hand should depend, in part, on whether such a solution is congruent with the principles and goals of these new approaches. Second, the specific proposal of adopting a middle variety of Arabic seems to be gaining appeal (Ryding 1991; Abu-Absi 1991), but it needs to be scrutinized more closely. As Ryding (1991, 214) observed, the notion of a "middle Arabic" suitable for teaching has been contemplated for a long time, but its formal characteristics and the extent of its use have only recently been investigated. These developments call for an evaluation of the claims concerning middle Arabic.

The following section of the article reviews briefly the major issues concerning variation in Arabic. Then, several arguments in favor of the integration of MSA and a vernacular in the AFL classroom, rather than the use of a "middle variety," are presented. Finally, procedures for implementing this integration as well as issues related to language interference and language testing which result from it are discussed.

Variation in Arabic

Accounts for the sociolinguistic situation in Arabic speaking communities are of two types. First, there is the diglossic model outlined in Ferguson, who defines diglossia as "a relatively stable language situation in which, in addition to the primary dialects. . . , there is a very divergent highly codified (often grammatically more complex) superposed variety of written literature, which is learned largely by formal education . . ." (1959, 336). According to this model, there exists a standard Arabic variety, commonly referred to as Modern Standard Arabic, which is shared by all Arab communities, alongside regional vernaculars (e.g., Egyptian Arabic, Moroccan Arabic). MSA is the written variety used in education, administration, literature, journalism, and so forth. Regional vernaculars are used in everyday informal transactions and are essentially spoken varieties. The following examples from MSA, Moroccan Arabic (MA), and Egyptian Arabic (EA) are intended to give the non-Arabic specialist a sense of the relatedness (or the lack thereof) of these Arabic varieties. The EA sentence (7) is taken from Omar (1976, 31).

(5) gaDiba li'annana: kunna: muta'axxiri:n. (MSA)

(6) tqalleq 9laHaqqaš kenna muxxri:n. (MA)

(7) zi9il 9ša:n iHna mit'axxari:n. (EA)

[he got angry because we were late]

The second model views Arabic variation in terms of a continuum of language varieties and contends that the dichotomous characterization of Arabic discussed above is oversimplified and inadequate because it fails to account for other varieties that are intermediate between the colloquial Arabic of the street, so to speak, and the highly complex and essentially written standard Arabic used in academia, for example. Thus, Blanc (1960, 85) claims that there are five different varieties of Arabic: Standard Arabic, Modified Classical, Elevated Colloquial, Koineized Colloquial, and Plain Colloquial. Meiseles (1980, 123), on the other hand, distinguishes four Arabic varieties: Literary Arabic, Oral Literary Arabic, Educated Spoken Arabic, and Plain Vernacular. Mitchell (1986, 17) uses the following diagram to illustrate the Arabic continuum:

ESA

		Unstigmatized		Stigmatized
High-flown	Formal	Informal		
		Careful	Casual	

At one end of the continuum is the high-flown variety exemplified by written Arabic prose. At the other end we find the stigmatized speech of illiterate people. The medium variety, Educated Spoken Arabic (ESA), is claimed to have three distinct styles: Formal, Informal-careful, and Informal-casual. Notice, however, that Mitchell's use of the term "continuum" to characterize the sociolinguistic reality represented in the above diagram is only partially accurate. The relationships between the various labels in the diagram are not solely linear, as the term continuum suggests, but hierarchical as well. The following is an alternative visual representation of the content of the diagram which highlights the hierarchical relationships.

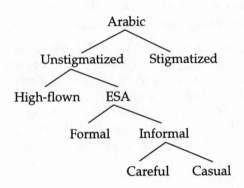

These attempts to come to grips with variation in Arabic reflect the complexity of the state of Arabic, and to some extent the inadequacy of the sociolinguistic models available. Thus, in addition to the problem of terminology indicated by the proliferation of terms that refer to the different varieties and the inconsistency in their use, the identification of many of these putative varieties of Arabic is extremely unsatisfactory. For example, Blanc's Elevated Colloquial has been defined as "any plain or koineized colloquial that is classicized beyond the 'mildly formal' range" (Mitchell 1986, 11). Statements like these, which include vague and ambiguous language ("mildly formal"), abound in the discussion of Arabic variation (see Parkinson 1991, 32–33 for a discussion of the problem of terminology for Arabic varieties in Egypt).

However, in spite of these divergent claims as to the number or the characteristics of Arabic varieties, researchers seem to agree that, in addition to the traditionally recognized dichotomy, MSA and vernacular, serious consideration must be given to an emerging Arabic variety which is "created and maintained by the constant interplay of written and vernacular Arabic" (Mitchell 1986, 13). Such a variety is alternatively termed Educated Spoken Arabic (ESA) or Formal Spoken Arabic (FSA) (Meiseles 1980, 123; Mitchell 1986, 8; Ryding 1991, 212).

It is only legitimate, then, that for the practical purpose of teaching AFL much of the detailed sociolinguistic analyses of Arabic variation must be set aside for the moment given their tentative and controversial nature. Instead, the focus should be on the somewhat simpler but usable view of Arabic variation which recognizes MSA, regional vernaculars, and the so-called Educated Spoken Arabic (Ryding 1991, 212). These varieties seem to be the only reasonable candidates for use in the AFL classroom. In what follows, I will argue that the integration of MSA and a regional vernacular in the AFL classroom is the soundest and most desirable option.

Integrating MSA and a Vernacular: The Rationale

At the outset, two clarifications have to be made. First, the term Arabic as a Foreign Language refers here to *general* courses of Arabic to nonnative speakers, such as those typically offered in foreign language departments of academic institutions. I am excluding, for example, courses of Arabic for specific purposes such as courses designed to help students to read Arabic literature or to decipher radio broadcasts. Second, it is assumed in this discussion that *authentic* language use as advocated by communicative, proficiency-oriented approaches is the ideal for language teaching (Omaggio 1986, 47).

Argumentation for the integration of MSA and the vernacular will be done in the following manner. First, it is shown that the traditional use of MSA alone is both psycholinguistically and sociolinguistically invalid and that the selection of a regional vernacular alone severely confines the learners' functional use of Arabic. Second, it is argued that the adoption of ESA in AFL programs is probably premature given the fact that the status of ESA is still unclear, in spite of the attention paid by scholars to this question.

The selection of MSA alone for AFL courses clearly fails to take into consideration crucial facts about Arabic. First, from a language acquisition perspective, MSA is the marked variety relative to the vernacular: a member of an Arabic speech community who knows MSA also knows the vernacular. In other words, there are no native speakers of Arabic who know only MSA. As Joseph points out, "while second language acquisition cannot directly reproduce the ideal patterns of first-language acquisition, neither should it run counter to them"

(1988, 31). Therefore, if the learners' ultimate aim is to achieve native-like competence in Arabic, they should be taught the vernacular in addition to MSA.

Second, from the point of view of language use, MSA is essentially a written formal variety. Thus, teaching speaking skills using this variety in dialogues involving informal topics (Abboud and McCarus, 1988, *passim*) is inappropriate, even though it is linguistically possible. The communicative competence of Arabic speakers includes the appropriateness of use of the language varieties available to them. For example, using MSA in an informal conversation about flight destinations and family members (Abboud and McCarus 1988, 209) is definitely inappropriate. Such interactions would normally be conducted in a regional vernacular.

Teaching a regional vernacular alone, however, has two obvious disadvantages for AFL students. First, these students will not be able to use the written medium since regional vernaculars are exclusively spoken varieties (Abu-Absi 1991, 119). Second, given the important differences between regional varieties of Arabic, they will encounter major difficulties when they attempt to communicate with speakers of a regional vernacular different from the one they have been taught. It is true that even with the approach advocated here, the integration of MSA and a regional variety, the second problem will subsist to some extent. However, the AFL student who learns both MSA and a regional vernacular will not be worse off in this respect than the majority of native speakers of Arabic, who also experience a great deal of frustration in their oral interaction with fellow Arabs who speak a different regional variety.

The other potential candidate for adoption in the AFL classroom is Educated Spoken Arabic (ESA). The selection of this variety is still not a viable option, however, because the extent of its use in different Arab countries and the identification of its formal characteristics are not clear. The claim that this variety is used as "a means of communication throughout the Arabic-speaking world" (Ryding 1991, 212) and that it serves "the everyday needs of interlocutors, from the manager and his reception clerks in the Hilton Hotels of the Arab world to the Arab diplomat chatting to colleagues at a reception" (Mitchell

1986, 9) is misleading. It is probably true that educated speakers in a particular region (e.g., Morocco) may exhibit speech which is noticeably different from that of illiterate people from the same region. However, this is markedly different from the claim that there exists a pan-Arab variety used throughout the Arab world. I believe that the emergence of a true pan-Arab educated Arabic would require, at least, substantial improvement in literacy rates, more intensive systems of communication, and more mobility in the Arab societies.

The identification of the features of what has been called Educated Spoken Arabic also raises some questions. Many of these features are either too general or too specific. For example, the reduction or elimination of inflectional marking of case and mood (in Arabic, 'i9ra:b') and the use of negative particles and numerals (Michell 1986, 10) are not peculiar to ESA. These exist in Moroccan Arabic, for example.[2] On the other hand, the majority of lexical items and expressions attributed to ESA by Ryding (1991, 215) are not used by all educated Arabic speakers. Educated Moroccans, for example, do not use terms such as *ba9deen* (afterwards), *kamaan* (also), *mish heek* (right), and may not even understand items such as *basiiTa'* (don't worry), *mish baTTaal* (not bad).[3]

The dubious status of the so-called ESA raises the following question: What do educated Arabic speakers from different regions, say a Moroccan, a Tunisian, a Syrian, a Bahreini, and a Saudi, speak when they encounter each other? The claim behind the ESA construct is that this heterogenous group has accessible to them a discrete variety of Arabic (namely, ESA) that they can use precisely in such encounters. As mentioned above, this claim has not been substantiated. Furthermore, it is plausible that in these encounters the participants do not necessarily use a single discrete language variety. Rather, each interlocutor tends to make necessary adjustments for the purpose of communication. Such adjustments may involve borrowing from MSA, avoidance of marked regional idioms, and even resorting to a foreign language (English or French, for example). Claims and counterclaims such as these need to be empirically tested before concluding that there is an Arabic variety used by educated Arab speakers, and that this variety should be adopted in the AFL classroom (Ryding 1991, 216).

Integrating MSA and a Vernacular: Procedures

This section suggests ways for integrating MSA and a vernacular.[4] The general guiding principle for this integration is that classroom activities and interaction, teaching techniques, language teaching materials, and the like should reflect as much as possible the respective functions of the two varieties. The first issue that will be discussed is the matching of "macro" language skills (i.e., reading, writing, speaking, and listening) with the language varieties. Second, a specific proposal concerning the use of Community Language Learning will be made and justified. Finally, I will address two main consequences of the integration of MSA and a vernacular: (a) the interference from one variety into the other; and (b) the problem of testing.

Table 1 presents the way in which the language varieties are matched with the language skills. The obvious aspect of this matching is that reading and writing concern MSA but not a vernacular. On the other hand, listening and speaking involve both varieties.

Table 1. Matching Language Skills
with Language Varieties

Skill	Language Variety	
	MSA	Vernacular
reading	+	−
writing	+	−
listening	+	+
speaking	+	+

However, the listening and speaking activities in the two varieties differ in terms of the type of discourse used: planned vs. unplanned (Ochs 1979, 51). Listening and speaking activities in MSA should focus on planned discourse such as newscasts and lectures, where the speaker reads aloud a prepared text, or at least heavily monitors his speech on the basis of extended written notes. Unplanned discourse as exhibited in spontaneous conversation is the domain of the vernacular.

Given the fact that the vernacular is used essentially for oral spontaneous communication, a version of Community Language Learning (Curran 1972) may be particularly appropriate for teaching this variety. The major role of the teacher ("counselor") in this approach to language teaching is to tell the students how to express in the target language whatever message they choose. Thus the learner is likely to receive authentic language input since the "counselor" is under time pressure to translate the learners' message into the target language without editing. This unedited, unmonitored input to the learner reflects the spontaneous speech of educated Arabic speakers more closely than the usual input which is prepared beforehand and consciously manipulated for putative pedagogical reasons.

The integration of MSA and a vernacular may lead to complications in the teaching process. Potential interference with one variety from the other is a legitimate concern for the AFL teacher, who must be prepared to deal with the possibility that students may be confused and unable to keep the two varieties apart. It should be noted, however, that the mutual influence of the two varieties would not always be negative. Overlaps between MSA and the vernacular, especially in the lexicon, may enhance the learning process. For example, learning a lexical item in the vernacular will likely facilitate the recognition of its cognate in MSA and vice versa. Furthermore, many of the differences between the two varieties are systematic and thus predictable, which will enable the learner to develop rules and strategies for telling the two varieties apart. The following contrastive terms from MSA and Moroccan Arabic (MA) clearly illustrate this point:

MSA	MA	Gloss
xaraža	xrəž	he went out
Daraba	Drəb	he hit
qatala	qtəl	he killed

On the basis of these patterns, a learner who encounters a verb form such as *saraqa* (he stole) should be able not only to identify it as a MSA form, but also to figure out what its MA equivalent is (i.e., srəq). Finally, some amount of mixing of the two varieties should be expected and tolerated since this is, after all, a major feature of educated native speech.

Now, a brief word about the implications of the integration of MSA and a vernacular for testing AFL. It is obvious that the evaluation of students should reflect the different functions of the two varieties studied. This can be achieved by *adapting* criteria such as those found in ACTFL proficiency guidelines. For example, the novice learner (Parkinson 1985, 17) should be able to tell the time, order a meal, and take a taxi *in the vernacular*, and fill out hotel guest forms and read train schedules *in MSA*. In other words, evaluation criteria should in part probe the communicative competence of the learner, which, as was argued earlier, includes the "knowledge" of the appropriate use of Arabic varieties.

Conclusion

The above discussion clearly indicates that, in order for AFL learners to achieve authentic communicative competence in the target language, they must be exposed to both MSA and a regional vernacular. It was shown that the integration of the two Arabic varieties is dictated by psycholinguistic and sociolinguistic considerations. The implementation of this integration requires that pedagogical decisions concerning language skills, teaching materials, classroom activities, and the like take into consideration the functions of the two varieties. This approach to teaching AFL may result in some problems such as interference with one variety from the other, or the inevitable complications concerning testing. However, as indicated above, such problems are not insurmountable, and should not detract from the viability of integrating MSA and a vernacular.

NOTES

1. The following symbols are used in the Arabic transcription:

'	glottal stop
H	voiceless pharyngeal fricative
9	voiced pharyngeal fricative
T	velarized voiceless dental stop
D	velarized voiced dental stop
ɤ	voiced uvular fricative

The rest of the symbols are standard and their phonetic values can be found in any American linguistics textbook.

2. The Moroccan Arabic plural form *rrža:l* (the men) corresponds to the following MSA forms: *arražula:ni* (dual, nominative), *arražulayni* (dual, genitive/accusative), *arriža:lu* (plural, nominative), *arriža:la* (plural, accusative), and *arriža:li* (plural, genitive).

3. It appears that the data presented in Ryding (1991, 214 ff.) represent the particular Arabic variety used by the teaching faculty at the Foreign Service Institute, rather than a variety common to all educated Arabic speakers. The author herself uses phrases such as "the FSI brand of F(ormal) S(poken) A(rabic)," which gives the impression that this is a teacher-made variety rather than a sociolinguistically real language variety.

4. I am assuming here that the vernacular selected would be one familiar to the instructor (e.g., an instructor of Egyptian origin would use Egyptian Arabic). If there are several instructors who know different regional vernaculars, the students may be allowed to study the vernacular of their choice.

Acquisition of Pragmatic Rules
The Gap between What the Language Textbooks Present and How Learners Perform[1]

Miyuki Takenoya

Abstract

This article reports on how selected language textbooks deal with pragmatic rules and how learners acquire such rules. The focus is on the acquisition of rules related to address terms by learners of Japanese as a foreign language (JFL). This article is divided into three parts. In the first, the learners' errors related to the acquisition of address terms in Japanese are introduced. Next, the presentation of address terms in textbooks is examined. In the final section, possible causes of learners' problems are discussed and some suggestions are presented to help solve them.

Introduction

In recent years, researchers in second-language acquisition have argued that pragmatic competence is an important factor for second- and foreign-language acquisition as well as linguistic competence (e.g., Bardovi-Harlig and Hartford 1990; Bardovi-Harlig et al. 1991; Beebe et al. 1990; Kasper 1989; Wolfson 1989). Pragmatics here is defined as "the ability of language users to pair sentences with the context in which they would be appropriate" (Levinson 1983, 24). In other words, learners need to know the appropriateness of expressions in context as well as the grammar, lexicon, and pronunciation of the expressions. The investigation of second-language learners' pragmatic competence has been developed in the field as "interlanguage pragmatics."

The major part of the previous research in interlanguage pragmatics has focused on the acquisition of pragmatics in English as a second language. Consequently, the focus of the field has been placed on the problematic aspects of pragmatics for learners of English. However, different issues are problematic in the acquisition of pragmatics in other languages, such as Japanese, which have linguistic encoding of the relative social ranks, age, and gender of participants and referents. In other words, different syntactic forms of verbs, adjectives, and nouns are used according to the social rank, age, and gender of the partner in the interaction.

The acquisition of address-term use will best illustrate the problems involved in Japanese language learning that do not occur in English language learning. As Wolfson (1989) claims, "the concept behind the use of appropriate forms of address [in English] is not difficult for language learners to grasp, since all languages make use of some kind of address forms, and many languages are much more complex than English with regard to respect forms" (85). However, the rules for address terms are rather complex in Japanese and the concept behind the use of appropriate forms of address is rather difficult to grasp for English-speaking learners of Japanese.

Address Terms in Japanese

Address terms will be defined as "words or phrases which denote a speaker's linguistic reference to his or her collocutor(s)" (Braun 1988, 7). For example, when a professor is addressed in

English, he or she can be denoted by, among others, any of the following: the second person pronoun 'you,' his or her first name, or his or her title and last name. According to Braun (1988), there are two forms of address: either free or bound. Free forms of address are forms "outside" the sentence construction, such as *Mr. Smith* in "Mr. Smith, may I talk to you, now?" Free forms can precede, succeed, or be inserted into the sentence. On the other hand, bound forms are syntactically integrated parts of sentences, such as *you* in "Do you like it?"

The address terms which can be used in Japanese are nouns and pronouns. Nouns include the first name, last name, full name, and their combinations with titles. As Harada (1976) illustrates, the Japanese titles consist of general titles and titles indicating institutionally defined positions (509). General titles approximate the use of Mr., Mrs., or Miss in English. Some examples of the general titles with phonetic transcriptions[1] and descriptions of use are listed below:

-sama[2] [sama]* (very polite)

-san [san] (average)

-tyan [tʃan] (diminutive)

-kun [kun] (mostly used by men)**

-sensee [sense:] (for teachers; details to be explained)

    * Phonetic transcription is provided by the author.
    ** This explanation is slightly modified.

Unlike Mr., Mrs., or Miss in English, the Japanese general titles do not have gender distinction or marital status distinction. In other words, they can be used for both men and women, and for both single and married people. For example, *Tanaka-san* can be used for Mr. Tanaka, Mrs. Tanaka, and Miss Tanaka. In addition, unlike Mr., Mrs., or Miss in English, these general titles can be attached to last names, first names, and full names.

The word *sensee* has a special usage as a title. According to Harada (1976), "contemporary usage of *sensee* confines it to a person who is respected for his or her capabilities, mainly in intellectual work" (509). The word *sensee* as a common noun means primarily "teacher"; as a title, it refers to authors, movie directors, artists, medical doctors, and politicians, as well as teachers and professors.

Other titles are formed from words indicating institutionally defined positions (Harada 1976, 509). Some examples are listed below:

In a company:

syatyoo   [ʃatʃɔ:]* "president"

butyoo   [butʃɔ:] "section chief"

In a university:

gakutyoo   [gakutʃɔ:] "president"

kyoozyu   [kjɔ:dju] "professor"

*Phonetic transcription is provided by the author.

These titles are used either independently or as a suffix to a name. Instead of using names, one can also address people by personal pronouns (Harada 1976, 511). Some examples of commonly used second person pronouns are listed below:

anata   [anata]* (standard and polite)

kimi   [kimi] (chiefly used by men to refer to men of
         equal or lower social status)

omae   [ɔmae] (informal and colloquial, somewhat
         pejorative)

*Phonetic transcription is provided by the author.

Although Japanese has nouns and pronouns that are used as address terms just as English does, the rules which operate in using them are different from the ones in English. Suzuki (1978, 131–132) proposed the following three rules relating to address-term use in Japanese:

1. A speaker cannot use a second person pronoun when addressing a superior.

2. A speaker cannot use just the individual's name when addressing a superior.

3. A speaker cannot use the status term (kinship term in family interaction) when addressing an inferior.

JFL Learners' Acquisition of Address Terms

In a previous study (1991), I reported on the frequency and systematic patterns of Japanese language learners' errors in address-term choice in Japanese. The learners who participated in the study were twenty-three American students who were enrolled in a third-year Japanese class. The results showed that learners of Japanese have two major problems related to the acquisition of address terms. One is the overuse and misuse of second person pronouns as a bound form of address. Sixty-six percent of the use of second person pronouns by subjects was inappropriate. In addition, learners used pronouns no matter whom they addressed. An example from the study of a learner's error in pronoun use is given below:

Situation: A student is talking to a professor asking whether the book belongs to the professor.

Student: Kore wa *anata no desu ka?

Translation: [This TM** you of is QM***; Is this yours?]

Key:
* = inappropriate speech
** TM = topic marker
*** QM = question marker

As Suzuki (1978) claimed, the use of second person pronouns is limited to addressing nonsuperiors. This use of the second person pronoun is inappropriate, therefore, since the addressee is in a socially higher position than the student is in. The student should have chosen the title *sensee*, meaning teacher or professor, instead of the second person pronoun *anata* as a bound form of address.

Another major problem in my 1991 study was students' choice of address terms for family members. The learners incorrectly used first names when addressing an older brother or sister, where native speakers of Japanese usually use kinship terms. As Suzuki claims, the use of first names is limited to addressing nonsuperiors. In Japanese society, older brothers or sisters have higher status than younger ones. An example of this type of error by a learner is shown below:

Situation: Talking to Keeko, older sister, to find out
whether a book belongs to her.

Student: Kore wa *Keeko no (desu ka)?

Translation: [This TM Keeko of (is QM); Is this Keeko's?]

Key:

* = inappropriate speech

QM = question marker

The use of the first name to the older family member is
inappropriate. Native speakers of Japanese usually use kinship
terms such as *oneesan* [ɔne:san] or *oneetyan* [ɔne:tʃan], meaning
"older sister" in this situation.

The results of the previous study provided the basis for the
present study. Because of the results of the previous study, I
decided to analyze the textbooks that the students used. Thus,
this analysis reported in this article investigates (1) whether the
textbooks provide pragmatically appropriate conversation
models regarding address term use; (2) how the meaning of
personal pronouns, occupational titles and usage rules are
explained; and (3) whether the pragmatically appropriate oral
exercises regarding address term use are provided.

The textbooks analyzed were volumes 1 and 2 of *Japanese:
The Spoken Language* by Jorden (1987, 1988). They are some of the
most widely used textbooks in universities in the United States.
They are also thorough and detailed in terms of sociocultural
information as well as grammatical patterns. Several other
textbooks of Japanese are used at the university level; however,
many of these are dated (e.g., *Learn Japanese: New College Text*
[Young and Nakajima-Okano 1967] and *An Introduction to
Modern Japanese* [Mizutani and Mizutani 1977]).[3] Thus, the
analysis reported on in this article concentrated on the textbooks
by Jorden.

Structure of the Textbooks

Volumes 1 and 2 of *Japanese: The Spoken Language* contain twelve
lessons each. The major components of each lesson are Core
Conversation with vocabulary lists and miscellaneous notes,

Structural Patterns, Drills, and Application Exercises, followed by review sections called Eavesdropping and Utilizations.

Core Conversations are short dialogues which are introduced at the beginning of the lesson to present new grammatical items and the vocabulary. Usually about five dialogues are listed and most of the dialogues contain two turns each, for a total of four turns. New grammatical items are usually introduced and explained in the Structural Patterns section. Usually three to five items are introduced and the explanation of the item is detailed and comprehensive. The Drills section usually contains ten to twenty different drills on new grammatical items, primarily substitution drills. Application Exercises are oral practice with situations that are presented after the drills.

The Eavesdropping section, one of the review exercises, is for listening comprehension practice. The learners are to listen to a tape and answer the questions written in the textbooks (Jorden 1987, xix). The Utilization section tests the learners' understanding and ability to use the learned items in the lesson by presenting typical situations in which expressions learners have studied might be utilized. According to Jorden, a situational orientation of this kind is intended to emphasize the importance of speaking a foreign language according to what is grammatically and culturally appropriate in a given setting, rather than through direct translation of what would be appropriate in a learner's native language in a similar setting (1987, xix).

Analysis

Core Conversation Dialogues

The Core Conversation sections in all the lessons were analyzed. From a total of twenty-four lessons, only one conversation included an address term. The conversation is listed below (Jorden 1987, 48):

a. Suzuki-san.

[Suzuki-Mr.; Mr. Suzuki.]

b. Nan desu ka?

[What is QM; What is it?]

a. Odenwa desu.

[Telephone is; It is the telephone.]

b. A, doo mo.

[Oh, well; Oh, thanks.]

Key:

QM = question marker

Suzuki-san, meaning "Mr. Suzuki" in the conversation, is the free form of address, which is the form used to attract Mr. Suzuki's attention. Since the free forms of address tend to be avoided in conversation both in English and Japanese, it makes sense even though the textbooks do not include them in the conversation. However, bound forms of address are unavoidable address forms. In addition, it is evident, from the results of the previous study by Takenoya (1991), that bound forms of address are a major part of the problem of learning address terms in Japanese. As Bardovi-Harlig et al. (1991, 4) claim, the appropriate conversation models are necessary for developing a learner's pragmatic awareness.

Structural Patterns Explanations

The Structural Patterns sections were analyzed to see how address terms were explained. The Japanese address term system was treated as important in grammatical explanation sections of the textbooks. The descriptions of address terms were precise and thorough. Most of the findings from sociolinguistic studies were covered in the explanation in the textbooks. For example, one entire page was devoted to the explanation of personal referent terms. *Anata*, which is one of the second person pronouns in Japanese, was also introduced as one of the personal referent terms. A summary of the explanation of *anata* is below (Jorden, 1987, 59):

a. *Anata* is a polite 'you' (singular).

b. *Anata* is used in addressing an equal or a subordinate.

c. *Anata* should be avoided in addressing superiors (including teachers).

d. *Anata* is used much less commonly in Japanese than corresponding words are used in English.

e. Surveys and questionnaires may address the anonymous reader as *anata*.

f. Wives may address their husbands as *anata*.

g. Foreign students of Japanese, in particular, should bring to an end their long-standing history of overuse of this word!

It is evident, if one compares the above explanation of *anata* with the earlier list, that all the major descriptions of the word *anata* by sociolinguists are covered in the explanation in the textbooks. In addition, Jorden's explanation points out one of the most common errors made by Japanese language learners and warns against such overuse of the word.

In other lessons, the kinship terms and rules of using them are also precisely described. The description emphasizes that whether one's brothers and sisters are older or younger is extremely important in recognition of the hierarchy in a Japanese family. The author of the textbooks presents the fact that the younger members of the family are addressed by their first name but older members are addressed with kinship terms. On the whole, the explanation of address terms in the textbooks is a complete and accurate one.

Drills and Application Exercises

After that, drills in the lessons which contained an explanation of address terms were analyzed. Only two drills using address terms were found. Although these two drills are related to address terms, they are substitution drills, and therefore have dubious value for developing learners' awareness of address term choice. One of the drills used in the textbook is below (Jorden 1988, 60–61):

Example: *Sensee* desu ka?
           [Teacher is QM*; Are you a teacher?]
1. *tomodati*   *Tomodati* desu ka?
           [Friend is QM; Are you a friend?]
2. *Satoo-san*   *Satoo-san* desu ka?
           [Satoo-Mr. is QM; Are you Mr. Satoo?]
   Key:
     QM = question marker

In this drill, learners are supposed to substitute the underlined word with the other words listed. It is evident that this drill is based on automaticity and does not provide practice for choosing the correct address term according to the addressee.

In developing the learners' pragmatic awareness of address terms, the drills in the textbooks have noticeable shortcomings. One of them is that they do not provide enough practice relating to address terms. Another is that the drills are based on substitution and do not make learners think about address term choices regarding the addressee.

Pedagogical Suggestions

Volumes 1 (1987) and 2 (1988) of the textbooks provide detailed and complete explanations regarding the complex system of address terms. However, they lack sufficient appropriate conversation models which draw the learners' attention to the different address terms according to the difference of social status, age, and gender of the participants in the interaction. In addition, they do not provide ample exercises to reinforce learners' understanding of the rules and encourage the application of the rules in real interaction.

In order to supplement the shortcomings of the textbooks, three types of activities will be presented. These activities are intended for intermediate learners who have finished the two volumes of the examined textbooks.

First of all, appropriate models of contextualized language use should be provided. This can be done through providing short dialogues in the classroom. Sample dialogues with bound forms of address are presented below:

Situation 1:	A student and a teacher converse.
Student:	*Sensee,* kore wa *sensee* no hon desu ka?
	[Teacher, this TM teacher of book is QM; Teacher, is this your book?]
Teacher:	Hai, soo desu.
	[Yes, so is; Yes, it is.]
Key:	
	TM = topic marker
	QM = question marker
Situation 2:	Two male students converse.
Student 1:	Oi, kore *kimi* no hon?
	[Hey, this you of book; Hey, is this your book?]
Student 2:	Aa, soo dayo.
	[Yeah, so is; Yeah, it is.]
Situation 3:	An older brother converses with his younger brother.
Older brother:	Oi, kore *omae* no hon?
	[Hey, this you of book; Hey, is this your book?]
Younger brother:	Un, soo dayo.
	[Yeah, so is; Yeah, it is]

In these dialogues the status of the participants is highlighted to draw the students' attention to the relationship between speaker status and address choice. Since the choice of pronouns changes according to the speaker and listener in the interaction, the dialogues are presented in contrast. The first dialogue shows the address term choice by one person talking to a higher status person. The second shows people of equal status, and the third shows a person in a higher status talking to a lower status person. By providing models in contrast, the learners' attention will be drawn to the address-term choice. Contrasting the models provides further evidence of the importance of speaker status on the choice of address terms.

Another activity to recommend is exercises for address-term use. The drills available in volume 1 of the examined textbooks can be modified in a manner that draws the learner's attention to the pragmatics. It can then be used as an exercise for intermediate learners. The example below presents the original drill in the textbook (Jorden 1987, 61) and a modified exercise.

Original drill (substitution):

Example:	Kore wa *anata* no desu ka?
	[This TM you of is QM; Is this yours?]
1. *gakusee*	Kore wa *gakusee* no desu ka?
	[This TM student of is QM; Is this the student's?]
2. *Satoo-san*	Kore wa *Satoo-san* no desu ka?
	[This TM Tanaka Mr. of is QM; Is this Mr. Tanaka's?]
3. *sensee*	Kore wa *sensee* no desu ka?
	[This TM teacher of is QM; Is this the teacher's?]

Key:
TM = topic marker
QM = question marker

Modified practice:
Ask the following people if this belongs to them.

1. your Japanese instructor, Yosio Tanaka
    Kore wa *sensee* no desu ka?
    [This TM teacher of is QM; Is this yours?]

2. your classmate, Kyooko Ono
    Kore wa *Ono-san* no (desu ka)?
    [This TM Ono–Ms. of is QM; Is this yours?]

3. your younger sister, Yooko
    Kore wa *Yooko* no (desu ka)?
    [This TM Yooko of is QM; Is this yours?]

4. your older brother, Takasi
    Kore wa *oniityan* no (desu ka)?
    [This TM older brother of is QM; Is this yours?]

The original drill is substitution. In the modified practice, learners are asked to choose the right bound form of address according to the addressee. For example, in addressing the Japanese instructor, "*Kore wa sensee no desu ka?*" is appropriate. In addressing a younger sister, in contrast, "*Kore wa Yooko no (desu ka)?*" is expected. By using this modification, the learners are encouraged to pay attention to the status difference of the addressee and to choose the right address terms accordingly.

Another type of practice that would be helpful to nurture the pragmatic awareness of learners is the use of role-playing activities in the classroom. In role-playing activities, the learners are provided with certain situations and asked to think what would be appropriate to say in the situation given. An example of a role-playing situation is below:

> When you go to visit Professor Iwamoto during his office hours, you find a Japanese book in front of the entrance to Goodbody Hall. You wonder whose it is and pick it up. You stop in front of Professor Iwamoto's office. The door is open, but he is reading a journal and does not notice that you are there. First attract his attention and ask him if the book is his.

In this situation, the learner taking the student role is expected to ask if the book belongs to Professor Iwamoto. When asking, "Does this book belong to you?" in Japanese, "*Kore wa sensee no hon desu ka?*" is appropriate. Whether the learner can produce an appropriate bound form of address for *sensee* ("teacher") is tested. As Bardovi-Harlig et al. (1991, 5) claim, the role of the teacher is not to teach about pragmatic rules, but to draw the learners' attention to the pragmatic rules and encourage learners to think about them.

Conclusion

To summarize, the examined textbooks include thorough explanations of the pragmatic rules, but they are short of both sufficient appropriate conversation models to nurture the learners' pragmatic awareness regarding address terms, and exercises that encourage learners to apply their pragmatic knowledge to real situations.

In the previous study by Takenoya (1991), learners of Japanese misused *anata* and kinship terms. However, how to use the word *anata* and kinship terms are very thoroughly and precisely explained in the examined textbooks in the Structural Patterns sections. Nevertheless, learners did not perform appropriately even after studying the lessons on address terms. It seems that the shortage of appropriate conversation models and ample practice plays a crucial role in limiting the learning of pragmatic rules. In short, learners lack natural input and practice.

The problems surrounding the introduction of pronouns as address terms in foreign language textbooks seem a common phenomenon in a number of languages, such as French, Italian, and Spanish (e.g., Uber 1985; Wieczorek 1991b, 1992). In this article, some options of classroom activities were presented to develop learners' pragmatic awareness. Although these suggestions are not meant to be exhaustive, they do illustrate some ways in which real-life activities can be constructed to supplement the shortcomings found in foreign language textbooks.

NOTES

1. In all transcriptions of phonetic values, IPA practices are followed.

2. All alphabetical denotations in the text follow the system used in *Japanese: The Spoken Language*, by Eleanor Jorden, Vols. 1 and 2, New Haven and London: Yale University Press.

3. Many new textbooks have been published after this paper was first written.

ACKNOWLEDGMENTS

I would like to express my thanks to Professor Kathleen Bardovi-Harlig for her valuable suggestions, encouragement and support. I would also like to thank Professor Beverly Hartford and students in her Sociolinguistics class for pointed comments and questions.

The Linguistic Effect of Foreign Language Learning on the Development of Mother Tongue Skills

István Kecskés
Tünde Papp

Abstract

This article describes how foreign language learning influences mother tongue development and use in a decisive period (ages 14–16) when the acquisition of the mother tongue skills is intensive, and individual writing, learning, and problem solving strategies and styles are being developed. It is argued that intensive and successful foreign language learning supports first language (L1) development significantly. Findings are based on a longitudinal experiment that was conducted in Hungary in 1988–1990 with native speakers of Hungarian learning either English, French, or Russian in different types of secondary schools. During the experiment only written language was examined; therefore, all the findings and conclusions refer only to the use of written language.

Although most linguists acknowledge that there must be a bidirectional interdependence between the first language (L1) and the foreign language (FL), only one side of this interaction has been emphasized in the relevant literature (Ellis 1985; Cook

1991; Larsen-Freeman and Long 1991). Much is known about the influence of L1 on the foreign language learning process but much less about the opposite direction: The effect foreign language learning (FLL) has on the development of the mother tongue. While educators have written about the possible coordination of mother tongue education and foreign language teaching, little has been done concretely to put this idea into practice.[1] Coordinating L1 and FL education makes sense only if we can prove that they are mutually supportive and in what ways. The aim of the 1988–1990 experiment was to find out how FLL influences mother tongue development and use in a decisive period (age 14–16) when the acquisition of the mother tongue is intensive, and individual writing, learning, and problem solving strategies and styles are being developed.[2]

We would like to emphasize here that in this article we concentrate only on foreign language learning that happens in classroom circumstances and involves some kind of instruction. Second-language acquisition in a natural setting and bilingualism are outside the scope of this work. During the experiment only written language was examined. Consequently, all of our findings refer only to the use of written language.

Hypotheses

Before the experiment the following hypotheses were set up:

1. Intensive and successful FLL can have a strong and beneficial influence on the development of L1.

2. Intensive FLL helps the internalization of L1 because linguistic operations based on conscious ways of thinking used in FLL can be transferred to L1 activities.

3. The transfer from a foreign language to L1 is especially intense and beneficial if L1 and the FL differ from each other in configuration, since synthetic and analytic languages develop different learning strategies. The combining of these strategies supports and even speeds up cognitive developmental processes.

Preliminary Studies

Our starting point was Bernstein's theory (Bernstein 1962, 1973), according to which an individual's system of communication is largely determined either by the restricted code or the elaborated code. The former belongs basically to the working class and the latter to the middle class, so the two codes are connected with the process of socialization. Several studies have proved the existence of these two different codes, but Bernstein's explanation connected with socialization has been partially rejected on the ground that the two codes do not necessarily represent different social classes (Lawton 1970; Papp and Pléh 1975; Biró 1984; Lawton 1986).

We hypothesized that the existence of the two codes could be explained by differences in the use of learning and task-solving strategies that are developed by controlled and conscious activities connected with school. In order to prove this, we had to measure the qualitative level of the use of the mother tongue. Mother tongue development is a very complex process including, among other factors, the acquisition of vocabulary, the use of different syntactic structures, and the application of communication strategies. In our work we concentrated mainly on the use of syntactic structures for two reasons: 1) well-structured sentences and the adequate use of more complex sentence structures are the best signs of the development of mother tongue use; and 2) because our starting point was Bernstein's theory, we tried to adapt the methods he and his followers and their critics used so that the results of our work could be legitimately compared to their results (Loban et al. 1961; Loban 1963; Bernstein 1962, 1973; Lawton 1970, 1986).

The Experiment

The longitudinal experiment was conducted in three different types of classes with fourteen-to-sixteen-year-old Hungarian students studying either English, French, or Russian as a foreign language. The locations of the experiment were three Hungarian high schools. All the students had had the chance to study

Russian for at least four years before entering high school, but English and French were entirely new to them.[3]

The three types of classes involved in the experiment were: immersion, specialized, and control classes. In the immersion classes, some school subjects such as math, and biology, chemistry were taught in the foreign language they were studying. Thirty-six students were involved in the immersion classes. Students in specialized classes studied English, French, or Russian. The students had six to eight foreign language classes a week and all the school subjects were taught in Hungarian. A total of thirty-five students took part in these classes. In control classes, students had two to three hours of foreign language instruction a week. All the school subjects were taught in Hungarian and thirty-three students were involved in the control classes. The students' social background and education were approximately the same in each of the three classes.[4]

The level of L1 use was tested at the beginning of the experiment. No significant differences were recorded in any of the three different types of classes. This is due mainly to the fact that each class used the same syllabus and books and had the same number of classes a week in Hungarian language and literature. Each class started to study FL (English or French) when the experiment began. The only exception was the Russian class that had had preliminary studies of their FL in elementary school.

Methods of Testing

Syntactic Structures

L1 and FL development and use were tested in writing twice during the two-year period. The tests always included creative activities in both L1 and FL, usually the production of a short text. For example, students were asked to do the following: 1) to write a composition on certain topics (family, future profession), 2) to describe the actions in a series of pictures, 3) to respond to advertisements, or 4) to finish incomplete stories. Students were usually expected to do the same task in FL and L1, but always had to produce first in the FL.[5] Research and teaching practice show that there is a strong influence from L1 on production in the foreign language. We wanted to find out if this effect could be brought about the other way around and how strong the influence of FL is on production in the mother tongue.

We used the Bernstein-Lawton-Loban method to measure the qualitative level of mother tongue development (Bernstein 1962, 1973; Lawton 1970, 1986; Loban 1961, 1963). Their method is based mainly on the use of complex sentences with particular emphasis on the frequency and types of subordinations therein. Linguists dealing with child language have proved that clauses of time, clauses of place, and noun clauses functioning as objects are acquired earlier than other types of subordinations (Limber 1973; Slobin 1973; Clark and Clark 1977). These constructions appear both in speech and writing more frequently than any other clauses. So in our survey, we distinguish these three types of clauses from the others.

The four following indexes were used to measure the level of conscious activities. These are interrelated, interdependent, and connected with the use of subordinations, and they show us what different kinds of strategies learners use when a task has to be solved, how they construct sentences, and how confidently they use linguistic structures.

1. Frequency Index

$$F = \frac{\text{total of subordinations}}{\text{total of finite verbs}}$$

This index shows us how frequently subordinate clauses are used in a text. As Lawton suggests, it is essential in an English text to use the total number of finite verbs instead of the total number of sentences (Lawton 1970). This type of analysis, however, is not as simple in Hungarian because the finite form of *lenni* (to be) is omitted in the present tense. This omission happens when the subject of the main clause or the subordinate clause is in third person (either singular or plural) and the predicate consists of a zero copula and a noun phrase (NP). For example:

A. *A lány,* akivel beszélgettél *még nagyon fiatal.*[6]
    The girl, whom with you talked still very young.
    [The girl you talked with is still very young.]

B. Azt hiszem, *hogy Péter katona.*[7]
    That believe I, that Peter soldier.
    [I believe that Peter is a soldier.]

Although this sentence type appears quite frequently in Hungarian, which could make the first indexes (frequency and unusual subordination) inaccurate on Hungarian data, we decided to keep it so that our findings could be compared with other works based on Hungarian data and using Lawton's method of analysis, which includes both the frequency index and the unusual subordination index.[8] In addition, all the students who took part in the experiments are Hungarian native speakers, and therefore, they use the sentence type in question according to their individual needs and competence. No significant conclusions can be made using only this index because the frequent use of the simplest subordinations (time, place, object) can produce very good results.

2. Unusual Subordinations Index

$$US = \frac{\text{total of unusual subordinations}}{\text{total of finite verbs}}$$

The simplest subordinate clauses (time, place, object) are acquired and used almost automatically (Lengyel 1981, Kecskés and Papp 1991). They function like formulaic chunks whose use does not require special kinds of conscious activity. The other types of subordinations are connected with a later stage of development, as they require special mental planning (Lengyel 1981). That is why this index tells us the most about the development of the student's creativity.

3. Loban Index

$$LI = \frac{\text{total number of B, C, D}}{\text{total number of A, B, C, D}}$$

Loban's weighted index of subordination is based on four categories of subordinate clauses:

A   (1 point): A subordinate clause that is directly dependent upon a main clause.

B   (2 points): A dependent clause modifying or placed within another dependent clause.

C   (2 points): A dependent clause containing a verbal construction (i.e., infinitive, gerund, participle).

D   (3 points): A dependent clause modifying or placed within another dependent clause which, in turn, is within or modifying another dependent clause.

This index shows how the student tries to use the potential of the language. If this value is high and the frequency index is low, it means that well-constructed sentences can be found in the text.

4. Loban Number

LN = (total point value of A + B + C + D)

As any of the four indexes can be misleading if used separately, evaluation was always based on an analysis of the numerical data of all the four indexes. This complex evaluation ensures the accuracy of the tests. In the appendix we demonstrate how the different kinds of indexes were used during the analysis of a text. The example is based on an English text so that the procedure will be clearer for the reader, but exactly the same procedures were used when Hungarian texts were analyzed.

Problem Solving Strategies

The experiment gave us the opportunity to examine several questions connected with problem solving strategies used by the students. What we wanted to analyze was how FLL can influence mental activities like memorization or planning and how much these activities are bound to L1 and FL systems. It is out of the realm of this article to describe all of the problem solving strategies, but an example is essential. At the end of the longitudinal experiment, one of the tasks the students had to work on was to describe what was happening in a series of pictures in the FL. Two pictures in the same series were then slightly modified and one picture that was in the FL version was removed. This time the students were to describe what was happening in the pictures in their mother tongue and recall the missing picture that was in the FL version, describing it in Hungarian. The purpose of the exercise was to find out the answers to the following questions:

1) to what extent students are bound to a language when doing different kinds of activities;

2) to what degree their mental processes are language specific;

3) what role linguistic memory and visual memory play in memorization and mental planning.

The answers to these questions are addressed below.

Questions 1 and 2

We would expect that if students do the same task first in L1 and then in FL, the FL production will be very similar to the one in L1. However, this is usually not the case when they have to do the task in FL first and then in L1. The experiment shows that the similarity or difference of the FL and L1 productions depends on how much the students are bound to a language when doing different kinds of activities and how much these activities are bound to the particular language they use when doing a task. Our findings show that the students basically used three types of strategies when describing the modified series of pictures in their mother tongue. Some students followed their FL language production in the mother tongue version and gave a kind of translation of the text they produced in the FL. Not even the modified pictures could make them change their FL version of the story very much. They reproduced the motives as well as the sentence types in the mother tongue version. Other students also followed the story line of their FL production but their mental planning was more language-specific, which means that they used sentence types other than the ones in their FL version. The motives in the story were similar, but the way they described them was different. In writing their compositions, they used their mother tongue potential better than the first group of students did. For a third group of students, the description of the modified pictures creates an essential part of the story and bears no resemblance to the FL version. Although these students produced the same story line in both languages, each production was an independent, well-written one that used the potential of the language in which it was written. Thus, the third group of students produced entirely different stories in their mother tongue that did not resemble their FL production. Not only the sentence types but the motives were entirely different.

An analysis of the data shows the following:

–immersion class:

8%	L1 text almost the same as FL not only in motives but in sentence types as well (Equal),
50%	L1 text is a developed version of FL text: motives are similar but description different (Variation),
42%	L1 text differs entirely from FL text (Independent).

–specialized class:

10%	L1 text almost the same as FL text (E),
19%	L1 text is a developed version of FL text (V),
71%	L1 text differs entirely from FL text (I).

–control class:

4%	L1 text almost the same as FL text (E),
10%	L1 text is a developed version of FL text (V),
86%	L1 text differs entirely from FL text (I).

Question 3

The second task the students were asked to do was to recall which picture from the first version of the series (when they wrote their composition in the FL) was missing in the second version of the series when the students had to use their mother tongue. When evaluating the answers, we distinguished linguistic memory from visual memory. If linguistic memory is used by the students, they recall the linguistic operations they did when writing the text in the FL. Consequently, when the missing picture has to be recalled, the students who use linguistic memory will translate that particular part of the FL text almost word by word into L1 or produce only a slightly different version of the FL text. When visual memory is used by the students, they recall only the pictures themselves without remembering the linguistic production in FL and usually produce a different description (text) of events in L1.

An analysis of the data shows the following:

–immersion class:

> 63% used linguistic memory; out of this 18% reproduced the FL text details and 45% recalled the plot

> 37% used visual memory

–specialized class

> 46% used linguistic memory; out of this 8% reproduced the FL text details and 38% recalled the plot

> 54% used visual memory

–control class

> 24% used linguistic memory; out of this 5% reproduced the FL text details and 19% recalled the plot

> 76% used visual memory

The analysis of these data shows that linguistic memory is based on linguistic operations. In the immersion and specialized classes, linguistic operations primarily direct the verbal planning and problem solving of students, and visual impulses are of secondary importance. When the students saw the same picture series with a slight change they recalled the text they had produced in FL, and according to the logical requirement of modification, they developed the same story later in the experiment. This shows that the difference in visual experience does not change the strategy students generally use when solving linguistic tasks. The findings of this study suggest that students studying foreign languages intensively are more bound to use linguistic operations in their mental activities than those who have less access to FLL.

Principal Findings of the Experiment

1. Intensive and Successful FLL Supports L1 Development Significantly.

    1.1. As stressed earlier, there was no significant difference among the three types of classes in the use of their mother tongue. This is due mainly to the fact that in the elementary school system the teaching of composition is based on rigid patterns, and the primary goal is not creativity itself but practicing and acquiring how to organize and construct a written composition. Creativity is important only within the acquired schemata. The students' productions are not characterized by individual approaches, style, and particular handling of the linguistic material, but by the use of learned patterns, which require activities that are carefully guided by the schemata themselves. Entrance to high school represents a dividing line. Since high school encourages creativity and the use of individual approaches and styles, the change in the school requirements is a real challenge for the students. Because they have no required schemata and guidelines to work from, students have to learn how to handle linguistic material independently. From this perspective, what the development of our three types of classes shows is of particular interest.

    1.2. The experiment showed two different kinds of tendencies in the use of L1. While the immersion and specialized classes developed in the direction of creative use of their mother tongue, the control class could not even maintain the previously reached level. Although the immersion groups (because their curriculum focused mainly on the FL) had fewer classes in L1 (Hungarian language and literature) than the specialized and control ones, their production in L1 exceeded that of the two other types of classes. The specialized and control classes had the same kind of instruction in L1 but by the end of the experiment the L1 level of the specialized class exceeded that of the control class. The results of the experiment show the reason for the two kinds of development very clearly.

1.3.   The immersion and specialized classes develop the previously learned patterns further and handle them not only as schemata, but as essential parts of their linguistic means and communicative competence by amalgamating them with the conscious knowledge conditioned by linguistic operations used in both L1 and FL activities. In the control class, an opposite process was recorded. Although these students had more instruction in L1 than the immersion class and as much instruction as the specialized class, the instruction in L1 itself was not enough for the students to adjust to the new requirement (i.e., the creative use of the language without schemata). Their written production became similar to their speech. It is more casual and spontaneous and resembles the dialogue format. (See Example 2 in Appendix.)

1.4.   The use of B, C, D sentences becomes sporadic in the control class (see Appendix). Student production is characterized by simplification on the one hand and by hypercorrection (Marcellesi and Gardin 1974, 131) on the other. Whenever these students try to use an unusual, not acquired, and not sufficiently practiced sentence construction, they usually fail to convey the meaning they want, and their production seems to be out of place and linguistically complicated in an unnatural way.

1.5. The findings of this experiment point out that the significant difference in L1 development is mainly conditioned by the intensive and successful FLL.

2. The Differences between the Restricted Code and the Elaborated Code Can Be Explained by the Ontogenesis and Development of Written Speech.

2.1. The experiment indicated that the differences between the restricted code and the elaborated code can be explained not by the different processes of socialization, but by the ontogenesis of written speech whose development is basically connected with schooling. This process requires a high level of abstraction and careful verbal planning and develops into special learning strategies based on conscious and controlled activities. That is why consequently, when combining subconscious mother tongue skills with conscious knowledge developed both in L1 and FL in school, learners can be expected to reach a higher level of development in L1.

2.2. The intensive FL learning in the immersion and specialized classes gives strong impulse to L1. The knowledge of the students in L1 can be activated, and L1 develops in the direction of creative language use. This means that the intensive and resultant FL learning can help mother tongue education to a significant extent by activating passive knowledge and making the use of L1 more conscious.

3. Written Planning in L1 Becomes Sophisticated and Develops More under the Influence of FLL.

3.1 By the end of the experiment the students in the immersion and specialized classes became quite confident in their use of complex sentences of different types. In most cases the influence of FL learning was obvious. The use of L1 in the immersion and specialized classes shows a strong developmental tendency in the direction of elaborated code. Subordinate clauses are better constructed than at the beginning of the experiment and embedded sentences are more frequently used and more complex. The semantics of subordination is characterized by the use of more unusual types. This tendency gets stronger no matter what kinds of style the students' tasks require. Written planning develops more and becomes sophisticated.

3.2. The control class did not show this development, which means that three hours of instruction a week is not enough to bring about this positive change. The beneficial effect of FLL on the development of mother tongue skills is just a potentiality—not a necessity. What is important is that this positive influence can be developed.

4. The Typological Difference of L1 and FL Can Have a Positive Effect on the Linguistic Development of the Student.

The influence of FLL on the development of mother tongue skills depends not only on paralinguistic factors like intensiveness, effectiveness of the learning process, and motivation of the students but on linguistic factors as well. One of them is connected with language typology (Kecskés and Papp 1991). Our results show that the positive effect on L1 was almost equally strong if FL was English or French, but less strong when it was Russian. Student motivation accounts for little here because all three languages had been voluntarily chosen by the students. In addition, Russian had already been studied previously by the members of the Russian specialized class. It is hypothesized, then, that the effect of FL is especially beneficial if L1 and FL differ in configuration.[9] Configurational languages and non–configurational languages develop different kinds of learning and problem solving strategies, and the ability to use both types in linguistic operations can have a positive effect on the linguistic development of students.[10] Further investigation is needed to prove this point, but our results in this particular experiment support it quite strongly.

Appendix

Pattern

Task: Describe what is happening in the series of pictures in the foreign language you are studying.

- Describe what you see in the series of pictures.
- Try to recall and describe the picture that was included in the previous series (that you had to describe in the foreign language) and that is now missing.

Class type: Specialized (Seven English classes a week)
Time: Second test at the end of the first year

Example 1: The following text is a copy of the original production of one of the students. It shows each mistake the student made. (Numbers denote clauses.)

1
Once upon a time a man was walking in a street and
2   3
suddenly he saw a very very pretty girl. She's got fair hair
                                    4
and wonderful eyes. The man immediately falled in love
              5   6   7
with the girl. And he decided to know her, so he began to
              8   9
shout. The girl falled in love with the man, too, because he
                                        10   11
looks like as her previous boyfriend. They decided to have
                              12
a dinner in a restaurant. But there was a difficult problem!
        13   14
The man's wife. Their marriage wasn't very succesful
              15   16
relationship, because the wife was a little fat, and she was

17   18
really very ugly. So, (to tell the truth) I can understand the
19   20
man, why he wanted to get marriage with the young, nice
21   22   23   24
girl. Because I've forgotten to say, that they diceded to get
25   26   27
marriage. I hope, it will be more succesful, than the

privious one.

Total of clauses: 27

Number of finite verbs: 20

Number of subordinate clauses, infinitive phrases, gerunds and participles: 13

Frequent clauses (clauses of time and place, infinitive clause functioning as object): 6, 11, 20, 22, 23, 24, 26

Unusual clauses (all the rest): 7, 9, 15, 17, 19, 27

Sentence types:

A   (1 point): a subordinate clause that is directly dependent upon main clause

B   (2 points): a dependent clause modifying or placed within another dependent clause

C   (2 points): a dependent clause containing a verbal construction (i.e. infinitive, gerund, participle)

D   (3 points): a dependent clause modifying or placed within another dependent clause which, in turn, is within or modifying another dependent clause

Indexes

F (frequency index):

total of subordinations	<u>13</u>
total of finite verbs	20

US (unusual subordination):

total of unusual subordination	<u>6</u>
total of infinite verbs	20

Loban index:

total number of B, C, D	<u>1</u>
total number of A, B, C, D	13

Loban number (total point value of A+ B+ C+ D): 24

Values: F = 0.65
US = 0.3
L = 0.077
LN = 24

Example 2: The following text, illustrating the restricted code, is a student production, reproduced exactly as written.

The man saw the girl, and thought: "She is very pritty."

He decided: I want to meet with the girl.

—Let's spend any time in a restaurant.

—Oh no, let's go home.

—Is there somebody?

—Just my mum.

The mum is cooking. They arrived.

—Hello mum, he's my new boy-friend.

The student was not confident enough to produce a description of events, so dialogue was used instead.

NOTES

This paper is based on a longitudinal experiment conducted in Hungary in 1988–1990 with native speakers of Hungarian learning either English, French, or Russian in different types of secondary schools.

The experiment is detailed in the dissertation of Tünde Papp for the candidate degree, defended at the Hungarian Academy of Sciences, Budapest, Hungary on September 10, 1991 (Papp 1991).

1. Immersion programs are exceptions. Recently there has been some development in the area of across-the-curriculum education as well.

2 There are several different views on cognitive development but "the major proponent of each would agree that preadolescent and adolescent cognition is characterized by growth in the following areas: (1) hypothetical reasoning that involves inductive and deductive processes; (2) the coordination of abstract ideas, rules, and systems; and

(3) the use of various abstract symbol systems, such as those that characterize mathematics, physics, formal logic, and language" (Kamhi and Lee 1988, 154).

3. Until 1989, Russian was compulsory from the 4th grade in Hungarian elementary schools.

4. At the time of the experiment, all Hungarian elementary schools were state-run and had the same curriculum.

5. Sometimes there was a slight difference between the two tasks, which is discussed in the part headed "Problem Solving Strategies."

6. The underlined part is the main clause.

7. The subordinate clause is underlined.

8. See, for example, Biró 1984.

9. Configurational languages (for example, English or French) have bound word order governed by grammatical rules. Nonconfigurational languages (such as Russian and Hungarian) have a relatively free word order governed by pragmatic rules (White 1989).

10. Canadian studies on immersion programs (Richard-Amato 1988, 266–80; Rehorick 1991) have demonstrated the beneficial interaction of French and English; however, they are both configurational languages.

The Development of the Japanese Speaking Test and the Preliminary Japanese Speaking Test

Margaret E. Malone
Sylvia B. Rasi

Abstract

This article discusses the development and validation of two different levels of simulated oral proficiency interviews (SOPIs) in Japanese. A SOPI is a semidirect test of oral proficiency that relies on a tape and test booklet in place of a live interviewer to test oral proficiency in a language. The Japaneses Speaking Test (JST) follows the model of earlier SOPIs, while the Preliminary Japanese Speaking Test (Pre-JST) employs a new version of the SOPI format, adapted for lower-level learners of Japanese. The new items for the Pre-JST were modelled according to the ACTFL guidelines. Following piloting and field-testing, it was discovered that the JST and Pre-JST are adequate measures of students' oral proficiency in Japanese.

Background of the Simulated Oral Proficiency Interview (SOPI)

Recent approaches to foreign language instruction have placed increasing emphasis on a proficiency-based curriculum (Stansfield et al. 1990). The work of Liskin-Gasparro (1987), Grosse and Voght (1991) and Milleret et al. (1991) reflects the involvement of foreign language researchers and practitioners in the proficiency movement whose basic tenets are described in detail by Omaggio (1986). The definition of oral proficiency adopted in this paper is that of Omaggio, who states that "general [oral] competence in a second language [is] independent of any particular curriculum or course of study" (1986, 9). In 1978, the American Council on the Teaching of Foreign Languages (ACTFL), the Educational Testing Service (ETS) and several government agencies combined efforts to organize the Federal Interagency Language Roundtable (FILR), which encourages proficiency teaching and supports its implementation in language testing (Stansfield et al. 1990). If a proficiency-based approach is to have an effect on both the teaching and learning of languages via a washback effect between language testing and teaching, the support of this proficiency-based approach to language teaching is crucial. In other words, if teachers focus on the speaking skill in the classroom, yet measure learner progress by administering only audiolingual or grammar-translation tests, then students will subsequently "learn for the test" and will not focus their energies on developing oral proficiency. Therefore, in order for proficiency-based teaching to be effective, testing methods must support classroom goals and activities by reflecting this proficiency-based approach.

As a result of this concern for proficiency-based testing in the language classroom, the Oral Proficiency Interview (OPI) was developed by ACTFL to measure oral proficiency, one of the four skills stressed in language proficiency. The OPI is a face-to-face interview which rates the learner's oral proficiency in a second language, conducted by trained interviewers and raters (Liskin-Gasparro 1987). The ACTFL proficiency guidelines (ACTFL 1986), which are based on earlier FILR guidelines, provide the criteria for the rating of language proficiency.[1]

Modelled closely on ACTFL's Oral Proficiency Interview, the Simulated Oral Proficiency Interview (SOPI), developed by the Center for Applied Linguistics (CAL), is a measurement-oriented language elicitation device. The major difference between the OPI and the SOPI lies in their testing methods; while the OPI relies on face-to-face contact with a trained interviewer, the SOPI rates speaking proficiency through a semidirect interview (Stansfield 1989, 1). The SOPI simulates a live interview by employing a test booklet and a test cassette tape to elicit and to record rateable speech segments produced by the examinee.

The SOPI was initially developed in response to a need for practical, accessible, and pedagogically up-to-date language tests expressed by practitioners in the less commonly taught languages, such as Chinese, Hausa, and Hebrew, in which few OPI raters have been trained. Furthermore, many teachers find that administering an OPI is impractical or impossible for large groups of students, while the semidirect format of the SOPI makes it accessible and appealing to practitioners in the less commonly taught languages.[2]

The SOPI: Uses and Relation to the OPI

The SOPI differs from other types of language tests because it is a proficiency test and not an achievement test. Achievement tests measure mastery of material from a particular set of curricula whereas proficiency tests measure mastery of certain skills in a language; in this case, speaking skills. Because the SOPI is not based on any particular language study curriculum, it may be employed by institutions for a variety of purposes, such as determining admission to a language study program or placement within a language program. A high SOPI rating could be used to qualify students for exemption from a foreign language requirement (Milleret et al. 1991). The SOPI may also be used for competency testing upon the completion of language studies. Test scores may also be used to determine qualification for scholarships or appointments and for admission to study abroad programs (Stansfield 1989).

The SOPI is also currently in use as a part of the teacher certification process in Texas. The Spanish and French forms of the Texas Oral Proficiency Test, developed in 1990 for the Texas Education Agency, are currently used as a part of the state certification requirements for French, Spanish, and bilingual education teachers.

Correlation of the SOPI with the OPI

The first test of this kind, the Chinese Speaking Test (CST), was developed by Clark and Li (1986). In order to establish the validity of the new test format, ratings received by examinees on the new, semidirect testing format were compared to ratings received by the same examinees on the Chinese OPI as scored by two different raters. A .95 correlation (p > .01) between the two tests was found. Subsequent SOPIs were developed in Portuguese (PST), Hebrew (HeST), Indonesian (InST) and Hausa (HaST). The PST, HeST, and InST showed correlations of .90 to .95 (p > .01) with the OPI (Stansfield 1989). Since the HaST could not be correlated with the OPI due to a lack of trained raters of Hausa, HaST examinee ratings were correlated for interrater reliability. A correlation of .91 (p > .01) was found (Stansfield 1989).

Table 1. Average SOPI/OPI correlations for previous SOPIs

Average SOPI/OPI Correlation	
Chinese Speaking Test	.93 (32 examinees)
Portuguese Speaking Test	.93 (30 examinees)
Hebrew Speaking Test (USA)	.93 (20 examinees)
Hebrew Speaking Test (Israel)	.89 (20 examinees)
Indonesian Speaking Test	.95 (16 examinees)

Format of the Multilevel SOPI

The multilevel SOPI has been designed to test examinees from the intermediate-high to superior levels as measured by the ACTFL Guidelines. The ACTFL novice level is not tested by the multi-level SOPI since at the novice level, examinees would only be able to produce lists of items and formulaic phrases, skills which cannot be adequately tested nor rated by the multilevel semidirect format. The Japanese Speaking Test (JST), the most recent multilevel SOPI, was completed in 1991.

The prototypical multilevel SOPI is divided into six parts designed to elicit language samples similar to those found in the OPI. The test begins with less challenging, intermediate-level items and gradually incorporates more advanced- and superior-level items. Thus, examinees must answer questions designed for varying levels of oral proficiency. Performance on the elicited speech segments as recorded on the examinee's cassette tape is rated to determine the examinee's level of speaking proficiency.

The first part of the multilevel SOPI consists of a warm-up that is contextualized with an initial encounter situation in order to allow the examinee to carry on a conversation in the target language with a speaker of that language. Since all directions and instructions on the SOPI are given in English, the warm-up is the only part of the multilevel test requiring the examinee to both listen to and respond in the target language only.

Parts two through six of the multilevel SOPI are designed to follow the OPI's level check and probe phases. Level checks are designed to ensure that the OPI interviewer checks to see if the examinee can handle a task at a particular level of difficulty successfully. If this is the case, the interviewer then probes the examinee's level by asking him or her to perform more challeng-ing tasks. Eventually, the examinee experiences a linguistic "breakdown" at which he or she cannot function at the level of the question being asked. It is then that the interviewer is able to determine the examinee's level. Because the SOPI consists of tasks at many different levels, the rater can determine the exami-nee's proficiency level by evaluating how well the examinee per-forms on tasks at different levels, and at which level of items the examinee experiences breakdown.

Parts two through four of the multilevel SOPI rely on pic-tures to elicit speech. Examinees are asked to perform intermedi-ate- and advanced-level tasks by using the pictures provided as a source of ideas (e.g., give directions using a map, narrate a se-quence of events occurring in the past). Parts five and six allow the examinee to talk about topics and hypothetical situations in the target language, such as the advantages and disadvantages of public transportation (Stansfield 1989). The SOPI concludes with a wind-down which draws the test to a conversational close.

Rating the Multilevel SOPI

Among the advantages of the SOPI is that the test proctor, who may be a language teacher, language laboratory assistant, or authorized individual, needs no special qualifications to administer the test. After administration, the examinees' speaking samples are listened to and rated according to the ACTFL proficiency guidelines by a trained ACTFL rater or by language professionals who have completed training to rate SOPIs in their respective languages. Experienced language teachers are quickly able to learn to recognize the salient characteristics of each speaking level. Thus, these factors result in less time-intensive SOPI training than the OPI, while retaining or even increasing test score reliability.

The Preliminary Japanese Speaking Test (Pre-JST): Its Genesis and Initial Considerations

Like most other foreign language students in the United States, the majority enrolled in Japanese as a foreign language are at or below the ACTFL intermediate level (Raffa 1991; see also Appendix A). In the United States, most students at intermediate-level range are high school and college students who have completed approximately three years of high school Japanese or two semesters of college Japanese (Brod 1988). While planning for the development of the multilevel JST, item writers noted that, although useful in determining the oral proficiency of examinees representing a wide range of proficiency levels, the multilevel format would nevertheless include many items too difficult for the potentially large number of intermediate-level learners. Therefore, the multilevel format might not adequately elicit rateable speech samples from the intermediate-level student population. In response to these issues, the Preliminary Japanese Speaking Test (Pre-JST), designed for intermediate-level speakers, was developed.

Speaking Tasks and Content Areas Pre-JST

The speaking tasks of the Pre-JST follow the ACTFL speaking proficiency guidelines (ACTFL 1986; see also Appendix A) for the intermediate level, which specify that a speaker should be able to perform specific tasks successfully, such as asking and answering simple questions, providing information, ordering meals, making purchases, and talking about personal routines.

The content areas covered in the Pre-JST also reflect the areas in which the ACTFL guidelines specify that intermediate-level speakers should be conversant (e.g., personal life, family, leisure time activities). Since the Pre-JST target audience is defined specifically as American high school and college students, items were written with content areas and situations appropriate to the examinees' general life experience (e.g., school life, holidays, health, leisure time, and travel). Recognizing that learners will encounter situations in which they will need to speak Japanese both in the United States and in Japan, situations are placed in both countries.

Language-Specific Considerations

As is the case with every SOPI developed, some potential language-specific difficulties were raised by members of the JST/Pre-JST external and internal review committees, which were composed of experienced Japanese language professionals. For example, it was agreed to exclude the intermediate-level task of giving directions since in Japanese, this task presents a higher level of complexity than can be successfully handled by an Intermediate-level speaker. Another difficulty was the use of highly formal settings in contextualizing the items, since such settings require the use of stylistic registers such as the nonpolite, the humble polite, and honorific polite registers, all of which require superior-level speech. These and other related issues were resolved through extensive meetings and consultation with committee members and the test development team.

Pre-JST Item Types and Format

Block Item

Each Pre-JST form includes two block items, compared to the multilevel SOPI, which consists entirely of these types of items. The block item provides a paragraph-length description of a situation or topic to which the examinee is asked to respond. Following the description of the situation, which is presented both orally and in written form, the examinee is given a short period of time to organize his or her response. After this time elapses, the examinee then hears a target language prompt and is given a longer time period to respond. An audio signal and a printed time limit serve to inform the examinee of the time limit for planning and executing each response. The block items on the Pre-JST probe the examinee's proficiency level by presenting only advanced-level tasks. This contrasts with the JST, whose multi-level format includes several advanced-, advanced-high- and superior-level items. With the inclusion of only a limited number of advanced items, intermediate-level examinees are adequately challenged yet not discouraged by many items far beyond their ability.

Table 2. Block Item

> Imagine that you have participated in a student summer exchange program. You have spent the summer at the home of the Nakamoto family in Kyoto, Japan. Before returning home to the U.S., you invite the family to a formal restaurant to express your thanks for their hospitality. Before the meal begins, you tell them that you have something to say. After you hear Mr. Nakamoto indicate that you have their attention, *express your appreciation to the Nakamotos for their hospitality during your stay.*

Exclusively Pre-JST Item Types

Because the Pre-JST is tailored to a specific proficiency range (intermediate) and to a particular audience (American high school and first-year college students learning Japanese), appropriate contextual settings were built into three new item types designed to elicit adequate speech samples from the targeted intermediate-level examinee audience. In order to prepare the examinees for the type of item presented in each section, each item type in the Pre-JST is modeled prior to the presentation of the test item types.

Dialogue-Response Item Type

The dialogue-response item type is designed to assess the oral proficiency of the Intermediate-level examinee, characterized by his or her ability to produce sentence-level discourse. The dialogue-response item is a discourse-oriented item type that provides the examinee with the opportunity to produce sentence-length speech segments in response to a series of questions generated in the context of a particular situation. To ensure comprehension of the task, each question is introduced by a brief oral description in English.

Table 3. Dialogue-Response Item

Imagine that you are staying with a host family, the Okagawas, in Japan. You are talking about your school in the United States with your host mother. Mrs. Okagawa tells you she has a few questions she would like to ask you about your classes in the U.S.   a. First Mrs. Okagawa asks you what courses you took last semester.   b. She now asks which course was your favorite.   c. Now Mrs. Okagawa asks what courses you plan to take next year.

Dialogue-Inquiry Item Type

The dialogue-inquiry item type evaluates the examinee's ability to ask questions, a task which an ACTFL intermediate-level speaker should be able to perform. The dialogue-inquiry item consists of a contextualized situation and a series of subsituations in English for which the examinee must produce an acceptable question (e.g., "What could you ask to find out where the rest rooms are?").

Table 4. Dialogue-Inquiry Item

Imagine that you and some American friends are visiting Tokyo,
Japan. You decide to go shopping at a local shopping center, but
you need to ask someone for some information. You approach a
man standing at a bus stop to ask him some questions.

   a. Since you don't know where you can find the nearest
      shopping center, what could you ask the man to find out?

   b. You would also like to know if you can reach the shopping
      center by bus or if you can walk. What could you say to
      find out?

   c. One of your friends would like to buy some souvenirs.
      How could you find out if souvenirs are sold at the
      shopping center?

   d. You decide that you have enough information to find the
      shopping center. What could you say to the man to thank
      him for helping you?

Free-Response Item Type

The free-response item type was designed to provide a more
flexible format for the elicitation of sentence-level discourse. This
item type consists of a setting followed by a series of open-ended
questions in the target language. The examinee answers each
question during the time provided between questions. Although
sentence-level discourse is targeted for elicitation in this item,
sufficient time is given to some questions to allow examinees to
speak at greater length if they so choose.

The questions featured on free-response items are asked in
simple Japanese, with no prior English equivalent translation. A
contributing element in the decision to develop the free-response
item type as an "all-Japanese" item was encouraged by feedback
on the pilot versions of the Pre-JST Forms A and B, which suggested that examinees strongly believe that more spoken
Japanese should be heard on the test, in spite of the fact that the
Pre-JST is a speaking and not a listening proficiency test.

Table 5. Free-Response Item

Imagine that you are registering for summer school at a university in Tokyo, Japan. You are in the office of the international student advisor, Mr. Yamada. He is asking you some questions about your studies and about your lodging in Japan.

    a. Amerika no daigaku wa dochira desu ka? [*What school do you attend in the United States?*]

    b. Nihongo wa donogurai benkyoo shimashita ka? [*How much Japanese have you studied?*]

    c. Samaa sukooru no aida doko ni sumimasu ka? [*Where are you planning to stay during summer school?*]

Picture Items

The Pre-JST features two picture items, one of which is included in the block item section and the other of which is a free-response item. Picture items present a contextualized setting and are accompanied by a page of line drawings arranged in a series or sequence depicting an event toward which the examinees must base their response.

JST and Pre-JST Pilot and Field Testing

The JST was piloted in April 1991 at Georgetown University and field-tested in January 1992 at various universities in the Washington, D.C. area. It has since undergone revision by two committees of experts in and professors of Japanese.

    The JST and Pre-JST were field-tested at two high schools and three universities in early 1992. Examinee feedback was generally positive, particularly with regard to the Pre-JST items. The test developers responded to feedback by eliminating some items and shortening the test. Examinees stated that the new discourse-oriented item types were appropriate and relevant, for such items allowed them to practice speaking Japanese in authentic situations. Most importantly, the majority of the examinees felt that they were able to manage most of the situations on the Pre-JST, indicating that the test is appropriate for learners with this level of proficiency.

Moreover, teachers of Japanese who participated in JST rater-training sessions expressed a great deal of interest in the Pre-JST, for they felt that an intermediate-level test is most appropriate for most of their students. The development of the Pre-JST as an intermediate-level SOPI represents an effort to advance the area of oral proficiency-based testing in Japanese by reaching the largest population of learners of Japanese, intermediate-level learners. Pre-JST may have implications for proficiency testing at lower levels of language instruction in other languages as well.

Conclusion

The development of the Pre-JST shows that the SOPI format can be adapted to meet the needs of intermediate-level students of Japanese. Field-testing has shown that this test can be successfully utilized in the language classroom. The Pre-JST has begun to address the issue of evaluating the oral proficiency of lower-level language learners by providing an alternative to the multi-level SOPI. Future research will show the applicability of the Pre-JST format to other languages.

The development of the JST and Pre-JST demonstrates that the SOPI format is appropriate for Japanese as well as the other languages in which SOPIs have been developed. The enthusiastic reception of the JST by Japanese language professionals and the positive response by students of Japanese indicate that the Japanese SOPI is filling a need in the Japanese language testing community. As the JST and Pre-JST are employed by Japanese instructors, we will discover more about the use of the multilevel SOPI for language evaluation as well as the importance of lower-level oral proficiency tests for lower-level students. Such tests will provide a model, not only for oral proficiency testing in general, but for smaller-scale classroom oral proficiency tests.

Appendix A

ACTFL Speaking Proficiency Guidelines: Intermediate (*Foreign Language Annals* 20 [1987]: 590–591).

The Intermediate level is characterized by the speaker's ability to:

- create with the language by combining and recombining learned elements, though primarily in a reactive mode
- initiate, minimally sustain, and close in a simple way basic communicative tasks; and
- ask and answer questions

Intermediate-Low

Generic. Able to handle successfully a limited number of interactive, task-oriented and social situations. Can ask and answer questions, initiate and respond to simple statements and maintain face-to-face conversation, although in a highly restricted manner and with much linguistic inaccuracy. Within these limitations, can perform such tasks as introducing self, ordering a meal, asking directions and making purchases. Vocabulary is adequate to express only the most elementary needs. Strong interference from native language may occur. Misunderstandings frequently arise, but with repetition, the Intermediate-low speaker can generally be understood by sympathetic interlocutors.

Japanese. Can ask and answer questions such as: Nan-ji desu ka? Hachi-ji desu. [*What time is it? It's 8:00 . . . okay.*]

Can engage in a simple, reactive conversation using the formal nonpast/past, affirmative/negative forms.

A: Boku wa kinoo futtoboorru o mi ni ikimashita.

[*I went to see a football game yesterday.*]

B: Soo desu ka. Boku mo ikimashita.

[*Oh, really. I did too.*]

Demonstratives: Kore/Sore/Are wa watashi no kuruma desu. [*This/that/that (over there) is my car*] and classifiers: Kami ga ni-mai arimasu [*There are two pieces of paper*].

Misunderstanding frequently arises from poor pronunciation, wrong pitch-accents and limited vocabulary.

Intermediate-Mid

Generic. Able to handle successfully a variety of uncomplicated, basic, and communicative tasks and social situations. Can talk simply about self and family members. Can ask and answer questions and participate in simple conversations beyond the most immediate needs, e.g., personal history and leisure time activities. Utterance length increases slightly, but speech may continue to be characterized by frequent long pauses, since the smooth incorporation of even the most basic conversational strategies is often hindered as the speaker struggles to create appropriate language forms. Pronunciation may continue to be strongly influenced by first language and fluency may still be strained. Although misunderstandings still arise, the Intermediate-Mid speaker can generally be understood by sympathetic interlocutors.

Japanese. Can ask and answer simple questions on topics such as

> *personal history*: Oniisan ga arimasu ka? [*Do you have an older brother?*]
>
> *leisure time activities*: Eiga ni yoku ikimasu ka? [*Do you like going to the movies?*]
>
> *simple transactions such as at the post office*: 100 en kitte go-mai kudasai. [*One hundred yen please.*]

Quantity of speech is increased and quality is improved. Greater accuracy in basic constructions and the use of high frequency and auxiliary verbs:

> A: Ima nani o shite imasu ka?
>
> [*What are you going to do now?*]
>
> B: Terebi o mite imasu.
>
> [*I'm going to watch T.V.*]

The Intermediate-Mid speaker is generally a less reactive and more interactive conversational partner.

A: Eiga ni ikimashoo ka?

[*Do you like to go to the movies?*]

B: Iie, watashi wa ongakkai ni ikitai desu.

[*No, I rarely go.*]

The use of classifiers is expanded, and the use of participles is more appropriate.

Intermediate-High

Generic. Able to handle successfully most uncomplicated communicative tasks and social situations. Can initiate, sustain, and close a general conversation with a number of strategies appropriate to a range of circumstances and topics, but errors are evident. Limited vocabulary still necessitates hesitation and may bring about slightly unexpected circumlocution. There is emerging evidence of connected discourse, particularly for simple narration and/or description. The Intermediate-High speaker can generally be understood even by interlocutors not accustomed to dealing with speakers at this level, but repetition may still be required.

Japanese. Emerging ability to distinguish between politeness and formality usage in most uncomplicated communicative tasks and social situations: Sensei, dochira e irasshaimasu ka? [*Teacher, where would you go?*]

There is emerging evidence of connected discourse, particularly for simple narration and/or description.

A: Kinoo nani o shimashita ka?

[*What did you do yesterday?*]

B: Kyooto ni itte, otera o mite arukimashita. Tenki ga yokute, tetotemo tanoshikatta desu.

[*Yesterday, I went to Kyoto and visited the temples. Because the weather was good, I enjoyed it very much.*]

NOTES

    1. For more information on the government-administered OPI, see Wilds (1975) and Sollenberger (1978). For information on the ACTFL oral interview, see Higgs (1984) and Stansfield and Harmon (1987).

    2. For more information, see Stansfield (1989).

Reinventing "Grammar" for Foreign Language Textbooks

Sharon L. Shelly

Abstract

In modern generative theory, "grammar" refers to the highly integrated system of knowledge underlying the behavior (e.g., production, comprehension, acceptability judgments) of the speakers of a language. However, many foreign language textbooks continue to assume a more traditional notion of "grammar" as a set of prescriptive rules applying only within the domains of syntax and inflectional morphology. This tendency is illustrated through an examination of eight recent French texts designed for first-year college study. The result is an artificial separation between "grammar" and "communication" that may actually impede the development of a true generative grammar of the target language.

Many applied linguists and foreign language pedagogues have probably never bothered to look up the word "grammar" in a standard dictionary. No doubt most of us are confident that we already know what grammar is and in our professional exchanges with colleagues in the field, we quite naturally assume that a broad consensus exists about such an elemental term. We therefore quickly proceed to those more specific theoretical and practical issues that provide us with something to argue about. In other words, a dictionary definition of grammar seems about as useful to language teachers as an elementary cookbook would be to Julia Child.

And yet it can be very instructive for us as professionals to remind ourselves of the usual "lay" definition of this ancient and infamous term. Consider, for example, the primary entry for "grammar" in Webster's 1971 *Third New International Dictionary*:

> a branch of linguistic study that deals with the classes of words, their inflections or other means of indicating relationships to each other, and their functions and relations in the sentence as employed according to established usage and that is sometimes extended to include related matter such as phonology, prosody, language history, orthography, orthoepy, etymology, or semantics. . . .

Two aspects of this definition are worthy of note. First, its prescriptive flavor: Words and sentences are to be studied within the context of "established usage." Traditional grammar, then, does not encourage us to explore the abundant structural possibilities available to us as users of a language; on the contrary, it seeks to limit our options by imposing upon us the constraints of some (official or officious) language authority.

Webster's definition also reflects another classic assumption about grammar: the notion that its principal domain is limited to "words," "inflections," and their "relations in the sentence." In other words, grammar is inflectional morphology and syntax. Phonology, etymology, semantics, and other aspects of the language are considered peripheral to grammar and are tpo be studied separately—perhaps in a less prescriptive, less coercive, atmosphere? This tendency to restrict the domain of grammar is confirmed by another standard definition, this one from the second edition of the *Random House Dictionary of the English Language* (1987): "the study of the way the sentences of a language are constructed; morphology and syntax. . . ."

The dictionary entries illustrate the traditional notion of grammar that is still held by many nonspecialists. Consider now the following definition from Chomsky's now-classic *Aspects of the Theory of Syntax*: "A grammar of a language purports to be a description of the ideal speaker-hearer's intrinsic competence. . . . Obviously, every speaker of a language has mastered and internalized a generative grammar that expresses his knowledge of his language" (1965, 4, 8). This conception of "generative grammar" has dominated much of the linguistic research of the past quarter-century. Terms such as "competence," "performance," and the "ideal speaker-hearer" have been widely discussed, occasionally ridiculed, and frequently misunderstood. In any case, it is clear that Chomsky's characterization describes a highly integrated system: grammar is quite simply everything you need to know about a language in order to function in it. Grammar, then, has become a dangerously ambiguous term. For nonspecialists, the word conjures up images of declensions, conjugations, and stern admonitions against dangling participles. For linguists, and in particular for those working within the generative framework, grammar describes what Chomsky now calls "internalized language," or "I-language": the interacting systems of phonological, morphological, syntactic, and semantic knowledge that underlie functional competence.

For foreign language teachers and textbook writers, this ambiguity has some rather serious consequences. On the one hand, recent developments in foreign language pedagogy have been strongly influenced by Chomsky's theory. The very notion of "communicative competence," which dominated discussion throughout the seventies, was a straightforward (if imperfect) adaptation of the concept of native linguistic competence defined by generative grammar. Moreover, since the establishment of the ACTFL Proficiency Guidelines in 1982, it has become possible to evaluate global foreign language proficiency in the areas of speaking, listening, reading, and writing.

On the other hand, the word "grammar" itself has not generally been used to describe the functional ability which we seek to foster in the foreign language, or L2. Most pedagogues prefer to discuss the "competence," or "proficiency," of the learner. In fact, teachers and textbook writers seem to retain a largely conventional notion of grammar which is remarkably similar to the dictionary definitions we have seen. The result, in many cases, has been an artificial separation between the grammar of a language and those factors which enable speakers to communicate in that language.

How is this separation effected in foreign language textbooks? And what are the consequences for L2 learning? The following observations are based on eight elementary French texts designed for first-year college study. All have been marketed since 1985: four as new programs, four as revised editions of earlier texts. Functional proficiency is identified as a primary goal in each of these programs.

A complete listing of the textbooks under consideration is provided in the bibliography. However, since it is not my intention to make claims about their relative merit, I will not refer to individual texts by name. It should also be emphasized that these books were selected as a representative sample of recent proficiency-oriented programs. My goal is to describe general tendencies in textbook writing—not to criticize specific texts.

Grammar Sections

All of the programs include some overt presentation of syntax and inflectional morphology under the heading of "grammar." Usually, these explanations are isolated within each chapter of the textbook, and labeled in such a way as to alert students to their serious and academic nature. Titles for these sections include "Grammaire" or "Notes grammaticales" (the honest approach), "Principes" (for moralists), and "Structures" (for the architecturally inclined). (In a refreshing deviation from this pattern, one textbook presents grammatical explanations under the promising epithet "Explorations.")

Two of the most recent texts have gone to greater lengths to separate grammar from the rest of foreign language study. The authors of one program have taken morphology and syntax out of the chapter altogether, and added a comprehensive reference grammar to the back of the text. No attempt has been made to design a pedagogical tool for teaching these structural notions in any sort of context: The reference grammar, as its name suggests, consists of exhaustive academic descriptions of each and every part of speech (pronouns, nouns, and so on). If the authors' goal is to persuade students that grammar is inherently tedious, and of marginal value to the foreign language learner, they have made their point quite effectively.

A variation on this theme is provided by the authors of the second textbook who, having designed a reference grammar similar to the one described above, detach it from the text itself and hide it at the back of the student workbook. In other words, grammar is no longer an integral part of the course at all, but is made available as a supplement for independent study.

Presentation of Vocabulary

As we saw in Webster's definition, the traditional notion of grammar is only "sometimes" extended to include "related matter" such as etymology and semantics. Indeed, the authors of many foreign language textbooks seem reluctant to make this extension: Vocabulary presentation is often carefully separated from structural discussions. In the French texts considered here, vocabulary items are virtually always taught "in context." Words to be learned in each chapter are organized according to communicative themes or situations ("the family," "student life") which are generally based on the content areas defined in the ACTFL Guidelines for novice and intermediate proficiency levels. These vocabulary sets are typically arranged in alphabetical order and presented in charts or boxes (perhaps with color background).

This presentation is enormously helpful to the L2 learner in many ways, and fosters the development of a practical lexicon organized along functional lines. Surely no one would argue that students should memorize lists of words without any context whatsoever. On the other hand, *communicative* context is not the only possible organizing principle for a lexicon. Words (or rather, morphemes) may also be grouped according to *structural* and *semantic* features. Whatever the communicative situation, it is very useful to know how bound and free morphemes are combined in L2 to form nouns, verbs, adjectives and adverbs. Conceivably, then, learners might profitably devote some attention to derivational morphology. Yet this approach has generally been avoided in French textbooks. And even when derivations are presented, the mechanics of word formations are studiously ignored.

Consider the case of nouns and adjectives of nationality. Typically, elementary students are provided with a number of vocabulary items such as *américain(e)*, *canadien(ne)* and *français(e)* in an early chapter. These words are to be used in simple dialogues in which students introduce themselves and their classmates. The corresponding geographical names *Amérique*, *Canada*, and *France* may be presented alongside the nationalities—or they may not. The actual place names are sometimes left for a later chapter, perhaps the one which includes the prepositional constructions *en Amérique*, *au Canada* and *en France*. Even when novice students do see pairs such as *Amérique/américain(e)*, *Canada/canadien(ne)*, *France/français(e)*, they are not encouraged to look for any derivational patterns. The list is likely to be arranged alphabetically—which effectively conceals potentially helpful groupings such as:

> *Amérique/américain(e)*
>
> *Mexique/mexicain(e)*
>
> *Afrique/africain(e)*
>
> *Canada/canadien(ne)*
>
> *Italie/italien(ne)*
>
> *Chili/chilien(ne)*
>
> *France/français(e)*
>
> *Irlande/irlandais(e)*
>
> *Thaïlande/thaïlandais(e)*

Perhaps, in the very early stages of L2 study, it is best to teach a few nationalities as unanalyzed units for immediate communicative use. On the other hand, beginning students overwhelmed by the volume of new L2 vocabulary might very well appreciate being given some general rules for word formation. More cognitive learners, who seek principles and paradigms, will be reassured to discover regularities. And eventually, all students can develop useful insights about the derivational patterns of French. (As an illustration of the ongoing nature of word formation in a natural language, students might be invited to guess the adjective coined for the recently-renamed nation of Burkina Faso: It happens to be *burkinabais*.)

In short, why not complement communicative word-learning with linguistic code-breaking strategies? If communication and grammar were not viewed as separate fields of study, textbook writers might be able to take a more integrative approach to the teaching of vocabulary.

The Sound System

Like semantics and etymology, phonology is peripheral to the conventional definition of grammar. And it is not surprising that the authors of proficiency-oriented texts find it difficult to integrate pronunciation into a functional syllabus: Discussion of the sound system of L2 may well seem even more abstract, and further removed from communicative goals, than the overt presentation of morphology and syntax. This general reluctance to "talk about the language" may be compounded by unhappy memories of the obsessive pronunciation drills of the audio-lingual method. Moreover, the textbook writers themselves (and foreign language teachers, for that matter) frequently have no specific training in phonetics or phonology. For these reasons, pronunciation is often the stepchild of L2 pedagogy.

The proficiency-oriented French texts considered here demonstrate a variety of responses to this dilemma. Only two of the programs have fully integrated the sound system with other aspects of language learning, devoting some of each chapter to specific practice of phonemes or suprasegmentals. At the other extreme, one text abdicates all responsibility for teaching pronunciation: the instructor (not the student) is simply referred to an appendix in which principles of French phonology are summarized. The other five texts have tried to find a middle road. In one case, pronunciation is addressed exclusively in a preliminary chapter that provides simple examples of the features most salient to English-speaking learners of French. Subsequent lessons do not reenter or expand upon this material. In the four remaining texts, pronunciation sections are included in the first few chapters, and then the whole issue is dropped. In general, then, the authors seem to be hoping that a few tips at the beginning of foreign language study will be sufficient to ensure the development of phonological competence.

As for the specific techniques used to address pronunciation in these elementary texts, the general tendency is to do as little real analysis as possible. The International Phonetic Alphabet is only occasionally presented, frequently in passing—or in the appendix. The contrastive approach may be used; still, in general, articulatory descriptions are kept to an absolute minimum. Students may simply be encouraged to imitate the instructor's (presumably accurate) production. Thus, in presenting the series of front rounded French vowels, one text points out that *"Ces voyelles n'existent pas en anglais,"* and then, without further explanation, directs students to pronounce a series of words containing these alien phonemes. If the instructor has provided a good model for repetition—and if the student is blessed with a good ear and a gift for mimicry—this approach may work reasonably well. But what if the teacher's own pronunciation is imperfect? Or the student cannot immediately reproduce the target sounds?

All eight programs considered here do include audiotape programs for additional oral/aural practice outside the class-room. These tapes closely follow the chapter organization of the textbook: If a chapter includes a specific unit on pronunciation, there is usually a corresponding section on the audiotape. In two cases, in fact, the material on tape is an exact duplication of the explanation and drill printed in the student text. Two other programs provide additional exercises, always in the form of repetition drills. Since the tapes are made by native French speakers, students are at least assured of good models for imitation. Still, if the authors are assuming that pure repetition is necessary (and sufficient) for acquiring acceptable pronunciation, one would expect the tapes to devote much more time to this activity. But of course, extensive repetition drills would be perceived by many as a reversion to our old nemesis, the audiolingual method. Instead, the current trend in audiotape programs is to emphasize dialogues and listening comprehension activities.

If elementary texts can include instructions for the formation of the *passé composé*, or for the placement of personal pronouns, why are they so hesitant to provide directions for the production of French sounds? Explicit presentation of a few rules of phonetics and phonology could be enormously helpful (and intellectually interesting) to many students. But for textbook writers, the teaching of "rules" is legitimate only in the context of teaching grammar—and the sound system of the language is not considered part of the grammar of that language.

Reinventing "Grammar"

Our survey of elementary French programs has revealed an organizational strategy that seems to be widespread in current textbook writing. Rather than adopting a generative, holistic definition of grammar, textbooks continue to fragment language learning into separate, arbitrarily-defined components while failing to show the interactions between the various systems. Grammar is presented as the only rule-governed domain of L2, and is often divorced from all communicative context. The structural organization of the lexicon is ignored: vocabulary items are taught as unanalyzed units. Meanwhile, phonology is given such short shrift that students often develop a completely fatalistic attitude toward pronunciation: Either you have a talent for French sounds, and catch on right away, or you are doomed to an eternal and embarrassing American accent.

If instructors and publishers were to rethink foreign language textbook design in terms of generative grammar, what might be done differently? Suppose we began with the assumption that *all* components of L2 are rule-governed systems, and that proficiency in L2 involves the constant interaction of all of these systems. It is simply incoherent, then, to single out inflectional morphology and syntax for structural treatment, while refusing to acknowledge the formal patterns of derivational morphology and phonology. Nor is it reasonable to teach the structural features of L2 separately from their functional uses, as if structure were only an academic ornament to natural language. Heny's observation seems particularly apropos:

> The fundamental problem and challenge for the language teacher is to bridge the gap between the desire to

communicate and the specific structures of language within which we are forced, as members of the human species, to conduct our business. Our inescapable use of specific language structures is why students have to be taught not communication, but Chinese, Japanese, Russian, or French. (1987, 209)

Heny's remarks suggest the key to resolving the pseudo-conflict between communicative proficiency and mastery of grammar. It is perfectly legitimate to design elementary-level courses around functional goals; at the same time, learners must grasp the essential fact that every L2 provides them with certain specific tools, and not others, with which to carry out these functions. The tools themselves are worthy of study, but they need not be artificially isolated from the context in which they operate. And perhaps it is time to do away entirely with traditional (and misleading) labels like "vocabulary," and "grammar." Instead, textbooks might do well to organize information about L2 according to the categories used by most linguists: phonology, morphology (both derivational and inflectional), syntax, semantics, pragmatics. In short, we need to design pedagogical "grammars" that contribute to the development of a true generative "grammar" of the target language.

Epilogue: Directions for Future Research in Foreign Languages

From Control to Chaos
Reflections on an "Unstylish" Research Paradigm

Vicki Galloway

Abstract

This article examines the common paths that have been taken by much of the existing research on foreign-language classroom learners and contends that some deviation from this well-traveled route may lead research efforts more directly to a knowledge of the complexities of the language learner as individual. Insights from chaos research suggest that traditional preoccupations with experimental control may have served more to limit than to advance our understanding of the learner.

Introduction

Implicit in definitions of research on foreign language learning (see, e.g., Clark 1993) is the potential for active participation of three human protagonists: 1) the teacher, who through formalized activities serves as the provider of language exposure; 2) the learner, who engages in the process of language acquisition; and 3) the researcher, who through disciplined inquiry investigates

separately and in their interaction, all of the above—the giver of
the exposure, as an individual or group; the nature of the exposure; the acquirer as an individual or group; the nature of the
learner/acquirer's engagement; the process of acquiring; and the
nature of the language itself.

The realities of U.S. academic culture have, however,
historically imposed definitions for these terms: Disciplined
inquiry has too often meant "a new experimental study that will
produce numerically significant results;" the process of
acquisition has come to mean "a student product or act that can
be measured quickly and easily by a test score;" and formalized
activities have been represented by countless types of intervention techniques and instructional treatments. Pressures of
academic communities combined with the privileged status traditionally accorded certain research methods and designs
(Johnson 1993) have not only driven an investigative agenda
focused on control, expediency, results, and new discovery, but
have also given rise to some pervasive, yet unspoken, assumptions. These assumptions relate to such things as the power of
"treatments" and manipulations; the notion of single variables;
the uniformity of individual learners, groups of learners, and
learning procedures; the equating of the ethnographically and
contextually different foreign-language learner with the second-
language learner (for discussion, see, e.g., Swaffar 1993); and the
facile derivation of process from product. What these more
prestigious research methods have, as yet, failed to capture and
reveal, are the real protagonists of the language learning drama
in its undeniable complexity—the persons, the processes, the
learning contexts, and how they change over time. Professional
"stylishness" has, in effect, focused investigation on the mere
outer edges of a potentially accessible and fascinating domain of
knowledge.

This article proposes the adoption of a new perspective
that, accompanied by more global applications of the principles
of investigative rigor, may afford a knowledge of the living
foreign-language classroom community as more than a static
excavation site, and a knowledge of the individual language
learner as more than an aggregate of artifacts or products. It
advocates some digging that may not be stylish in terms of

accepted research methodology, that may not be in vogue in its instruments or procedures, its controllability or variable isolation, its predictions or expectations, its generalizability, or its ability to produce the fast "answers" that are so desired. It suggests that new styles, new ways of thinking, new order, and new hopes may be found in turning from traditional preoccupations with treatment and control to find excitement in and comfort in chaos. What is proposed is the application of new frameworks derived from work in chaos theory to a renewed and more thorough study of the *learner* and of what is meant by the strangely redundant mix of words "learner-centered teaching and research."

Learner-Centered Research

Our present knowledge of the foreign language learner is principally derived from two types of research, both of which have as their core the requirement of variable isolation: 1) experimental treatments and 2) correlational studies between traits and performance. In both types of investigations, researchers have been limited only by their imaginations in variables selected for study, for human behavior presumably presents an infinite number of potentially explorable aspects. Yet, since imagination proceeds from and is, to a great extent, bounded by experience, our very knowledge base may serve to narrow and confine the possibilities for acquiring new knowledge.

Pedagogical treatment experiments have followed an input-output model—prompted by expectation of effect, conducted with the goal of encountering newsbreaking, mathematically "significant" relationships to student outcomes, and evaluated in terms of implications for change in the classroom. The problems of this experimental model have been cited frequently in professional literature. From the motivation angle, pure inquiry is rejected in favor of rapid results and direct transportability to pedagogical implementation; from the purpose angle, description is rejected in favor of explanation and proof of the expected; and from the design angle, selection of variables derives from assumptions born of previous assumptions, not from an extensive observational data base, for such a data base does not exist for classroom foreign language acquisition:

> ... in seeking to detect the effects of a single variable, the researcher was implicitly making the assumption that it was such a powerful variable that its effects would not be masked by the thousands of other variables that would presumably be held constant across several levels of the independent variable.... This research strategy can therefore be used only with the most influential of variables and we typically have little a priori basis for identifying them. (Jarvis 1991, 299–300)

Without a data base, the practices of experimental research are much akin to those of the home repairman who tinkers with a little-understood machine: his fondlings and fiddlings may, through trial and error, produce an effect in the performance of the machine, but without furthering his understanding either of the machine or of the true nature of his intervention in its functioning.

The expectation-isolation-control-outcome-prediction paradigm, for all its respected rigor, has often effectively bypassed what we perhaps most seek to understand: the learner, the process, the teaching-learning relationship. Johnson (1993), for one, notes that while experimental studies have offered information regarding particular groups of students in particular sociocultural settings, their generalizability to other students, tasks, and settings has been severely limited: Such studies often fail to provide insights into why different instructional practices produce different results, since the descriptive background of treatment conditions, learning contexts, and student participants is generally reported in the briefest terms. She recommends, in particular, the incorporation of richer descriptions of the students we study—"their cultural experiences, their dynamic multilingualism, their personal characteristics, and their approaches to learning" (5).

To date, the bulk of research focusing on these students we study and on their characteristics has been undertaken with the major purpose of identifying relationships between various learner characteristics and such things as achievement, proficiency, or rate of progress in the target language (O'Malley and Chamot 1993). Of these studies, characteristics most frequently studied are those relating to a student's *cognitive style*. However, while cognitive style refers to sets of traits that shape *how* one perceives and organizes information and concepts, an assumption underlying much of the research in this area is that certain assumed style traits may serve as predictors of *how well* one will perform overall. Of these assumed traits, perhaps the most commonly researched is that of field independence, as measured by a generic instrument called the GEFT (Group Embedded Figures Test) (Oltman et al. 1971). The term "field independence" refers to the facility with which an individual distinguishes relevant from less relevant information, sees patterns and sub-patterns and perceives analytically. Other commonly researched aspects of learning style include reflectivity, tolerance of ambiguity, environmental and modality preferences, and traits such as risk-taking and competitiveness. However, as O'Malley and Chamot (1993) note, no unifying theoretical framework exists for this aggregate of variables studied under the rubric of learning style.

The characteristic bent of this learning style research has been that of 1) accepting the existence of a trait as defined by the instrument used to measure it; 2) categorizing the learning styles of individuals based on this instrument; 3) correlating the products of individuals to these traits and 4) comparing learners deposited in distinct learning trait categories, with the aim of 5) predicting which style will succeed in performance of a particular discrete task.

Several problems lie, however, in this type of abstraction, not the least of which is the perpetuation of the notion that learning style (how) can be understood in terms of learner performance (what), without regard for the nature of the task and the learner's interaction with it. Learner typing precludes study of the instability and contextual variability of learning style. Correlational studies reduce complex constructs to sets of numbers. And generic instruments ignore the nature of the learning task, the type of materials, and the specifics of the situation. Johnson (1993) notes that the value of such correlational studies hinges on the initial definition of the construct itself and on the validity of the instrument used to measure it. Yet in some cases, the true construct of the trait becomes lost in its own instrument of measurement. Assumed traits such as "field independence" easily become *reified*, converted from abstract concepts into concrete entities. Reified traits are then used to create more reified traits whose association is then sought in the attempt to relate learner *products* to an artificial construct of trait composites. The result is that a particular assumed trait often becomes stretched beyond its initial definition to become inextricably entwined in an acquired associational network. The cognitive trait of field independence, for example, has become a caricature of reality, an entity complete with its own assigned personality traits (Brown 1980), of "coldness," "competitiveness," and "individualism." Ironically, a mere "trait" has often assumed more dimension than the humans who purportedly possess it. [For a summary of research in this area, including critical examination of other researched aspects of learning style, see Galloway and Labarca 1990.]

As with pedagogical treatment research, the model of these studies is still input-output, and as Long (1983) notes, we have still not said anything about classroom language learning: " . . . the research bypasses the effect (if any) of the instructional component. . . . Learner characteristics have replaced "method" variables, but the contribution of teaching and learning is not so much studied as *controlled for*" (27) (emphasis added).

In terms of implications for the classroom, it is here that speculation and distortion abound, if Jarvis's assessment is accurate:

> "Enormous leaps are made from paradigms such as
> nonsense-syllable research to language classrooms. . . .
> Faith has become more important than understanding"
> (1991, 296–97).

Even casual observation of teaching practice provides a plethora of like examples in the classroom, where cooperative learning is the label too often applied to pairing students for drill, and where the notion of "learning style" has been collapsed into a sorting system that provides the justification for ability tracking—"low groups" being those with a "poor learning style."

Whereas the concept of learning style addresses abstractly the notions of both *learner* and *process*, much research to date has ignored both. From the outset, the learner presents himself to the researcher not as an individual, but merely as a piece of a mass; not as real, but as an artificial construct; not as a dynamic and variable whole whose traits may exist in ranges and in infinitely complex combination with other traits, but as fixed and immutable parts and elements that can be categorized and compared, and whose performance can be used to predict the likely success or failure of future groups and masses. Since many of the traits measured have no physical existence apart from their instrument of measurement, we might suspect that not only do they embody scores of other traits, but that similar correlations might be achieved by choosing at random *any other* trait—say, the ability to draw a straight line, the slant of one's handwriting, the perception of shades of green. Given our existing knowledge base, one trait seems as worthy as any other.

Much of current research, in its convenient avoidance of individuals and their learning process and development, may be actually counterproductive, contributing more to a semblance of knowledge, to conformity of models, and to perpetuation of myths than to true inquiry and advancement of understanding. Garrett (1991), for one, observes that

> . . . aggregating data across learners obscures individual patterns of development to the point where the average data are meaningless. . . . Research must also preserve the integrity of data from individual subjects, since there is ample reason to believe that language processing is a highly individual matter, even among very similar learners in the same classroom situation (76; 82).

In order to understand learners and learning, we may have to begin by getting to know *individual* learners. And here, we may have to accept the notion that the individual is not only "one of many," but also "many in one." The possibility exists of finding not only more variability within a group than between groups, but more variability within an individual than among individuals. However, a research community that seeks rapid and demonstrable outcomes and demands *control* and manipulation of variables has not traditionally embraced this type of idiosyncratic exploration, for such study invites "fuzziness," a phenomenon long eschewed by classical research methodology.

> As psychologists adopted physical science methods, they also imported the presuppositions and assumptions under-girding them (causal regularity, law-like generalizations, predictability and near perfect confirmation). To make these methods work, behaviorists either had to ignore the telic properties of human behavior, or deny that human beings had the capacity to act with purpose (including the capacity to act stupidly or inconsistently). (Fenstermacher 1986, 41–42, as cited in Jarvis 1991, 302).

While notions of inconsistency, randomness, and seeming disorder have long played havoc with linear thought, groups of researchers are beginning to find comfort, even excitement, in a new framework of inquiry, one which crosses the stifling confines of statistics to delve into the very nature of events themselves and of the seeming chaos that is often a chief attribute of these events. What they are finding is a heretofore unseen order and pattern and what they are seeking is neither explanation nor manipulation, but *description*.

Chaos: An Orderly Disorder

Michael Crichton's bestselling novel *Jurassic Park* posits one of the most fascinating and ingenious experiments imaginable—the effort of scientists and technicians to create life and control biology technologically. A complete, true-to-scale, living replica of a prehistoric milieu serves as home to several species of man-made dinosaurs. The grand plan of these scientists has accounted for every conceivable behavior of their living specimens in a "nature manipulated to be more natural than the real thing" (1990, 133). To control for population growth, only female dinosaurs have been created, and their whereabouts are tracked at all times by computer. By every scientific calculation, the experiment should have worked. But the rapid outcome was, instead, chaos. For one thing, the scientists had tracked only the *expected* number of dinosaurs so they could be advised instantly of loss. But loss wasn't the problem. The problem was they had *more* than the expected number. The scientists' obsession with control and forced patterns of behavior had summarily closed the door on observation of any real patterns that might reveal themselves; expectation and assumption had obstructed viewing of real events. One of the major characters of the novel, Malcolm, delivers a stinging indictment of the scientists' efforts: "You cannot make an animal and not expect it to act alive . . . to be unpredictable." He also denigrates scientists in general: "They can't just watch, they can't just appreciate, they can't just fit into the natural order. They have to make something unnatural happen" (284). Malcolm is a self-proclaimed advocate of *chaos theory*.

Since chaos began to emerge as a field of study in the 1970s, groups of mathematicians, physicists, biologists, and chemists have been reframing traditionally held notions of order, control, and predictability in their focus on the heretofore unexplainable. Because chaos is a science of *process*, rather than product or state, and because its focus is on the *whole* rather than constituent parts, chaos theorists across disciplines are countering linear thought and reductionist research trends. Their study is that of real-world phenomena and everyday events as dynamic systems within whose variability and seeming randomness can be found order, pattern, and internal rhythms. Even the lexicon of chaos theorists depicts their real-world orientation and pattern-hunting focus in its "smooth noodle maps," "folded towel diffeomorphisms," "ropes and sheets," and "sponges and foams."

According to these researchers, if one looks, chaos, or seeming randomness, is evident in the shapes of clouds, the swirl of smoke, the flutter of a flag, the drip of a faucet, the behavior of the weather, the human heart, or the eye movements of schizophrenics. Indeterminacy and irregularity are everywhere—from the stock market, to brain waves, to rioting crowds, to insomnia. The randomness and unpredictability of events such as these has always played havoc with classical science, which has trusted linear explanations of cause and effect, and relied on statistical reporting systems that discard quirks, peculiarities, and incongruities as experimental error. As Gleick notes (1987), where chaos begins, classical science stops: "For as long as the world has had physicists inquiring into the laws of nature, it has suffered a special ignorance about disorder. . . . The irregular side of nature, the discontinuous and erratic side—these have been puzzles to science, or worse, monstrosities" (3).

It is both beyond the scope of this paper and vastly beyond the author's humble expertise to delve into the intricacies of research in this area, for chaos theory has captured attention across nearly every discipline. What is suggested, rather, is that its message may offer us a fresh and intriguing perspective in our approach to understanding the learner, and that both its mindset and its openmindedness may offer exciting possibilities for more profound exploration of the mysteries of foreign language learning.[1]

The first message of chaos theorists is that in the real world there is disorder and ambiguity. Phenomena and events are stable and unstable; change, often sudden and seemingly irrational, is a characteristic of existence, not an anomaly. And even the smallest wrinkle of change can have large consequences for the total fabric. The natural world is dynamic and remarkably resistant to human manipulation. And humans, as willful living beings, are the most elusive creatures of all.

The second message is that before we explain behaviors, and well before we expect or seek to predict these behaviors, we must attempt to describe our unbiased observations of them as they occur naturally. Chaos is a science of real-world mapping. Computer-generated graphic depictions of natural events and behaviors rarely display straight lines, evenness, and uniformity. They are characterized, rather, by elaborate loops and spirals, twists, splinters, tangles, bumpy surfaces, holes, fractures, and brambles—they have texture.

A third, and most profound message, is that disorder and randomness lie only in appearance, and appearance is a matter of perspective and of time. Chaos theory holds that isolated events appear random, but if we look long enough and deep enough, order begins to emerge—a new order, a nonlinear order. The most well-known illustration of this concept is that of the

Lorenz Butterfly, a graphic depiction of weather turbulence tnat resembles a butterfly's wings. The image, which has became an emblem of chaos theory, reveals a structure embedded in a stream of data over time. This shape is not captured by a static point, nor is a shape like this produced by a single event. The shape lies, rather, in the fabric of the whole, in the variability of the motion and direction of each event—in process. Although the pattern of the data is random, never following the same line twice, its randomness is patterned. In this image can be found boundaries—delineations between happenings and non-happenings or never-happenings. These boundaries set the broad outer limits of predictability. Over the long term, an accumulation of events shows "attractor areas," points of looping and crossover. These boundaries and attractor areas, together, form the image. This combination of traits allows the perception of a pattern in randomness, a harmony of order and disorder.

The notion of scale and scaleable things has also been a persistent preoccupation of chaos theorists, for the question, "How big is it?" has always been one of scientists' most prominent inquiries. Some things in nature possess a self-similarity trait; others do not. The problem is one of both real and perceived proportions. The human body, for example, is not really scaleable. If a human could be scaled up twice its size, the resulting bone structure would not support its weight; scale does not produce self-similarity. Nor does perception of this human body show scaleability, for viewing it close up one loses certain information about it, while gaining other, new information. While self-similarity was once a powerful notion in science, the trend toward breaking things apart, isolating their properties, then combining them to examine their interaction had contributed to a rejection of this notion. Chaos theorists, however, have revived it, but with a new perspective. As Gleick (1987) notes, "the power of self-similarity . . . begins at much greater levels of complexity. It is a matter of looking at the whole" (115). And this perspective calls into question a great many other impositions on perception:

> *Hurricane.* By definition, it is a storm of certain size. But the definition is imposed by people on nature. In reality,

atmospheric scientists are realizing that tumult in the air
forms a continuum, from the gusty swirling of litter on a
city street corner to the vast cyclonic systems visible from
space. Categories mislead. The ends of the continuum are
of a piece with the middle. (108)

It is in looking at the pattern of the whole that one finds
scaleability: "A day is like a whole life—it has the same hap-
hazard quality. Your whole life has the same shape as a single
day" (Crichton, 171). One of the missions of chaos researchers is
to look for "scaling structures" that relate the big details to the
little details, for these are the only things that can ever be
universal.

A final message to be gleaned from chaos research is that
of the fallacy of singularity of effect. Events and elements in the
natural world display "sensitive dependence on initial
conditions" (23). It has long been recognized that in any chain of
events a point of crisis can magnify a small change. But, as
Gleick notes, chaos tells us this is not one point, but many:
" . . . chaos meant that such points were everywhere. In systems
like the weather, sensitive dependence on initial conditions was
an inescapable consequence of the way small scales intertwined
with large" (23). The true beauty and complexity of this notion
comes to life in the following history of a snowflake. One may
wonder whether, if nature's design can bestow such indivi-
duality on such a tiny, short-lived particle as a snowflake, can we
ever presume to understand, much less control, her proudest
creation, a human being, by subsuming in masses and assuming
sameness. The lesson is a powerful one:

As a growing snowflake falls to earth, typically floating in
the wind for an hour or more, the choices made by the
branching tips at any instant depend sensitively on such
things as temperature, the humidity, and the presence of
impurities in the atmosphere. The six tips of a single
snowflake, spreading within a millimeter of space, feel the
same temperatures, and because the laws of growth are
purely deterministic, they maintain a near-perfect
symmetry. But the nature of turbulent air is such that any
pair of snowflakes will experience very different paths.
The final flake records the history of all the changing

weather conditions it has experienced, and the combinations may as well be infinite. (Gleick 1987, 311).

Conclusion: Charting Trends in the Foreign Language Learner

In reading the chronicles of chaos research, one is struck by something even more penetrating, however, than the messages themselves. It is the contagion of the researchers' awe and humility as they pull back the curtain of "respectable" scientific tradition to expose the real world around them, to see art and science at one with each other. It is their joy in starting over, to build a new and richer understanding.

The framework for this new understanding has been an attitude of wonder toward and acceptance of natural "order"—a true desire to learn. The chaos researchers' focus on describing pattern in the dynamic whole as it appears over time has run counter to the politics of a science that seeks to deposit real-world events into neat, crisp categories and formulae. On–off, black–white, true–false, 0–1 approaches fall apart when applied to nature and to even the most apparently simple of naturally occurring phenomena.

Perhaps foreign language researchers also may find new freedom to learn through an altered perspective, a new attitude. Looking back on our research on foreign language learning, it appears that much of our effort has been applied to defining, even defying the makeup of the learner. Yet in education in general, it is the human as learner whom we seek to know. In foreign language education in particular, we seek to know these learners as they engage in what must be the most amazing of all human processes—the acquisition of language—in what can only be the most complex of contexts—interaction with other humans for what, beyond doubt, is the most superbly awesome accomplishment the human mind can imagine—communication. In our trend toward learner-centeredness, if all our research focuses on mass student performance as the result of a seemingly controlled pedagogical practice, or on deriving conclusions from categories of abstract attributes and comparison of student products, we might well question how much we really know about the learner and how "centered" our research really is. Our desire to be quick and to the point may be ignoring the continuum and thus missing the point entirely.

Hand in hand with ongoing efforts, we might also explore the learner—a learner—through multiple observations as he or she engages in a variety of complex acts, makes choices from a variety of options, and acts and reacts in a variety of contexts over time. The chaotic nature of humans in a chaotic world may require that we look for ranges and levels and depths in the individual—cognitive ranges, interactional ranges, comfort ranges, developmental ranges, interest ranges. Qualitative methods (case studies, diaries, ethnographies, and so on), alone and in combination with quantitative methods, hold promise in this area in their potential for capturing the richness and complexity of the context and the wholeness of the person as learner.

This new image of the learner as individual is bound to be as magnificently complex as that of the Lorenz Butterfly. It will not be captured on the spot through one glance at one act or product, one microsegment of one context at one moment of the day. Rather, the image will be formed by patterns over time, within ambiguity and contradiction. It is perhaps only by looking long and deep that the boundaries and attractor areas will allow a sense of an individual's profile. In other words, we must devote attention to depicting what actually happens before we can presume to predict, much less attempt to manipulate, these happenings. Garrett contends that to study language learning, the first domain of our research must be the nature of language-learner mapping. This research must be directed to process and language processing and to idiosyncratic meaning-form connections *over time*.

> Language acquisition per se can be assessed and understood only through research over time on individual learners' ability to create, access, and deploy form-meaning connections. The crucial importance of preserving individual data militates heavily against cross-sectional studies of acquisitions, since the aggregation of

data across learners inevitably confuses individual
variation with acquisition patterns (1991, 83).

For this type of research agenda, she believes the computer to be
the sine qua non. Its ability to elicit, analyze, and map individual
interactions in real time, as individuals engage in different tasks
with different sets of language data, may provide us with a new
beginning in our look at the language learner. Research in this
area is already under way and is providing a window into
learners' processing strategies (Noblitt and Bland 1991, 11).
Much more will be needed for patterns and internal rhythms to
begin to emerge.

Chaos theorists have achieved a new vantage point in their
view of the world, simply by allowing themselves to see what
other scientists had learned *not* to see. In foreign language
research, it seems we have skipped this fundamental step in the
evolution of knowledge. We have not yet developed the
descriptive data base that, according to Jarvis, is the primary role
and responsibility of research:

> We have asked in many different ways what happens to Y
> when we manipulate X in particular ways. We have not,
> however, accomplished the prerequisite steps of
> describing what happens typically in classrooms with X
> and Y. Does X have a thousand different renditions . . . or
> does it vary little? We need to know what X is before we
> can hypothesize how to manipulate it (300).

The title of this book, *The Foreign Language Classroom:
Bridging Theory and Practice* (1995) speaks to the true center of our
being as a profession: the "real world" of the classroom. At
present, however, it seems we have nothing to link to it. We have
no real image of the learner, therefore, no real description of
language learning. We also lack a cohesive, mutually satisfying
theory of foreign language learning that integrates language
acquisition and cognition; that can account for, among other
phenomena, automaticity and flexibility; that can integrate more
general learning theory with the richness of language and the
uniqueness of foreign language learning; and that applies to not
only the novice but the sophisticated language user. We have no
theory of foreign language education, then, that operationalizes
it—that guides us in studying, planning, implementing, and

evaluating our efforts as educators, or that even allows us to conceive of the seamless sequence of instruction that we so desire.

Traditionally, the domain of the researcher and the domain of the classroom practitioner have been viewed as distinct islands whose bridging has often been a mere leap of faith. Yet a common sea breaks the shores of both domains, and it is this sea that we must begin to know. We will not know it by trying to span it, bypass it, fight its currents, or control its movement. We will only know it, cooperatively and collaboratively, through a new relationship with it—by observing it, charting it, accepting it; by moving with its natural trend.

NOTE

1. The basis for description of these concepts of chaos theory is Gleick (1987) who chronicles the movement across disciplines.

Bibliography

Abboud, Peter, and Ernest McCarus, eds. 1988. *Elementary Modern Standard Arabic*. Cambridge, England: Cambridge University Press.

Abraham, Roberta G., and Roberta J. Vann. 1987. "Strategies of Two Language Learners: A Case Study." In *Learner Strategies in Language Learning*, ed. Anita Wenden and Joan Rubin. Englewood Cliffs, N.J.: Prentice Hall, 85–102.

Abu-Absi, Samir. 1991. "The Simplified Arabic of *Iftah Yaa Simsim*: Pedagogical and Sociolinguistic Implications." *Al-9Arabiyya* 24: 111–22.

Adams, Dennis, and Mary Hamm. 1990. *Cooperative Learning: Critical Thinking and Collaboration Across the Curriculum*. Springfield, Ill: C.C. Thomas.

Albert, Martin L., and Loraine K. Obler. 1978. *The Bilingual Brain: Neuropsychological and Neurolinguistic Aspects of Bilingualism*. New York: Academic Press.

Allen, Edward D., Elizabeth B. Bernhardt, Mary Therese Berry, and Marjorie Demel. 1988. "Comprehension and Text Genre: An Analysis of Secondary School Foreign Language Readers." *The Modern Language Journal* 72: 163–72.

American Council on the Teaching of Foreign Languages. 1983. *Provisional Proficiency Guidelines*. Hastings-on-Hudson, N.Y.: American Council on the Teaching of Foreign Languages Materials Center.

American Council on the Teaching of Foreign Languages. 1986. *ACTFL Proficiency Guidelines*. Hastings-on-Hudson, NY: American Council on the Teaching of Foreign Languages.

"American Council on the Teaching of Foreign Languages Japanese Proficiency Guidelines." *FLA* 20, 6 (December 1987): 589–603.

Applebee, Arthur N. 1981. *Writing in the Secondary School*. NCTE Research Report no. 21. Urbana, Ill.: National Council of Teachers of English.

Arens, Katherine. 1991. "Training Graduate Students to Teach Culture: A Case Study." *ADFL Bulletin* 23.1: 35–41.

Armbruster, Bonnie B., and Beth Gudbransen. 1986. "Reading Comprehension Instruction in Social Studies Programs." *Reading Research Quarterly* 21.1: 36–48.

Asher, James. 1966. "The Learning Strategy of the Total Physical Response: A Review." *The Modern Language Journal* 50: 79–84.

———. 1981. "The Extinction of Second-language Learning in American Schools: An Intervention Model." In *The Comprehension Approach to Foreign Language Instruction*, ed. H. Winitz. Rowley, Mass.: Newbury House, 49–68.

Asher, James, J. Kusudo, and R. de la Torre. 1974. "Learning a Second Language through Commands: The Second Field Test." *The Modern Language Journal* 58: 24–32.

Aston, G. 1986. "Trouble Shooting in Interaction with Learners: The More the Merrier?" *Applied Linguistics* 7: 128–43.

Azevedo, Milton M. 1976. "Preservice Training for Graduate Teaching Assistants." *The Modern Language Journal* 60: 254–58.

Bailey, Leslie F. 1986. "A Role for the Language Laboratory." In *Planning and Using Language Learning Centers*, ed. Jerry W. Larson. Provo, Ut: The CALICO Monograph Series 1, 74–77.

Bakker, Dirk J. 1981. "A Set of Brains for Learning to Read." In *Individual Differences and Universals in Language Learning Aptitudes*, ed. K. Diller. Rowley, Mass: Newbury House, 65–71.

Baltra, Armando. 1992. "Breaking with Tradition: The Significance of Terrell's Natural Approach." *Canadian Modern Language Review / Revue canadienne des langues vivantes* 483: 565–93.

Bardovi-Harlig, Kathleen, and Beverly Hartford. 1990. "Congruence in Native and Nonnative Conversations: Status Balance in the Academic Advising Session." *Language Learning* 40: 467–501.

Bardovi-Harlig, Kathleen, Beverly Hartford, Rebecca Mahan-Taylor, Mary Morgan, and Dudley Reynolds. 1991. "Developing Pragmatic Awareness: Closing the Conversation." *ELT Journal* 45: 4–15.

Barnett, Marva. 1989. "Writing as Process." *French Review* 63: 31–44.

———. 1991. "Language and Literature: False Dichotomies, Real Allies." *ADFL Bulletin* 22.3: 7–11.

Beauchesne, André, and Hélène Hensler. 1987. *L'école française à clientèle pluriethnique de l'île de Montréal.* Québec: Editeur officiel du Québec.

Beebe, Leslie, Tomoko Takahashi, and Robin Uliss-Weltz. 1990. "Pragmatic Transfer in ESL Refusals." In *On the Development of Communicative Competence in a Second Language*, ed. R. Scarcella, E. Andersen, and S.D. Krashen. Cambridge, Mass: Newbury House, 55–73.

Behrens, Susan J. 1985. "The Perception of Stress and Lateralization of Prosody." *Brain and Language* 26: 332–48.

Bernstein, Basil B. 1962. "Linguistic Codes, Hesitation Phenomena, and Intelligence." *Language and Speech* 5: 31–46.

———. 1973. *Class, Codes and Control.* London: Routledge and Kegan Paul.

Besse, Henri, and Rémy Porquier. 1984. *Grammaire et didactique des langues.* Paris: Collection langues et apprentissage des langues, Hatier-Crédif, Paris.

Bialystok, Ellen. 1979. "The Role of Conscious Strategies in Second Language Proficiency." *Canadian Modern Language Review/Revue canadienne des langues vivantes* 35: 372–94.

———. 1981. "The Role of Conscious Strategies in Second Language Proficiency." *The Modern Language Journal* 65: 24–35.

———. 1983. "Inferencing: Testing the 'Hypothesis-Testing' Hypothesis." In *Classroom Oriented Research in Second Language Acquisition*, ed. Herbert W. Seliger and Michael Long. Rowley, Mass.: Newbury House, 104–23.

Bialystok, Ellen, and Maria Frohlich. 1977. "Aspects of Second Language Learning in Classroom Settings." *Working Papers on Bilingualism* 13: 1–26.

Biró, Zoltan. 1984. *Beszéd és környezet.* [Speech and Environment.] Bucharest: Kriterion Könyvkiadó.

Bisaillon, Jocelyne. 1992. "La révision des textes: un processus à enseigner pour l'amélioration des productions écrites." ["Rewriting texts: a teaching process for the improvement of writing productions."] *Canadian Modern Language Review/ Revue canadienne des langues vivantes* 48.2: 277– 91.

Black, Janis H. 1993. "Learning and Reception Strategy Use and the Cloze Procedure." *Canadian Modern Language Review/Revue canadienne des langues vivantes* 49: 418–45.

Blanc, Haim. 1960. "Style Variations in Spoken Arabic: A Sample of Interdialectal Educated Conversation." In *Contributions to Arabic Linguistics*, ed. Charles Ferguson. Cambridge, Mass.: Harvard University Press, 81–156.

Block, Ellen. 1986. "The Comprehension Strategies of Second Language Learners." *TESOL Quarterly* 20: 463–94.

Bochart-Fiévez, J. and J. Delahaut. 1991. "Préface," *Richesse du vocabulaire*. Tôme 1. Belgique: Duculot.

Brannon, Lil, and C.H. Knoblauch. 1982. "On Students' Rights to Their Own Texts: A Model of Teacher Response." *College Composition and Communication* 33: 157–66.

Braun, Friederike. 1988. *Terms of Address: Problems of Patterns and Usage in Various Languages and Cultures*. Berlin: Mouton de Gruyter.

Brod, Richard I. 1988. "Foreign Language Enrollments in U.S. Institutions of Higher Education, Fall 1986." *ADFL Bulletin* 19: 39–45.

Brodkey, Dean, and Howard Shore. 1976. "Student Personality and Success in an English Language Program." *Language Learning* 26: 153–59.

Brown, H.D. 1980. *Principles of Language Learning and Teaching*. Englewood Cliffs, NJ: Prentice Hall.

Brown, Joan Lipman. 1986. "¡Diga! Telephone Protocols and Strategies in the Intermediate Conversation Course." *Hispania* 69: 413–17.

Brown, P., and S. Levinson. 1978 "Universals in Language Usage: Politeness Phenomena." In *Questions and Politeness: Strategies in Social Interaction*, ed. E. Goody. Cambridge, England: Cambridge University Press, 56–310.

Brown, Thomas H. 1991. *Pas à pas*. New York: John Wiley and Sons.

Brownell, Hiram H. 1988. "Appreciation of Metaphoric and Connotative Word Meaning by Brain-damaged Patients." In *Right Hemisphere Contributions to Lexical Semantics*, ed. C. Chiarello. Berlin: Springer-Verlag, 1–18.

Brumfit, Christopher. 1984. *Communicative Methodology in Language Teaching*. Cambridge: Cambridge University Press.

Byrnes, Heidi. 1983. "Discourse Analysis and the Teaching of Writing." *ADFL Bulletin* 15: 30–36.

Canale, Michael, and Merrill Swain. 1980. "Theoretical Bases of Communicative Approaches to Second Language Teaching and Testing." *Applied Linguistics* 1: 1–47.

Carrell, Patricia L., and Joan C. Eisterhold. 1983. "Schema Theory and ESL Reading Pedagogy." *TESOL Quarterly* 17: 553–73.

Carroll, Fairlee W. 1981. "Neurolinguistic Processing of a Second Language: Experimental Evidence." In *Research in Second Language Acquisition*, ed. Stephan Krashen and Robin Scarcella. Rowley, Mass: Newbury House, 81–86.

Carroll, John B. 1960. "The Prediction of Success in Intensive Foreign Language Training." Mimeographed. Quoted in Wallace Lambert, 1963, "Psychological Approaches to the Study of Language," *The Modern Language Journal* 47: 51–62.

———. 1973. "Implications of Aptitude Test Research and Psycholinguistics for Foreign Language Teaching." *International Journal of Psycholinguistics* 2: 5–14.

Cauvin, Jean-Pierre, and Mary Baker, eds. 1990. *Panaché littéraire*. New York: Harper and Row.

Chafe, Wallace L., ed. 1980. *The Pear Stories: Cognitive, Cultural, and Linguistic Aspects of Narrative Production*. Norwood, Mass.: Ablex.

Chary, Prithika. 1986. "Aphasia in a Multilingual Society: A Preliminary Study." In *Language Processing in Bilinguals: Psycholinguistic and Neuropsychological Perspectives*, ed. J. Vaid. Hillsdale, N.J.: Erlbaum, 183–197.

Chastain, Kenneth. 1986. "On Methods Theory and Practice: Response to Ms. Losiewicz." *Hispania* 69: 173–75.

———. 1987. "Examining the Role of Grammar, Explanation, Drills, and Exercises of Communication Skills." *Hispania* 70: 160–66.

———. 1990. "Characteristics of Graded and Ungraded Compositions." *The Modern Language Journal* 74: 10–14.

Chaudron, Craig. 1984. "The Effects of Feedback on Students' Composition Revisions." *RELC Journal* 15: 1–14.

———. 1988. *Second Language Learning: Research on Teaching and Learning*. Cambridge, England: Cambridge University Press.

Chiarello, Christine, ed. 1988. *Right Hemisphere Contributions to Lexical Semantics*. Berlin: Springer-Verlag.

Chomsky, Noam. 1965. *Aspects of the Theory of Syntax*. Cambridge, Mass.: MIT Press.

——. 1986. *Knowledge of Language: Its Nature, Origin and Use*. New York: Praeger.

Clark, Herbert H., and Eve V. Clark. 1977. *Psychology and Language*. New York: Harcourt Brace Jovanovich.

Clark, John L.D. and Fred Davidson. 1993. "Language-learning Research: Cottage Industry or Consolidated Enterprise?" In *Research in Language Learning: Principles, Processes, and Prospect*, ed. Alice Omaggio Hadley. Lincolnwood, IL: National Textbook Co, 254–278.

Clark, John L.D., and Ying-che Li. 1986. *Development, Validation, and Dissemination of a Proficiency-Based Test of Speaking Ability in Chinese and an Associated Assessment Model for Other Less Commonly Taught Languages*. Washington, D.C.: Center for Applied Linguistics; ERIC Document Reproduction Service, no. ED 278 264.

Cohen, Andrew D. 1987a. "Student Processing of Feedback on Their Compositions." In *Learner Strategies in Language Learning*, ed. Anita Wenden and Joan Rubin. Englewood Cliffs, N.J.: Prentice Hall, 57–69.

——. 1987b. "Studying Learner Strategies: How We Get the Information." In *Learner Strategies in Language Learning*, ed. Anita Wenden and Joan Rubin. Englewood Cliffs, N.J.: Prentice Hall, 31–39.

Cook, Vivian. 1991. *Second Language Learning and Language Teaching*. London: Edward Arnold.

Corder, S. Pit. 1967. "The Significance of Learner's Errors." *International Review of Applied Linguistics in Language Teaching* 5: 161–70.

Crichton, Michael. 1990. *Jurassic Park*. NY: Ballantine Books.

Cumming, Alistair H. 1985. "Responding to the Writing of ESL Students." In *Patterns of Development*, ed. A. Pare and M. Maguire. Ottawa: Canadian Council of Teachers of English, 58–75.

Curran, Charles. 1972. *Counseling Learning*. New York: Grune and Stratton.

Day, R., N. Chenoweth, A. Chun, and S. Leppescu. 1984. "Corrective Feedback in Native-Nonnative Discourse." *Language Learning* 34.2: 19–45.

Dennis, Maureen, and Harry Whitaker. 1977. "Hemispheric Equipotentiality and Language Acquisition." In *Language Development and Neurological Theory*, ed. S. Segalowitz and F. Gruber. New York: Academic Press, 93–106.

Devens, Monica S. 1986. "Graduate Education in Foreign Languages and Literatures: A View from Five Universities." *ADFL Bulletin* 17.3: 14–18.

Devens, Monica S., and Nancy J. Bennett. 1986. "The MLA Surveys of Foreign Language Graduate Programs, 1984–85." *ADFL Bulletin* 17.3: 19–31.

Dinneen, David A., and Madeleine Kernen. 1989. *Chapeau! First Year French.* New York: John Wiley.

Di Pietro, Robert J. 1987. *Strategic Interaction: Learning Languages through Scenarios.* Cambridge, England: Cambridge University Press.

Dougill, John. 1987. *Drama Activities for Language Learning.* London: Macmillan.

Doughty, C., and T. Pica. 1986. "Information Gap Tasks: Do They Facilitate Second Language Acquisition?" *TESOL Quarterly* 20: 305–25.

Doukanari, Elli. 1995. "Student Videotaped Output: A Valuable Input and Resource of Input in L2 Learning." Unpublished manuscript.

Dvorak, Trisha R. 1986. "Writing in the Foreign Language." In *Listening, Reading, Writing: Analysis and Application,* ed. Barbara H. Wing. Middlebury, Vt.: Northeast Conference on the Teaching of Foreign Language, 145–63.

Ehrman, Madeline, and Rebecca Oxford. 1989. "Effects of Sex Differences, Career Choice, and Psychological Type on Adult Language Learning Strategies." *The Modern Language Journal* 73: 1–13.

Elling, Barbara. 1988. "National Trends: Implications of Graduate Student Training and Career Placement." *ADFL Bulletin* 19: 45–48.

Ellis, Rod. 1985. *Understanding Second Language Acquisition.* Oxford: Oxford University Press.

Emig, Janet A. 1971. *The Composing Processes of Twelfth Graders.* NCTE Research Report no. 13. Urbana, Ill.: National Council of Teachers of English.

Erickson, Frederick. 1984. "Rhetoric, Anecdote, and Rhapsody: Coherence Strategies in a Conversation among Black American Adolescents." In *Coherence in Spoken and Written Discourse,* ed. Deborah Tannen. Norwood, Mass.: Ablex, 81–154.

Ericsson, K. Anders, and Herbert A. Simon. 1980. "Verbal Reports as Data." *Psychological Review* 87: 215–51.

——. 1984. *Protocol Analysis*. Cambridge, MA: The MIT Press.

Ervin, Gerard L. 1981. "A Training Program for New TAs in Russian." *Russian Language Journal* 35: 27–33.

Ervin, L.G., ed. 1991. *International Perspectives on Language Teaching*. Lincolnwood, Ill.: National Textbook.

Feldmann, Ute, and Brigitte Stemmer. 1987. "Think aloud a_ retrospective da__ in C-te__ taking: diffe_ languages - diff__ learners - sa__ approaches?" In *Introspection in Second Language Research*, ed. Claus Faerch and Gabriele Kasper. Clevedon, Avon, England: Multilingual Matters, 251–67.

Fenstermacher, Gary D. 1986. "Philosophy of Research on Teaching: Three Aspects." In *Handbook of Research on Teaching*, ed. Merlin C. Wittcock. NY: Macmillan Publishing Co., 3rd. ed, 37–49.

Ferguson, Charles. 1959. "Diglossia." *Word* 15: 325–40.

Ferguson, Charles A., and Dan I. Slobin, eds. 1973. *Studies of Child Language Development*. New York: Holt, Rinehart and Winston.

Flower, Linda. 1988. "The Construction of Purpose in Writing and Reading." *Occasional Paper No. 4*. Berkeley, Calif.: Center for the Study of Writing.

Flower, Linda, and John R. Hayes. 1981. "A Cognitive Process Theory of Writing." *College Composition and Communication* 32: 365–87.

Freed, Barbara F. 1987. "Preliminary Impressions of the Effects of a Proficiency-Based Language Requirement." *Foreign Language Annals* 20: 139–46.

Freedman, Sarah W., ed. 1985. *The Acquisition of Written Language: Response and Revision*. Norwood, N.J.: Ablex.

Friend, J.A. 1971. *Writing English as a Second Language*. Glenview, Ill.: Scott Foresman.

Fulwiler, Toby. 1980. "Journals across the Disciplines." *English Journal* 69: 14–18.

Galloway, Linda. 1978. "Language Impairment and Recovery in Polyglot Aphasia: A Study of a Heptalingual." In *Aspects of Bilingualism*, ed. M. Paradis. Columbia, S.C.: Hornbeam Press, 139–48.

Galloway, Linda, and Stephen Krashen. 1981. "Cerebral Organization in Bilingualism and Second Language." In *Research in Second Language Acquisition*, ed. Stephen Krashen and Robin Scarcella. Rowley, Mass: Newbury House, 74–80.

Galloway, Vicki and Angela Labarca. 1990. "From Student to Learner: Style, Process, and Strategy." In *New Perspectives and New Directions in Foreign Language Education,* ed. Diane W. Birckbichler. Lincolnwood, IL: National Textbook Co., 117–158.

Gangi, P. A. 1986. *Draft Revision: Systematic Development of Instruction for First Year Composition Dissertation.* Ph.D. Diss., Arizona State University.

Gardner, Robert C. 1990. "Attitudes, Motivation, and Personality as Predictors of Success in Foreign Language Learning." In *Language Aptitude Reconsidered,* ed. Thomas S. Parry and Charles W. Stansfield. Englewood Cliffs, N.J.: Prentice Hall Regents, 179–221.

Gardner, Robert C., and Wallace Lambert. 1972. *Attitudes and Motivation in Second Language Learning.* Rowley, Mass. Newbury House.

Garrett, Nina. 1991. "Theoretical and Pedagogical Problems of Separating 'Grammar' from 'Communication.'" In *Foreign Language Acquisition Research and the Classroom,* ed. Barbara F. Freed. Lexington, MA: D.C. Heath and Co., 74–87.

Gass, Susan, and Carolyn Madden. 1985. *Input in Second Language Acquisition.* Rowley, Mass.: Newbury House.

Gass, Susan, and E. Varonis. 1985. "Task Variation and Nonnative/Nonnative Negotiation of Meaning." In *Input in Second Language Acquisition* ed. Susan Gass and Carol Madden. Rowley, Mass.: Newbury House, 149–161.

Gattegno, Caleb. 1962. *A Teacher's Introduction to the Cuisenaire-Gattegno Methods of Teaching Arithmetic.* New York: Cuisenaire Co. of America.

Gattegno, Caleb. 1976. *The Common Sense of Teaching Foreign Languages.* New York: Educational Solutions.

Gaudiani, Claire. 1981. *Teaching Composition in the Foreign Language Curriculum.* Language in Education: Theory and Practice Series 43. Washington, D.C.: Center for Applied Linguistics.

Genesee, Fred. 1982. "Experimental Neuropsychological Research on Second Language Processing." *TESOL Quarterly* 16: 315–22.

Germain, Claude. 1990. *Les grands courants en didactique des langues.* Recueil de textes LIN3680. Montréal: Université du Québec.

Gleick, James. 1987. *Chaos: Making a New Science.* NY: Penguin Books.

Glisan, Eileen W. 1989. "Teaching Grammar and Vocabulary for Proficiency." In *Perspectives in Foreign Language Teaching.* Proceedings of the Annual Conference on the Teaching of Foreign Languages and Literatures. ERIC Document Reproduction Service, no. ED 318 224. Youngstown, OH: Youngstown State University, 106–120..

Goffman, Ervin. 1967. *Interaction Ritual*. New York: Anchor Books.

Goldberg, Elkhonon, and Louis D. Costa. 1981. "Hemisphere Differences in the Acquisition and Use of Descriptive Systems." *Brain and Language* 14: 144–73.

Goldstein, Lynn M., and Susan M. Conrad. 1990. "Student Input and Negotiation of Meaning in ESL Writing Conferences." *TESOL Quarterly* 24: 443–60.

Goring Kepner, Christine. 1991. "An Experiment in the Relationship of Types of Written Feedback to the Development of Second-Language Writing Skills." *The Modern Language Journal* 75: 305–313.

Graham, Carolyn. 1978. *Jazz Chants: The Rhythms of American English for Students of English as a Second Language*. New York: Oxford University Press.

Graves, Donald H. 1984. *A Researcher Learns to Write*. Exeter, N.H.: Heinemann Educational Books.

Grosse, Christine U., and Geoffrey M. Voght. 1991. "The Evolution of Languages for Specific Purposes in the United States." *Modern Language Journal* 75: 181–95.

Guiora, Alexander Z., Robert C.L. Brannon, and Cecelia Y. Dull. 1972. "Empathy and Second Language Learning." *Language Learning* 22: 111–30.

Hafner, Lawrence E., and Robert G. Stakenas. 1990. *A Study of the Social Studies Reading Achievement and Reading Interests of a Group of Eighth Graders*. Tallahassee: The Florida State University; ERIC Document Reproduction Service, no. ED 317 957.

Hammond, Robert M. 1988. "Accuracy versus Communicative Competency: The Acquisition of Grammar in the Second Language Classroom." *Hispania* 71: 408–17.

Hansen, Jacqueline, and Charles Stansfield. 1982. "Student-Teacher Cognitive Styles and Foreign Language Achievement: A Preliminary Study." *The Modern Language Journal* 66: 263–73.

Harada, S. I. 1976. "Honorifics." In *Syntax and Semantics 5: Japanese Generative Grammar*, ed. Masayoshi Shibatani. New York: Academic Press, 499–561.

Hardy, Marguerite, and Maria Joly. 1991. *Intermède: Guide de l'enseignant intermédiaire et avancé*. Laval, Québec: Editions FM.

Hargis, C.H., M. Terhaar-Yonkers, P. Couch Williams, and M. Testerman Reed. 1988. "Repetition Requirements for Word Recognition." *Journal of Reading* 31.4: 320–27.

Harris, David P., and Leslie A. Palmer. 1986. *A Comprehensive English Language Test for Learners of English*. New York: McGraw-Hill.

Hatch, Evelyn M. 1983. *Psycholinguistics: A Second Language Perspective*. Rowley, Mass.: Newbury House.

Hatch, Evelyn, and Anne Lazaraton. 1991. *The Research Manual: Design and Statistics for Applied Linguistics*. New York: Newbury House.

Hatch, Evelyn, and Michael H. Long. 1980. "Discourse Analysis, What's That?" In *Discourse Analysis in Second Language Research*, ed. Diane Larsen-Freeman. Rowley, Mass.: Newbury House, 1–40.

Heaton, J.B. 1975. *Writing English Language Tests*. London: Longman.

Henderson, Ingeborg. 1985. "Training Teaching Assistants in the Yearlong Methods Course." *ADFL Bulletin* 16: 49–52.

Heny, Frank. 1987. "Theoretical Linguistics, Second Language Acquisition, and Language Pedagogy." In *Foreign Language Instruction: A National Agenda*, ed. Richard D. Lambert and Alan W. Heston. The Annals of the Academy of Political and Social Science 490. Newbury Park, Calif.: Sage.

Higgs, Theodore V., ed. 1984. *Teaching for Proficiency, the Organizing Principle*. Skokie, Ill.: National Textbook.

Hill, Jennifer. 1986. *Using Literature in Language Teaching*. London: Macmillan.

Hillocks, George. 1987. "Synthesis of Research on Teaching Writing." *Educational Leadership* 44: 71–82.

Hollaway, Becky L. 1989. *Improving Elementary LD Students' Recall of Social Studies and Science Vocabulary Using Mnemonic Instruction*. Practicum Report. Fort Lauderdale, Fla.: Nova University ERIC Document Reproduction, no. ED 315 962.

Hope, Quentin. 1988. *L'art de lire*. New York: Macmillan.

Horwitz, Elaine K. 1986. "Some Language Acquisition Principles and Their Implications for Second Language Teaching." *Hispania* 69: 684–89.

———. 1990. "Attending to the Affective Domain in the Foreign Language Classroom." In *Northeast Conference Reports*, ed. Sally

Sieloff Magnan. Middlebury, Vt.: Northeast Conference on the Teaching of Foreign Languages, 13–15.

Hosenfeld, Carol 1977. "A Preliminary Investigation of the Reading Strategies of Successful and Nonsuccessful Second Language Learners." *System* 5: 110–23.

———. 1979. "A Learning-Teaching View of Second Language Instruction." *Foreign Language Annals* 12: 51–54.

———. 1984. "Case Studies of 9th Grade Readers." In *Reading in a Foreign Language*, ed. J. Charles Alderson and A.H. Urouhavet. London: Longman, 231–249.

Jacobs, Holly L., S. Zingraf, D. Wormuth, V. Hartfield, and J. Hughey. 1981. *Testing ESL Composition: A Practical Approach*. Rowley, Mass.: Newbury House.

James, Dorothy. 1989. "Re-shaping the 'College-level' Curriculum: Problems and Possibilities." In *Northeast Conference Report: Shaping the Future: Challenges & Opportunities*. Middlebury, Vt: Northeast Conference on the Teaching of Foreign Languages, 79–110.

Jarvis, Ana C., and Raquel Lebredo. 1987. *Entre amigos Video Program*. Lexington, Mass.: D.C. Heath.

Jarvis, Ana C., and Raquel Lebredo. 1990. *¿Cómo se dice?* 4th ed. Lexington, Mass.: D.C. Heath.

Jarvis, Gilbert A. 1991. "Research on Teaching Methodology: Its Evolution and Prospects." In *Foreign Language Acquisition Research and the Classroom*, Barbara F. Freed, ed., Lexington, Mass. D.C. Heath and Co., 295–306.

Jarvis, Gilbert A., Thérèse M. Bonin, Donald E. Corbin and Diane W. Birckbichler. 1988. *Invitation*. 3rd ed. New York: Holt, Rinehart and Winston.

Jerald, Michael, and Raymond Clark. 1983. *Experiential Language Teaching Techniques*. Brattleboro, Vt.: Pro Lingua.

Joanette, Yves, and Pierre Goulet. 1988. "Word-Naming in Right-Brain Damaged Subjects." In *Right Hemisphere Contributions to Lexical Semantics*, ed. Christine Chiarello. Berlin: Springer-Verlag, 1–18.

———. 1990. "Narrative Discourse in Right-Brain Damaged Right-handers." In *Discourse Ability and Brain Damage: Theoretical and Empirical Perspectives*, ed. Y. Joanette and H. Brownell. New York: Springer-Verlag, 131–53.

Joanette, Yves, Pierre Goulet, and Didier Hannequin. 1990. *Right Hemisphere and Verbal Communication*. New York: Springer-Verlag.

Johnson, Donna M. 1993. "Classroom-Oriented Research in Second-Language Learning." In *Research in Langauge Learning: Principles, Processes, and Prospects*, ed. Alice Omaggio Hadley. Lincolnwood, IL: National Textbook Co. 1–23.

Johnson, Leonard W. 1983. *Grading the Advanced Placement Examination in French Language*. Princeton, N.J.: Advanced Placement Program of the College Board.

Jones, Ken. 1982. *Simulations in Language Teaching*. Cambridge, England: Cambridge University Press.

Jorden, Eleanor. 1987. *Japanese: The Spoken Language*. Vol. 1. New Haven:, Conn. Yale University Press.

———. 1988. *Japanese: The Spoken Language*. Vol. 2. New Haven, Conn.: Yale University Press.

Joseph, John E. 1988. "New French: A Pedagogical Crisis in the Making." *The Modern Language Journal* 72: 31–36.

Kamhi, Alan G., and René F. Lee. 1988. "Cognition." In *Later Language Development: Ages 9 through 19*, ed. Marilyn A. Nippold. Boston: Little Brown, 127–59.

Kasper, Gabriele. 1989. "Variation in Interlanguage Speech Act Realization." In *Variation in Second Language Acquisition*, Vol. 1, *Dixcourse and Pragmatics*, eds. S. Gass, C. Madden, D. Preston, and L. Selinker. Clevedon, England: Multilingual Matters, 37–59.

Kassen, Margaret Ann. 1990. "Responding to Foreign Language Student Writing: A Case Study of Twelve Teachers of Beginning, Intermediate and Advanced Level French." Ph. D. Diss., University of Texas at Austin.

Kaufman, Margo R. 1977. "A Training Program for Teaching Assistants." *Foreign Language Annals* 10: 659–61.

Kecskés, István, and Tünde Papp. 1991. *Elméleti nyelvészet, alkalmazott nyelvészet, nyelvoktatás* [Theoretical linguistics, applied linguistics, language teaching]. Budapest: Ts-Programiroda.

Keirsey, David, and Marilyn Bates. 1978. *Please Understand Me: Character and Temperament Types*. Del Mar, Calif.: Prometheus Nemesis Books.

Keung, Ho Sai, and Rumjahn Hoosain. 1989. "Right Hemisphere Advantage in Two-Character Chinese Words." *Brain and Language* 37: 606–15.

Kinginger, Celeste. 1990. *Task Variation and Classroom Learner Discourse.* Ph.D. Diss., University of Illinois at Urbana-Champaign.

Kirby, Dan, and Tom Liner. 1981. *Inside Out: Developmental Strategies for Teaching Writing.* Montclair, N.J.: Boynton/Cook.

Klein, Ilona. 1990. "Teaching in a Liberal Arts College: How Foreign Language Courses Contribute to 'Writing Across the Curriculum' Programs." *The Modern Language Journal* 74: 28–35.

Knapp, Donald. 1972. "Focused, Efficient Method to Relate Composition Correction to Teaching Aims." In Harold B. Allen and Russel N. Campbell (Eds.) *Teaching English as a Second Language.* 2nd Ed. New York: McGraw Hill International, 213–221.

Kolich, E.M. 1988. "Vocabulary Learning—What Works? Perspectives from the Research Literature." *Reading Improvement* 25: 117–24.

Konopak, Bonnie C. 1988a. "Effects of Inconsiderate vs. Considerate Text on Secondary Students' Vocabulary Learning." *Journal of Reading Behavior* 20: 25–41.

Konopak, Bonnie C. 1988b. "Using Contextual Information for Word Learning." *Journal of Reading* 31: 334–39.

Kraetschmer, Kurt. 1986. "Current Trends in Neurolinguistics Studies of Bilingualism." *International Review of Applied Linguistics in Language Teaching* 24: 1–11.

Kramsch, Claire J. 1981. *Discourse Analysis and Second Language Teaching.* Washington, D.C.: Center for Applied Linguistics.

———. 1985. "Classroom Interaction and Discourse Options." *Studies in Second Language Acquisition* 7.2: 169–83.

———. 1986. "From Language Proficiency to Interactional Competence." *The Modern Language Journal* 70: 366–72.

———. 1987. "The Missing Link in Vision and Governance: Foreign Language Acquisition Research." *Profession*: 26–30.

———. 1993. *Context and Culture in Language Teaching.* Oxford, England: Oxford University Press.

Krashen, Stephen D. 1982. *Principles and Practice in Second Language Acquisition.* New York: Pergamon Press.

———. 1985. *The Input Hypothesis: Issues and Implications.* London: Longman.

———. 1986. "We Acquire Vocabulary by Reading." In *Teaching Our Students a Second Language in a Proficiency-Based Classroom*, ed. A. Papalia. New York: Schenectady, 51–59.

Krashen, Stephen D., and Tracy D. Terrell. 1983. *The Natural Approach—Language Acquisition in the Classroom*. Hayward, Calif.: Alemany Press.

Kreeft, Joy, R.W. Shuy, J. Staton, L. Reed, and R. Morroy. 1984. *Dialog Writing: Analysis of Student-Teacher Interactive Writing in the Learning of English As a Second Language*. Washington, D.C. Center for Applied Linguistics (ERIC Document ED 252 097).

Kroeger, Otto, and Janet M. Thuesen. 1981. *MBTI Type-Watching Qualifying Workshop*. Fairfax, Va.: Otto Kroeger Associates.

———. 1988. *Type Talk*. New York: Delta.

Lalande, John F. 1982. "Reducing Composition Errors: An Experiment." *The Modern Language Journal* 66: 140–149.

———. 1991. "Advancing the Case for an Advanced Methods Course." In *Challenges in the 1990s for College Foreign Language programs*, ed. Sally Sieloff Magnan. Boston: Heinle & Heinle, 151–66.

Lalonde, R.N., and Robert C. Gardner. 1984. "Investigating a Causal Model of Second Language Acquisition: Where Does Personality Fit?" *Canadian Journal of Behavioral Science* 16: 224–37.

Larsen-Freeman, Diane. 1980. *Discourse Analysis in Second Language Research*. Rowley, Mass.: Newbury House.

———. 1990. "On the Need for a Theory of Language Teaching." In *Linguistics, Language Teaching and Language Acquisition: The Interdependence of Theory, Practice and Research*, Georgetown University Round Table on Languages and Linguistics, ed. James E. Alatis. Washington, D.C.: Georgetown University Press, 261–70.

Larsen-Freeman, Diane, and Michael H. Long, eds. 1991. *An Introduction to Second Language Acquisition Research*. London: Longman.

Lawton, Denis. 1970. *Social Class, Language and Education*. London: Routledge and Kegan Paul.

———, ed. 1986. *School Curriculum Planning*. London: Hodder and Stroughton.

Lengyel, Zsolt. 1981. *A gyermeknyelv* [Child Language]. Budapest: Gondolat.

Levinson, Stephen. 1983. *Pragmatics*. Cambridge, England: Cambridge University Press.

Limber, John. 1973. "The Genesis of Complex Sentences." In *Cognitive Development and the Acquisition of Language*, ed. T.E. More. New York: Academic Press, 171–182.

Linde, Charlotte, and William Labov. 1975. "Spatial Networks as a Site for the Study of Language and Thought." *Language* 51: 924–39.

Liskin-Gasparro, Judith. 1987. *Testing and Teaching for Oral Proficiency*. Boston: Heinle and Heinle.

Littlewood, William. 1981. *Communicative Language Teaching: An Introduction*. Cambridge, England: Cambridge University Press.

Livingstone, Carol. 1983. *Role Play in Language Learning*. Essex, England: Longman.

Loban, Walter. 1954. *Literature and Social Sensitivity*. Champaign, Ill.: National Council of Teachers of English.

——. 1963. *The Language of Elementary School Children*. NCTE Research Report no. 1. Champaign, Ill.: National Council of Teachers of English.

Loban, Walter, M. Ryan, and J.R. Squire. 1961. "Teaching Language and Literature, Grades 7– 12." In *Teaching Language and Literature*, ed. W.B. Spalding. New York: Harcourt Brace and World.

Lonergan, Jack. 1984. *Video in Language Teaching*. Cambridge, England: Cambridge University Press.

Long, Donna Reseigh. 1989. "Second Language Listening Comprehension: A Schema-Theoretic Perspective." *The Modern Language Journal* 73: 32–40.

Long, Michael H. 1983. "Inside the Black Box: Methodological Issues in Classroom Research on Language Learning." In *Classroom-Oriented Research in Second Langauge Acquisition*, eds. Herbert W. Seliger and Michael H. Long. Rowley, MA: Newbury House, 3–35.

——. 1983. "Native Speaker/Nonnative Speaker Conversation and the Negotiation of Comprehensible Input." *Applied Linguistics* 4: 126–141.

——. 1985. "Input and Second Language Theory." In *Input in Second Language Acquisition*, eds. Susan Gass and Carolyn Madden. Rowley, Mass. Newbury House, 377–393.

Long, M., and P. Porter. 1985. "Group Work, Interlanguage Talk and Second Language Acquisition." *TESOL Quarterly* 19.2: 207–228.

Lozanov, Georgi. 1978. *Suggestology and Outlines of Suggestopedy*. New York: Gordon and Breach.

Magnan, Sally S. 1985. "Teaching and Testing Proficiency in Writing: Skills to Transcend the Second-Language Classroom." In *Proficiency, Curriculum, Articulation: The Ties that Bind*, ed. Alice C. Omaggio. Middlebury, Vt.: Northeast Conference on the Teaching of Foreign Languages, 109–36.

Maley, Alan, and Alan Duff. 1989. *The Inward Ear: Poetry in the Language Classroom*. Cambridge, England: Cambridge University Press.

Maley, Alan, Alan Duff, and Françoise Grellet. 1980. *The Mind's Eye: Using Pictures Creatively in Language Learning*. Cambridge, England: Cambridge University Press.

Manghubai, Francis. 1987. "The Processing of Input by Beginning L2 Learners: Five Case Studies." Ph.D. Diss., University of Toronto.

Mansoor, Menahem. 1959. "Arabic: What and When to Teach." In *Report of the Tenth Annual Round Table Meeting of Linguistics and Language Studies*, ed. Richard S. Harrell. Washington, D.C.: Georgetown University Press, 83–96.

Marcellesi, J. B., and B. Gardin. 1974. *Introduction à la sociolinguistique*. Paris: Librairie Larousse.

McCarthy, Bernice. 1987. *The 4MAT System: Teaching to Learning Styles with Right/Left Mode Techniques*. Barrington, Il.: Excel.

McHoul, A. 1978. "The Organization of Turns at Formal Talk in the Classroom." *Language in Society* 7: 183–213.

Meiseles, Gustav. 1980. "Educated Spoken Arabic and the Arabic Language Continuum." *Archivum Linguisticum* 11: 118–43.

Milleret, Margo, Charles W. Stansfield, and Dorry M. Kenyon. 1991. "The Validity of the Portuguese Speaking Test for Use in a Summer Study Abroad Program." *Hispania* 74: 778–87.

Mitchell, Terrence. 1986. "What is Educated Spoken Arabic?" *International Journal of the Sociology of Language* 61: 7–32.

Mizutani, Osamu, and Nobuko Mizutani. 1977. *An Introduction to Modern Japanese*. Tokyo: The Japan Times.

Moffett, James. 1981. *Active Voice: A Writing Program Across the Curriculum*. Portsmouth, N.H.: Boynton/Cook.

Molloy, Raymond, Hiram H. Brownell, and Howard Gardner. 1990. "Discourse Comprehension by Right-Hemisphere Stroke Patients: Deficits of Prediction and Revision." In *Discourse Ability and Brain Damage: Theoretical and Empirical Perspectives*, ed. Y. Joanette and H. Brownell. New York: Springer-Verlag, 113–30.

244 *Bibliography*

Morain, Genelle. 1990. "Preparing Foreign Language Teachers: Problems and Possibilities." *ADFL Bulletin* 21: 20–24.

Morocco, Glenn and Margot Soven. 1990. "Writing Across the Curriculum in the Foreign Language Class: Developing a New Pedagogy." *Hispania* 73: 845–849.

Murphy, Joseph A. 1990. "The Graduate Teaching Assistant in an Age of Standards." In *Challenges in the 1990 for College Foreign Language Programs*, ed. Sally Sieloff Magnan. Boston: Heinle & Heinle, 129–49.

Murphy, Sandra, and Leo Ruth. 1988. *Designing Writing Tasks for the Assessment of Writing*. Norwood, N.J.: Ablex.

Murray, M. Donald. 1984. *Write to Learn*. New York: Holt, Rinehart and Winston.

Myers, Isabel Briggs. 1962. *Myers-Briggs Type Indicator*. Palo Alto, Calif.: Consulting Psychologists Press.

Myers, Isabel Briggs, and Mary H. McCaulley. 1985. *Manual: A Guide to the Development and Use of the Myers-Briggs Type Indicator*. Palo Alto, Calif.: Consulting Psychologists Press.

Naiman, Neil, Maria Fröhlich, Hans Heinrich Stern, and Angela Todesco. 1978. *The Good Language Learner*. Toronto, Ontario: Institute for Studies in Education.

Nemni, M. 1986. "Les maux des mots." *Canadian Modern Language Review* 41.6: 1020–40.

Nippold, Marilyn A., ed. 1988. *Later Language Development: Ages 9 Through 19*. Boston: Little Brown.

Nisbett, Richard E., and Wilson, Timothy D. 1977. "Telling More Than We Know: Verbal Report on Mental Processes." *Psychological Review* 84: 231–259.

Noblitt, James S. and Susan K. Bland. 1991. "Tracking the Learner in Computer-Aided Language Learning." In *Foreign Language Acquisition Research and the Classroom*, ed. Barbara F. Freed. Lexington, Mass: D.C. Heath and Company, 120–132.

Noel-Gaudrault, Monique. 1990. "Didactique du discours expressif." *Bulletin de l'AQEFLS* 12.1: 119–32.

Nunan, David. 1989. *Designing Tasks for the Communicative Classroom*. Cambridge, England: Cambridge University Press.

———. 1991. *The Learner-Centered Curriculum*. Cambridge: Cambridge University Press.

Obler, Loraine K. 1981. "Right Hemisphere Participation in Second Language Acquisition." In *Individual Differences and Universals in Language Learning Aptitudes*, ed. Karl Diller. Rowley, Mass.: Newbury House, 53–64.

Obler, Loraine K., Robert J. Zatorre, Linda Galloway, and Jyostna Vaid. 1982. "Cerebral Lateralization in Bilinguals: Methodological Issues." *Brain and Language* 15: 40–54.

Ochs, Elinor. 1979. "Planned and Unplanned Discourse." In *Syntax and Semantics 12: Discourse and Syntax*, ed. Talmy Givon. New York: Academic Press, 51–80.

Oller, John W., Jr. 1991. "Foreign Language Testing, Part 2: Its Depth." *ADFL Bulletin* 23: 5–13.

Oltman, Philip K., Evelyn Raskin and Herman A. Witkin. 1971. *Group Embedded Figures Test*. Palo Alto, Calif.: Consulting Psychologists Press.

Omaggio, Alice C. 1986. *Teaching Language in Context: Proficiency-Oriented Instruction*. Boston: Heinle and Heinle.

O'Malley, J. Michael and Anna Uhl Chamot. 1993. "Learner Characteristics in Second-Language Acquisition." In *Research in Language Learning: Principles*, ed. Alice Omaggio Hadley. *Processes, and Prospects*, Lincolnwood, Ill.: National Textbook Co., 96–123.

O'Malley, J. Michael, Anna Chamot, Gloria Stewner-Manzanares, Lisa Kupper, and Rocco Russo. 1985. "Learning Strategies Used by Beginning and Intermediate ESL Students." *Language Learning* 35: 21–46.

Omar, Margaret K. 1976. *Levantine and Egyptian Arabic: A Comparative Study*. Washington, D.C.: Foreign Service Institute.

Osterholm, Kathryn K. 1986. "Writing in the Native Language." *In Listening, Reading, Writing: Analysis and Application*, ed. Barbara H. Wing. Middlebury, Vt.: Northeast Conference on the Teaching of Foreign Language, 117–143.

Otto, Sue E.K. 1989. "The Language Laboratory in the Computer Age." In *Modern Technology in Foreign Language Education: Applications and Projects*, ed. William Flint Smith. Lincolnwood, Ill.: National Textbook, pp. 13–41.

Oxford, Rebecca. 1989. "Use of Language Learning Strategies: A Synthesis of Studies with Implications for Strategy Training." *System* 17: 235–47.

———. 1990. *Language Learning Strategies: What Every Teacher Should Know*. New York: Newbury House.

Oxford, Rebecca, and Martha Nyikos. 1989. "Variables Affecting Choice of Language Learning Strategies by University Students." *The Modern Language Journal* 73: 291–300.

Palmer, Barbara C. 1989. *An Investigation of the Effects of Newspaper-Based Instruction on Reading Vocabulary, Reading Comprehension and Writing Performance of At-Risk Middle and Secondary School Students* (Final Report). Tallahassee: The Florida State University; ERIC Document Reproduction Service, no. ED 315 732.

Papp, Mària, and Csaba Pléh. 1975. "A szociális helyzet és a beszéd összefüggései az iskoláskor kezdetén." [The relationship of social environment and speech at the beginning of schooling.]*Valóság*. XV. évf. 2: 52–58.

Papp, Tünde. 1991. *Az anyanyelvi tudás és az eredményes idegennyelv tanulás összefüggései egy többszintu longitudinális vizsgálat alapján.* [The interrelation of L1 and FL on the basis of a multi-level longitudinal experiment.] Unpublished diss. for the candidate degree, Hungarian Academy of Sciences, Budapest.

Paribakht, Tahereh. 1985. "Strategic Competence and Language Proficiency." *Applied Linguistics* 6: 132–45.

Parkinson, Dilworth. 1985. "Proficiency to Do What? Developing Oral Proficiency in Students of Modern Standard Arabic." *Al-9Arabiyya* 18: 11–43.

———. 1991. "Searching for Modern Fusha: Real Life Formal Arabic." *Al-9Arabiyya* 24: 31–64.

Patrie, J. 1989. "The Use of the Tape Recorder in an ESL Composition Programme." *TESL Canada Journal* 6: 87–89.

Peters, Ann M. 1981. "Language Learning Strategies: Does the Whole Equal the Sum of the Parts?" In *Individual Differences and Universals in Language Learning Aptitudes*, ed. Karl Diller. Rowley, Mass.: Newbury House, 37–52.

Peyton, Joy K. 1990. "Dialogue Journal Writing." In *Bilingual Education: Issues and Strategies*, ed. A.M. Padilla, H.H. Fairchild and C.M. Valadez. Newbury Park, Calif.: Sage, 184–94.

Phillips, Elaine M. 1992. "The Effects of Language Anxiety on Students' Oral Test Performance and Attitudes." *The Modern Language Journal* 76: 14–26.

Phillips, June K. 1984. "Practical Implications of Recent Research in Reading." *Foreign Language Annals* 17: 285–96.

Pica, Teresa. 1987. "Second Language Acquisition, Social Interaction and the Classroom." *Applied Linguistics* 8: 3–21.

Pica, Teresa, and Catherine Doughty. 1985a. "The Role of Group Work in Classroom Second Language Acquisition." *Studies in Second Language Acquisition* 7.2: 233–48.

———. 1985b "Input and Interaction in the Communicative Classroom: A Companion of Teacher-Fronted and Group Activities." In *Input in Second Language Acquisition*, eds. S. Gass and C. Madden. Rowley: Newbury House, 115–132.

Pimsleur, Paul. 1966. *The Pimsleur Language Aptitude Battery*. New York: Harcourt Brace Jovanovich.

Pinsonneault, Lise. 1985. *Accueillir un allophone*. Québec: Ministère de l'Education, Direction générale des régions, Services éducatifs aux communautés culturelles.

Politzer, Robert L., and Mary McGroarty. 1985. "An Exploratory Study of Learning Behaviors and Their Relationship to Gains in Linguistic and Communicative Competence." *TESOL Quarterly* 19: 103–23.

Porter, P. 1986. "How Learners Talk to Each Other: Input and Interaction in Task-Centered Discussions." In *Talking to Learn*, ed. R. Day. Rowley, Mass.: Newbury House, 200–224.

Proulx, Lucie. 1988. *Profil des enseignants et enseignantes, accueil, secondaire, 1987–1988*. Montréal: C.E.C.M., Service des études.

Raffa, Rosemary M. 1991. Personal communication to Charles W. Stansfield, October 25.

Raimes, Ann. 1983. *Techniques in Teaching Writing*. New York: Oxford University Press.

Redfield, James. 1989. "The Politics of Language Instruction." *ADFL Bulletin* 20: 5–12.

Rehorick, Sally. 1991. "The New Meaning of Creativity in the Foreign Language Classroom: A Canadian Perspective." In *International Perspective on Foreign Language Teaching*, ed. G.L. Ervin. Lincolnwood, Ill.: National Textbook Co. 108–20.

Rice, Donald B. 1991. "Language Proficiency and Textual Theory: How the Twain Might Meet." *ADFL Bulletin* 22: 12–15.

Richard-Amato, Patricia A. 1988. *Making It Happen: Interaction in the Second Language Classroom*. New York: Longman.

Riley, Peggy. 1989. "Imagery: Thinking with the Mind's Eye." *The Quarterly of the National Writing Project and the Center for the Study of Writing* 11.1: 23–26.

Robb, Thomas, Steven Ross, and Ian Shortreed. 1986. "Salience of Feedback on Error and Its Effect on EFL Writing Quality." *TESOL Quarterly* 20: 83–93.

Rochester, Myrna B., Judith A. Muyskens, Alice C. Hadley, Claudine Convert-Chalmers, and Patricia Westphal. 1991. *Bonjour, ça va?* 3rd ed. New York: McGraw-Hill.

Rogers, Carmen Villegas. 1987. "Improving the Performance of Teaching Assistants in the Multi-Section Classroom." *Foreign Language Annals* 20: 403–08.

Rubin, Joan. 1975. "What the 'Good Language Learner' Can Teach Us." *TESOL Quarterly* 9: 41–51.

———. 1981. "Study of Cognitive Processes in Second Language Learning." *Applied Linguistics* 2: 117–31.

———. 1987. "Learner Strategies: Theoretical Assumptions, Research History and Typology." In *Learner Strategies in Language Learning*, ed. Anita Wenden and Joan Rubin. Englewood Cliffs, N.J.: Prentice Hall, 15–30.

Rutherford, W.E. 1987. *Second Languages Grammar: Learning and Teaching*. New York: Longman.

Ryding, Karin. 1991. "Proficiency Despite Diglossia: A New Approach for Arabic." *The Modern Language Journal* 72: 212–18.

Sacks, Harvey, Emanuel A. Schegloff, and Gail Jefferson. 1974. "A Simplest Systematics for the Organization of Turn-Taking in Conversation." *Language* 50: 696–735.

St. Onge, Susan S., and Robert M. Terry. 1990. *Vous y êtes!* 2nd ed. Boston: Heinle and Heinle.

Sandberg, Karl C., Georges Zak, Anthony A. Ciccone, and Françoise Defrecheux. 1990. *Ça marche! Cours de français communicatif*. New York: Macmillan.

Savignon, Sandra J. 1972. *Communicative Competence: An Experiment in Foreign Language Teaching*. Philadelphia: Center for Curriculum Development.

———. 1983. *Communicative Competence: Theory and Classroom Practice*. Reading, Mass.: Addison-Wesley.

———. 1985. "Evaluation of Communicative Competence: The ACTFL Provisional Proficiency Guidelines." *The Modern Language Journal* 69.2: 129–134.

———. 1991. "Communicative Language Teaching: State of the Art." *TESOL Quarterly* 25: 261–77.

Schegloff, M.G. Jefferson, and H. Sacks. 1977. "The Preference for Self-Correction in the Organization of Repair in Conversation." *Language* 53 (2): 361–382.

Schiffrin, Deborah. 1994. *Approaches to Discourse*. Cambridge, Mass.: Basil Blackwell.

Schneiderman, Eta I. 1986. "Learning to the Right: Some Thoughts on Hemisphere Involvement in Language Acquisition." In *Language Processing in Bilinguals: Psycholinguistic and Neuropsychological Perspectives*, ed. J. Vaid. Hillsdale, N.J.: Erlbaum, 233–51.

Schneiderman, Eta I., and Marjorie B. Wesche. 1983. "The Role of the Right Hemisphere in Second Language Acquisition." In *Second Language Acquisition Studies*, ed. K. Bailey, M. Long, and S. Peck. Rowley, Mass.: Newbury House, 162–74.

Schultz, Jean Marie. 1991a. "Mapping and Cognitive Development in the Teaching of Foreign Language Writing." *French Review* 64: 978–88.

———. 1991b. "Writing Mode in the Articulation of Language and Literature Classes: Theory and Practice." *The Modern Language Journal* 75: 411–17.

Schwartz, J. 1980. "The Negotiation for Meaning: Repair in Conversations between Second Language Learners of English." In *Discourse Analysis in Second Language Research*, ed. D. Larsen-Freeman. Rowley, Mass.: Newbury House, 138–153.

Schwartz, R.M. 1988. "Learning to Learn Vocabulary in Content Area Textbooks." *Journal of Reading* 32: 108–19.

Scovel, Thomas. 1982. "Questions Concerning the Application of Neurolinguistic Research to Second Language Learning/ Teaching." *TESOL Quarterly* 16: 323–31.

———. 1988. *A Time to Speak: A Psycholinguistic Inquiry into the Critical Period for Human Speech*. New York: Newbury House.

Seiferling, Mary. 1981. "A Real Voice and Audience for the Classroom Writer," *Teaching, Writing, Learning*. Ed. Ian Pringle and Aviva Freedman. Ottawa: The Canadian Council of Teachers of English.

Seliger, Herbert W. 1982. "On the Possible Role of the Right Hemisphere in Second Language Acquisition." *TESOL Quarterly* 16: 307–14.

———. 1983. "The Language Learner as Linguist: Of Metaphors and Realities." *Applied Linguistics* 4: 179–91.

Semke, Harriet D. 1984. "Effects of the Red Pen." *Foreign Language Annals* 17: 195–202.

Shumway, Nicolas. 1990. "Language Teaching in Literature Departments: Natural Partnership or Shotgun Marriage?" *ADFL Bulletin* 21: 40–43.

Slavin, Robert, and Nancy Madden. 1979. "School Practices That Improve Race Relations." *American Educational Research Journal* 16: 169–80.

Slobin, Dan I. 1973. "Cognitive Prerequisites for the Development of Grammar." In *Studies of Child Language Development*, ed. Charles A. Ferguson, and Dan I. Slobin. New York: Holt, Rinehart and Winston, 175–208.

Sollenberger, Howard. 1978. "Development and Current Use of the FSI Oral Interview Test." In *Direct Testing of Speaking Proficiency: Theory and Application*, ed. John L.D. Clark. Princeton, N.J.: Educational Testing Service, 1–12; ERIC Document Reproduction Service, No. ED 172 523.

Spack, Ruth, and Catherine Sadow. 1983. "Student-Teacher Working Journals in ESL Freshman Composition." *TESOL Quarterly* 17: 575–93.

Stansfield, Charles W. 1989. *Simulated Oral Proficiency Interviews. ERIC Digest.* Washington, D.C.: ERIC Clearinghouse on Languages and Linguistics.

Stansfield, Charles W., Dorry Mann Kenyon, Ricardo Paiva, Fatima Doyle, Ines Ulsh, and Maria A. Cowles. 1990. "The Development and Validation of the Portuguese Speaking Test." *Hispania* 73: 641–49.

Stansfield, Charles W., and Richard W. Harmon, eds. 1987. *ACTFL Proficiency Guidelines for the Less Commonly Taught Languages.* Washington, D.C.: Center for Applied Linguistics; Hastings-on-Hudson, N.Y.: American Council on the Teaching of Foreign Languages; ERIC Document Reproduction Service, no. ED 289 345.

Stern, Hans Heinrich. 1975. "What Can We Learn from the Good Language Learner?" *Canadian Modern Language Review/Revue canadienne des langues vivantes* 31: 304–18.

Stevick, Earl. 1980. *Teaching Languages: A Way and Ways*. Rowley, Mass.: Newbury House.

Sussman, Harvey M., Philip Franklin, and Terry Simon. 1982. "Bilingual Speech: Bilateral Control?" *Brain and Language* 15: 125–42.

Suzuki, Takao. 1978. *Japanese and the Japanese: Words in Context*. Tokyo: Kodansha International.

Swaffar, Janet K. 1988. "Readers, Texts, and Second Languages: The Interactive Processes." *The Modern Language Journal* 72: 123–49.

———. 1989. "Curricular Issues and Language Research: The Shifting Interaction." *Profession* 89: 32–38.

Swaffar, Janet and Susan Bacon. 1993. "Reading and Listening Comprehension: Perspectives on Research and Implications for Practice." In *Research in Language Learning: Principles, Processes, and Prospects*, ed. Alice Omaggio Hadley. Lincolnwood, Ill.: National Textbook Co., 124–155.

Swain, Merrill. 1985. "Communicative Competence: Some Roles of Comprehensible Input and Comprehensible Output in its Development." In *Input in Second Language Acquisition*, ed. Susan M. Gass and Carolyn G. Madden. Cambridge, Mass.: Newbury House, 235–53.

Takenoya, Miyuki. 1991. "Investigation of Negative Politeness: Acquisition of pronouns as address terms in Japanese." Paper presented at Fifth Annual International Conference on Pragmatics and Language Learning, University of Illinois at Urbana-Champaign, April 3–5.

Tannen, Deborah. 1984. *Conversational Style: Analyzing Talk among Friends*. Norwood, Mass.: Ablex.

———. 1987. "Repetition in Conversation: Toward a Poetics of Talk." *Language* 63: 574–605.

———. 1989. *Talking Voices: Repetition, Dialogue, and Imagery in Conversational Discourse*. Cambridge, England: Cambridge University Press.

Terrell, Tracy D. 1987. "Approche naturelle en enseignement des langues: une mise à jour." *Le français langue seconde; de la théorie à la pratique*. Special edition, *Canadian Modern Language Review/ Revue canadienne des langues vivantes* 43.1: 110–32.

———. 1990. "Trends in the Teaching of Grammar in Spanish Language Textbooks." *Hispania* 73: 201–11.

———. 1991. "The Role of Grammar Instruction in a Communitive Approach." *The Modern Language Journal* 75: 52–63.

Terry, Robert M. 1989. "Teaching and Evaluating Writing as a Communicative Skill." *Foreign Language Annals* 22: 43–54.

Therrien, Michel. 1990. "L'enseignement du français à des clientèles allophones: aspects discursifs de la langue écrite." Article présenté au Congrès mondial de linguistique appliquée, Thessalonika, Grèce. [Talk presented to the World Congress of Applied Linguistics, Thessalonika, Greece.]

Todorov, Tzvetan. 1970. *Introduction à la littérature fantastique*. Paris: Seuil.

Uber, Diane. 1985. "The Dual Function of *usted*: Forms of Address in Bogota, Colombia." *Hispania* 68: 388–92.

Valdman, Albert, Marva A. Barnett, Elizabeth Holckamp, Michel Laronde, Sally Sieloff Magnan, and Cathy Pons. 1986. *En Route*. New York: Macmillan.

Valette, Jean-Paul, Rebecca M. Valette, and Teresa Carrera-Hanley. 1988. *Situaciones*. Lexington, Mass.: D.C. Heath.

Valette, Jean-Paul, and Rebecca Valette. 1989. *¡Adelante!* Lexington, Mass.: D. C. Heath.

van Lier, Leo. 1988. *The Classroom and the Language Learner*. New York: Longman.

———. 1991. "Inside the Classroom: Learning Processes and Teaching Procedures." *Applied Language Learning* 2.1: 29–68.

Vann, Roberta J., and Roberta G. Abraham. 1990. "Strategies of Unsuccessful Language Learners." *TESOL Quarterly* 24: 177–98.

Vigner, Gerard. 1984. *L'exercice de français*. Paris: Hachette.

Wagner-Gough, Judy, and Evelyn Hatch. 1975. "The Importance of Input Data in Second Language Acquisition Studies." *Language Learning* 25: 297–308.

Walz, Joel C. 1982. *Error Correction Techniques for the Foreign Language Classroom*. Language in Education: Theory and Practice Series no. 50. Washington, D.C.: Center for Applied Linguistics.

Walz, Joel, and Jean-Pierre Piriou. 1990. *Rapports*. 2nd ed. Lexington, Mass.: D.C. Heath.

Wanner, E., and L.R. Gleitman, eds. 1982. *Language Acquisition*. Cambridge, England: Cambridge University Press.

Watson-Gegeo, Karen A., and David W. Gegeo. 1986. "Calling Out and Repeating Routines in Kwara'ae Children's Language Socialization." In *Language Socialization across Cultures*, ed. Bambi Schieffelin and Elinor Ochs. Cambridge, England: Cambridge University Press, 17–50.

Webb, N. M. 1982. "Student Interaction and Learning in Small Groups." *Review of Educational Research* 52: 421–45.

Wenden, Anita. 1986a. "Helping L2 Learners Think about Learning." *English Language Teaching Journal* 40: 3–12.

———. 1986b. "What Do Second-language Learners Know about their Language Learning? A Second Look at Retrospective Accounts." *Applied Linguistics* 7: 186–205.

———. 1987. "Conceptual Background and Utility." In *Learner Strategies in Language Learning*, ed. Anita Wenden and Joan Rubin. Englewood Cliffs, N.J.: Prentice Hall, 3–13.

Wesche, Marjorie Bingham. 1979. "Learning Behaviors of Successful Adult Students on Intensive Language Training." *Canadian Modern Language Review/Revue canadienne des langues vivantes* 35: 415–30.

Westhoff, Gerard J. 1991. "Increasing the Effectiveness of Foreign Language Reading Instruction." *ADFL Bulletin* 22: 28–32.

White, Lydia. 1989. *Universal Grammar and Second Language Acquisition*. Amsterdam: John Benjamins.

Widdowson, Henry G. 1978. *Teaching Language as Communication*. Oxford: Oxford University Press.

———. 1979. *Explorations in Applied Linguistics*. Oxford: Oxford University Press.

Wieczorek, Joseph A. 1991a. "Error Evaluation, Interlanguage Analysis, and the Preterit in the Spanish L2 Classroom." *Canadian Modern Language Review/Revue canadienne des langues vivantes* 47: 497–511.

———. 1991b. "Spanish Dialects and the Foreign Language Textbook: A Sound Perspective." *Hispania* 74: 175–81.

———. 1992. "Classroom Implications of Pronoun (Mis)use in Spanish." *The Modern Language Journal* 76: 34–40.

Wilds, Claudia. 1975. "The Oral Interview Test." In *Testing Language Proficiency*, ed. Randall Jones and Bernard Spolsky. Arlington, Va.: Center for Applied Linguistics, 29–44.

Wolfson, Nessa. 1989. *Perspectives: Sociolinguistics and TESOL*. New York: Newbury House.

Young, Dolly Jesusita. 1991. "Creating a Low-Anxiety Classroom Environment: What Does the Language Anxiety Research Suggest?" *The Modern Language Journal* 75: 426–37.

Young, John, and Kimiko Nakajima-Okano. 1967. *Learn Japanese: New College Text.* 4 vols. Honolulu: University of Hawaii Press.

Yule, George 1991. "Developing Communicative Effectiveness through the Resolution of Referential Conflicts." *Linguistics and Education* 3: 31–45.

Yule, George, and Doris MacDonald. 1990. "Resolving Referential Conflicts in L2 Interaction: The Effect of Proficiency and Interactive Role." *Language Learning* 40: 539–556.

Zamel, Vivian. 1982. "Writing: The Process of Discovering Meaning." *TESOL Quarterly* 16: 195–209.

———. 1985. "Responding to Student Writing." *TESOL Quarterly* 19: 79–101.

Ziv, Nina D. 1984. "The Effect of Teacher Comments on the Writing of Four College Freshmen." In *New Directions in Composition Research*, ed. R. Beach and L. Bridwell. New York: Guilford Press, 362–80.

Contributors

JANIS H. BLACK teaches in the Department of French and Spanish at Memorial University of Newfoundland. She obtained a B.A. (Hons.) degree in French Studies from the University of Reading, England and her P.G.C.E. at the University of London. She began her career as a teacher of French at the secondary level, and worked for a number of years as a university language laboratory supervisor. She earned an M.Ed. degree in Curriculum and Instruction from Memorial University of Newfoundland and has taught French language and writing courses at the university level for the past ten years. Her research focuses on the process of second-language learning—in particular, on learning strategies, individual differences in learners, and strategy training for weaker learners.

MARY EMILY CALL currently teaches linguistics, English as a second language (ESL) and language teaching methodology courses at Montclair State University, where she chairs the Linguistics Department. She received her B.A. from Case Western Reserve University, majoring in French and minoring in Spanish, and taught French and Spanish for six years at the junior and senior high levels. She earned an M.A. in Spanish and a Ph.D. in linguistics at the University of Pittsburgh, where she taught courses in Spanish and ESL as a graduate assistant. In addition, she spent an academic year teaching English as a foreign language in Greece as a Fulbright exchange teacher. Her research interests include exploring the role of personality in language learning, the teaching and learning of listening comprehension, and the development of proficiency-oriented exit criteria for ESL programs.

ELLI DOUKANARI is currently a doctoral candidate in linguistics at Georgetown University, where she received her M.S. in 1989. She obtained a B.A. degree in Greek and English language and literature from the University of Athens. She taught English as a foreign language in Greece, and Greek as a foreign language at Georgetown University. Her research interests include the designing of new teaching materials and classroom activities for the teaching of Greek, discourse analysis of narratives and conversations, sociolinguistic analysis of *Kipriaka chattista* (rhymes improvised by Greek-Cypriots), and the effect of diglossia on contemporary Greek. She has presented numerous papers at professional conferences, and has published on Greek diglossia. She is currently completing her dissertation on Kipriaka chattista.

AHMED FAKHRI currently teaches Linguistics, ESL Theory and the Structure of Modern French at West Virginia University. He received his M.A. and Ph.D. in Linguistics from the University of Michigan in 1985 and taught Linguistics, Second Language Acquisition and Methodology, Arabic and French both in the United States and abroad. He published in *Language Learning, the International Review of Applied Linguistics*, and *Pragmatics and Lan-uage Learning*. His research interests include second language acquisition and pedagogy and discourse analysis.

MICHEL GAGNON is a teacher and researcher in the field of second-language instruction. He taught the high-school-aged Inuit of Nunavik (Northern Québec); since 1987, he has been teaching French to English-speaking students at Centennial Regional High School near Montréal, Québec. His master's thesis focused on the writing process in a second-language classroom. Since 1990, he has been giving lectures and workshops at various conventions and pedagogical meetings.

VICKI GALLOWAY is a professor of Spanish at the Georgia Institute of Technology, where she also serves as associate director of the institute's program in Spanish for Business and Technology. She has taught at all levels of instruction and has served as state supervisor of foreign languages for South Carolina, as project director for the American Council on the Teaching of Foreign Languages, and as editor of *Foreign Language Annals*. She is the author of instructional materials and several textbooks for middle school, high school, and college levels, and her professional articles have appeared in *The Modern Language Journal*, *ACTFL Language Education Series*, *Northeast Conference Reports*, and publications of the *American Education Research Association*.

MARGARET ANN KASSEN received her Ph.D. from the University of Texas at Austin. She is assistant professor and language coordinator in the Department of Modern Languages at The Catholic University of America in Washington, D.C. In addition to her work with second-language writing, she is interested in teacher/teaching assistant development and the use of technology in foreign language instruction.

ISTVÁN KECSKÉS is professor of linguistics in the English Department at the University of Montana. He teaches second-language acquisition, pragmatics, and computer-assisted language learning. He received his Ph.D. in linguistics from Kossuth University, Debrecen, Hungary, in 1976 and his candidate degree in applied linguistics from the Hungarian Academy of Sciences in 1986. He is the author of several textbooks, including *English for Computer Users*, CALL programs in English, Russian, and Hungarian, and a book titled *Theoretical Linguistics, Applied Linguistics and Language Teaching* (coauthor Tünde Papp).

CELESTE KINGINGER is assistant professor in the Department of French and Italian, University of Maryland at College Park. She supervises teaching assistants, directs the French language program, and teaches courses in applied linguistics and second-language acquisition. She is interested in the applications of discourse analysis to the study of classroom language learning, including communicative approaches to teaching and computer-aided instruction.

MARGARET E. MALONE is a Research Associate at the Evaluation Assistance Center East at the George Washington University. She has taught graduate-level courses in language testing and assessment and language teaching methodology at Georgetown University and the American University. She is currently a Ph.D. candidate in applied linguistics at Georgetown University.

TÜNDE PAPP received her Ph.D. in linguistics from Eötvös University, Budapest, Hungary in 1981 and her candidate degree in psycholinguistics from the Hungarian Academy of Sciences in 1991. She taught general linguistics, psycholinguistics, and French at Kossuth University, Debrecen, Hungary, until 1990. Since then she has been teaching psycholinguistics and French in the Foreign Language Department at the University of Montana. Her main research interest is in language acquisition, psycholinguistics and French linguistics.

SYLVIA B. RASI is Assistant Professor of Spanish and ESL at Pacific Union College in Angwin, CA. She is currently a Ph.D. candidate in applied linguistics at Georgetown University.

JEAN MARIE SCHULTZ is director of the second-year program in French at the University of California at Berkeley, where she received her Ph.D. in comparative literature with a concentration in French, Russian, and English literature. Within the field of language acquisition, she specializes in the teaching of foreign language writing, and has published articles in *The Modern Language Journal* and *The French Review*. She has given numerous workshops on the use of literature in the language classroom and on the teaching of writing. She is currently working on a book on these topics, as well as on the revision of a major grammar book and the development of the Educational Testing Service Achievement Test in French.

SHARON L. SHELLY is a native of Cleveland, Ohio, and completed a B.A. in music and French at Case Western Reserve University. She earned an M.A. from the University of North Carolina at Chapel Hill, and a Ph.D. in romance linguistics from Harvard University. She has been teaching college-level French for thirteen years. She has also spent three years in France as *lectrice d'anglais* in the *Grandes Ecoles* system (Hautes études commerciales, Ecoles normale supérieure). More recently, she has worked in the Department of French, and the program in linguistics, at the University of Kentucky. Sharon Shelly is currently an assistant professor of French at the College of Wooster in Ohio.

MIYUKI TAKENOYA is currently an assistant professor of Japanese language and Japanese linguistics at Eastern Michigan

University. She also taught Japanese at Indiana University and other institutions. She has been working on sociolinguistics and pragmatics in second-language acquisition. Her current research interests include address term systems in Japanese and English. She is interested in how second/foreign language learners acquire sociocultural rules such as the address term system in the target language.

THERESA A. WALDSPURGER is assistant professor of Teaching English as a Second Language (TESOL) and director of the Master of Arts in TESOL program at The American University in Washington, D.C. Her interests lie in adult second-language acquisition and English as a second language classroom interaction.

About the Editors

MARGARET AUSTIN HAGGSTROM (Ph.D., University of Minnesota-Minneapolis, 1986) is assistant professor at Loyola College in Maryland, where she teaches French. She has published in *The French Review*, *The Canadian Modern Language Review*, *Foreign Language Annals*, *ADFL* and *Clio*, and is coauthoring a first-and second-year college French text. She is currently a vice president of the Maryland Foreign Language Association. Her areas of interest are foreign language pedagogy, computer assisted language learning, and eighteenth-century French theater.

LESLIE ZARKER MORGAN (Ph.D., Yale University, 1983) is associate professor at Loyola College in Maryland, where she teaches Italian and French. She has published in *The Canadian Journal of Linguistics*, *The Canadian Modern Language Review*, *Forum Italicum*, *Foreign Language Annals*, and *Literary and Linguistic Computing*, and has articles forthcoming in *Italica* and *Italian Culture*. She has served as vice president of the American Association of Teachers of Italian, Long Island chapter. Her areas of research interest are contrastive structures of English and the romance languages, multiple language interference (historical and pedagogical), and computational philology.

JOSEPH A. WIECZOREK (Ph.D., Georgetown University) teaches French, Spanish, and interactive teledistance Russian at Centennial High School in Howard County, Maryland. He is also an adjunct professor of Spanish and education at Loyola College in Maryland as well as adjunct professor of Spanish at the University of Maryland, Baltimore County. He has published in *Word*, *Hispania*, *The Georgetown Journal of Languages and*

Linguistics, The Canadian Modern Language Review, The Modern Language Journal, Proceedings from the Georgetown Round Table (1993), *Foreign Language Annals,* and *Polish Linguistics.* He has written the lab manual and testing program for *Poco a poco,* a first-year Spanish language program published by Heinle and Heinle, and the testing program for *Intercambios* (Heinle and Heinle). He is currently a vice-president of the Maryland Foreign Language Association. He is also chief editor for the *Mid-Atlantic Journal of Foreign Language Pedagogy.* His areas of research interest are pedagogy and second-language acquisition.

Index

Source Books on Education